Open Office Planning

Open Office Planning

A Handbook for
Interior Designers
and Architects

By John Pile

WHITNEY LIBRARY OF DESIGN
an imprint of Watson-Guptill Publications/New York

THE ARCHITECTURAL PRESS LTD/LONDON

First Published 1978 in the United States and Canada by the Whitney Library of Design
an imprint of Watson-Guptill Publications,
a division of Billboard Publications, Inc.,
1515 Broadway, New York, N.Y. 10036

Library of Congress Cataloging in Publication Data
Pile, John F
   Open office planning.
   Bibliography: p.
   Includes index.
   1. Office layout—Handbooks, manuals, etc.
I. Title.
HF5547.P522   651'.32   78-883
ISBN 0-8230-7401-3

First published 1978 in Great Britain by The Architectural Press Ltd.,
9 Queen Anne's Gate, London SW1H 9BY
ISBN 0 85139 507 4

Manufactured in U.S.A.

First Printing, 1978
Second Printing, 1979

Contents

Acknowledgments

I want to thank the many designers and manufacturers who have contributed information and illustrative material for this book. Dr. Rudolpho Planas of the Quickborner Team (now retired) has been particularly helpful in presenting and explaining the basic ideas of open planning and in providing illustrative material. Among manufacturers, Herman Miller with Carl Ruff and Knoll International with Carolann Cioffi have been particularly generous with information and illustrations. Every effort has been made to give full and accurate credit to planners, designers, manufacturers, and photographers. In some cases information has been missing or supplied through indirect sources so that credits may be incomplete. A general apology is offered for any errors or omissions that may exist.

Introduction

For many years, office planning was a specialized form of architectural or interior design practice in which the only specialized qualities resulted from the rather narrow realities of office needs. Around 1958 to 1960, first in Europe and then a little later in the U.S., a new kind of office planning surfaced under the German name of *Bürolandschaft*, literally, "office landscape" and as it became Americanized, under the name of "open planning."

I first became aware of this phenomenon when I saw in an issue of the *Architectural Review*, the foremost British architectural magazine, a plan so shocking in character as to make me assume that I was in the presence of some sort of British joke. The text that accompanied the plan was, however, too serious to really encourage the idea that this was a humorous effort. I was, in fact, confronting an example of "office landscape" and the commentary that supported it. Since I happened to be working on a book on office planning at that time (to be completed in 1969 as *Interiors Second Book of Offices*), I felt that it was necessary to look into this strange and eccentric kind of planning.

I succeeded in tracking down the originators of this astonishing approach to office planning and before long managed to assemble enough information to put together an article: "Clearing the Mystery of the Office Landscape" for *Interiors* magazine in January 1968. This article, which was to become a chapter in my 1969 book, was the first full exposure of the idea of open planning in the U.S. and became a basic reference in the controversies about the approach that have continued until the present. Open planning is a departure from familiar norms so drastic that it generates controversy. It offers promises of advantages so significant that any office planning project must include some consideration of whether this new approach deserves some serious consideration. "Should we use open planning?" is a serious question that can only be dealt with in the light of reasonable knowledge of what open planning is and what its record of success (or failure) has been.

There is a growing literature of commentary on this approach to office design and a growing body of examples of installations in use for substantial periods of time. There is not, however, as yet, any significant body of writing that tries to clarify the actual *process* of open planning in any detail. The practitioners of this kind of planning are vocal in presenting its advantages, but tend to be reserved in describing the process, hinting, in many cases, that certain techniques are involved that are too complex for general understanding or that are, perhaps, simply trade secrets that require that the expert in question be employed so that he can make his special knowledge available.

In the course of collecting material for publication, I found that I had become a kind of ad hoc expert on the subject of office landscape, and so found myself involved in a number of planning projects that were developing with this approach as a basis. Eventually, I had clients who asked me to plan offices using this method or not, as might be best. I was led to develop criteria for decisions about the use of open planning and when this approach seemed best, to plan for them using the method that my own analysis of landscape techniques generated.

This book is addressed to any office planner, interior designer, architect, or other planning professional who is interested in becoming knowledgeable about landscape planning, who is prepared to have an open mind about its applicability, and who wants to be able to use this approach in a reasonable way wherever it may be appropriate. I am not interested in selling this approach as a universal solution to all office problems, but I believe that any intelligent planner will recognize that it can have significant applicability. I am also anxious to avoid any suggestion of a mystique involving difficult and mysterious techniques, not readily available or perhaps beyond the understanding of the average professional.

It is true that open plan methods suggest the use of mathematical techniques—possibly techniques that are well adapted to computer processing. As a result, the practitioners of open planning tend to suggest that this approach *must* be tied to use of data processing involving complex and highly specialized programming and methodological steps not readily accessible to understanding by the typical designer or client. Without questioning the possible usefulness of computer-related techniques, it is the intention here to explain the methods of open planning in terms that can be dealt with entirely on a pencil-and-paper level, at least in connection with projects of modest size. The need to resort to the computer arises when complex method is applied to large projects in which the management of the vast masses of data and their manipulation gets beyond the scale of pad-and-pencil dealing. What needs to be done and how it can best be done is, in such large projects, only different in magnitude from what is involved in more modest projects. The approaches described here in terms that can be understood by anyone are the same as those which, when projects are sufficiently large, become the basis for data processing techniques.

Anyone involved in an office planning project should be aware of the developments discussed in this book. The detailed discussion of step-by-step processing of a typical project is offered as background information for understanding of open planning, but is also intended as a specific outline for processing a project in accordance with this approach. The bases for decision about whether this approach is right for a given project are discussed quite fully, and there is no intention to urge that this is the only approach or even the best approach for *every* project. Indeed, deciding about *when* to use open planning is probably the most important issue discussed here. Given the decision to take this direction, the methods outlined here are applicable, but there is no question that each planner, designer, or planning team will find that certain variations on the routines suggested will be advantageous.

My aim is to be specific, not vague, so that anyone who follows the steps set forth here will find it practical and easy to manage a project effectively according to the open planning techniques that have become well accepted. At the same time, the reader is encouraged to notice the range of alternatives that are discussed and to recognize that there is no *one* perfect way of planning. Every planner must, in the end, find his or her own method which may even change from one project to the next, and may constantly develop in accordance with new insights that surface with each new project.

At this time it is hardly possible for anyone to insist that open planning is totally unworkable. With hundreds of projects in continuing daily use (some for as long as 18 years) and with *no* histories of abandonment or reconstruction on conventional lines, it is surely clear that open planning does *work* at least at some level of practicality. It is still possible to debate whether it is or is not the *best* way of planning offices in general or of planning any one, particular office. Intelligent debate must be based on knowledge, and it is the intention of this book to provide full knowledge of this approach—knowledge sufficient to make the formation of sound decisions possible.

What Is Open Planning?

1

A New System

The term "open planning" has become the usual English language designation for a way of laying out office space without using partitions. As it is usually used (and as it is used in this book), it refers to a rather specific way of doing such planning, not just to the use of unpartitioned space. For many years there have been some offices without partitions—one thinks of the clerical pools of insurance companies' headquarters or the platform area of a typical bank—but the literal openness of these older offices does not qualify them for the description "open plan" in the new and specific sense.

The new open plan is based on a closely reasoned theory that suggests that partitioning is, in almost all cases, not only unnecessary in offices, but detrimental to ideal office functioning. This applies not only to clerical or general office uses, but also to office space for managerial and executive personnel that until recently would have certainly been provided with private office accommodation. In settling for the term "open planning," several other terms are being put aside. These alternatives need to be defined to avoid some semantic confusions that often clutter discussion of this subject.

Office Landscape

The curious term "office landscape" is often used for open planning. It is a translation of the German term *"Bürolandschaft,"* which was coined by the first open planners when the idea first surfaced in the late 1950s. It makes reference to openness (the out-of-doors is, above all, open) and was probably further suggested by the extensive use of plants in the first (and most subsequent) open offices. It probably also refers to the highly irregular arrangements of furniture that were characteristic of those first landscaped offices. Because the originators of office landscape were extremely specific about the details of their method, it seems reasonable to confine the term to examples of their work or at least to work that follows their methods and policies very closely.

In this book, office landscape, then, will mean only one, very special form of open planning: that done by its originators or their immediate followers (or imitators). Office landscape is one kind of open planning. Open planning that departs from the originators' approach (fully discussed in the following chapter) is often called landscape, but is not really correctly described by that term.

Action Office

Another new concept in office design has emerged concurrently with *Bürolandschaft*. This is an approach that centers on the needs of the individual office worker and the furniture and equipment that will best serve work processes. "Action Office" is the name given by Robert Propst and his client furniture manufacturing company, Herman Miller, Inc., to a group of office furniture components developed on the basis of Propst's research in this area. Many furniture systems have appeared in imitation of Action Office, but strictly speaking the term applies only to the originator's products. Propst did not, originally, intend his furniture for use in any specific kind of planning. In fact, when he was developing his ideas, open planning had not yet emerged and it was his expectation that Action Office furniture would be used in conventional offices

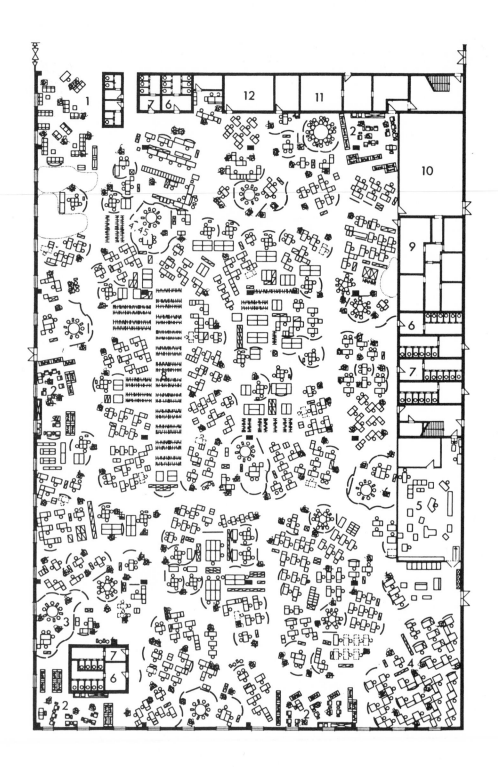

Above: A typical office landscape plan from a project in Germany planned by the Quickborner Team: GEG-Versand, Kamen, 1963-1964. Opposite page top: An American open plan without fixed partitions, but geometrically ordered. Weyerhaeuser Co. Headquarters, Tacoma, Wash., 1971; designed by Skidmore, Owings & Merrill, architects; Sydney Rogers Associates, space planners. Opposite page bottom: Action Office furniture as developed by Robert Propst for Herman Miller, Inc., 1964.

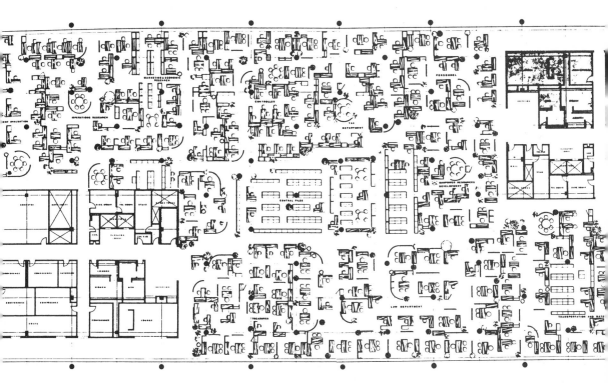

which were then the only offices in use. By an interesting coincidence, however, Action Office furniture turned out to be quite suitable to open plan offices— indeed, it seemed to offer solutions to some of the problems that open planning introduces. As Propst became aware of open planning, he modified and extended his approach to make Action Office particularly suitable for use in such plans.

Since both Action Office and open planning are new approaches, still somewhat experimental and even controversial, it is natural that they appeal to the same kinds of planners and users. Their relationship is, therefore, a natural one although not in any way a necessary one. It is not surprising, however, that some confusion has developed in terminology. Visitors who may inspect an open plan office equipped with Action Office furniture (or one of its imitations) may assume that all open planning is dependent on such furniture or may assume that this furniture can only be used in open planning. Neither of these assumptions is correct. In fact, use of Action Office will almost certainly modify planning in a way that leads away from the original *Bürolandschaft* concept. An open plan office *may* be equipped with Action Office furniture, but it may just as well not; Action Office furniture *may* be used in an open office, but it can also be used in conventional offices. In the end, the clearest definition of open planning is probably derived from comparison with the planning that we do not call open.

Conventional vs. Open

All offices before the late 1950s were planned (if they were planned at all) in a way that is now called "conventional." The profession of "office planner" developed in the use of this way of working and the great majority of existing offices are examples of it. It has its basis in the logic of architectural planning as it is practised in the design of buildings and in some assumptions that were probably made without seriously considering their validity. Office work, "desk work" as it is often called, is assumed to be a form of study. It involves reading and writing and occasional conversation, usually one-to-one person conversation conducted face to face or on the telephone. These are all activities that are often conducted at home and the ideal home setting for them is a room called a "study," or even a "den." The business office then emerges as a grouping of such studies or offices. Sizing of offices and their location is largely based on rank hierarchy and on the departmental make-up of the organization. The top executive will have the largest office in the best location, usually a corner of an upper floor. His secretary will have a guardian position, limiting access to the top man. Other executives will be close by in rooms carefully graded in size and other amenities to match the rank of the occupant.

Functional departments (accounting, sales, etc.) will often be remotely removed from the executives who direct them, but also will include private offices for their managers. Unpartitioned space is used for "pools" or "bull pens" in which a number of clerical workers sit in a large room, usually with the related managers in adjacent, glass-enclosed private spaces. Walls separate departments and differing pools within departments. Access is by a system of corridors that lead from entrances, stairs, elevators, and utilities to the individual offices.

The origins of this kind of planning date back to the days when large organizations were unusual and when the typical organization had only a few people as its office staff. The typical office building of the 1890s had a plan much like that of a hotel: small rooms were lined up along a window wall with an access corridor running the length of the building. Each room was an office, each to be rented individually. The typical tenant, a lawyer, broker, or salesman, occupied one private office. An assistant or secretary (then probably male and not designated by that term) might share the office or a part of it, cut off by a railing or glazed partition. Other assistants, bookkeepers or stenographers, as they were added to the organization, would be assigned other office rooms,

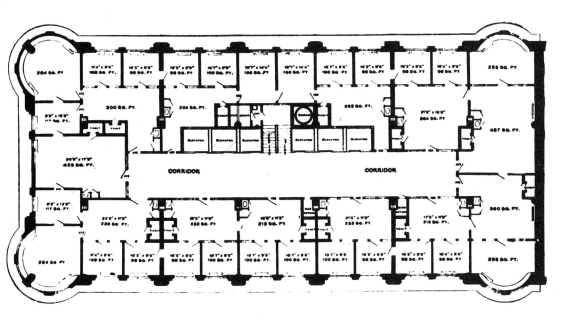

Plan of a typical older office building with individual office rooms constructed as part of the building and rented to any tenant. The Old Colony Building, Chicago, 1894, designed by Holabird & Roche, architects.

possibly adjacent, but if the adjacent rooms were occupied by other tenants, possibly at some distance up or down the hall or even in another building. This pattern can be traced still extant in many office buildings constructed even as late as the 1930s. Larger organizations simply rented a large number of office rooms (possibly including some that could be thrown together to make a larger general office or pool) and assigned them according to rank and departmental organization.

In Europe, where office buildings are often converted from those with other uses and where office space appears in older buildings to a greater extent than is true in America, the pattern of many small rooms along a corridor has remained prevalent. In the United States, particularly after World War II, a boom in construction of new office buildings produced a large stock of office space in which the availability of air conditioning and satisfactory artificial lighting has reduced dependence on windows and has so led away from the pattern of narrow bands of office space along outside walls. Instead, many modern office buildings offer large, open floors, similar to industrial or warehouse space. Conventional planning in such buildings still lines up private offices along window walls and then locates pools in the inner space, sometimes with a glimpse of window borrowed through the use of glass partitions.

In recent years the changing nature of office work has tended to reduce the activities that formerly were carried on in pool spaces. Computers have taken over many such tasks, while the desire of the office worker for increased dignity and status has generated an increasing pressure for privacy for every office worker. As a result, many modern conventional office plans offer private, or at least semiprivate, spaces for virtually everyone. A large proportion of the private spaces in such a plan are small and windowless. Indeed office plans of this type sometimes suggest the lower decks of older ocean liners where hundreds of second class passengers were packed into tiny windowless rooms lined up along labyrinthine corridors. First class passengers, like the office executives, had windowed rooms in suites on an upper deck.

At its best, this kind of conventional planning gives every member of an organization the kind of space in which he or she can best work and arranges these spaces in a logical way that makes it possible to find one's way about and that gives people who need to work together reasonable ease in getting back and forth to each others' work places. When skillfully designed, conventional offices can also be attractive and comfortable and can emphasize visually qualities of order, organization, and stability. Skilled planners, interior designers, and architects produced a steady flow of distinguished conventional projects during the 1950s and 1960s. One thinks of Skidmore, Owings, & Merrill's Connecticut General office (with the Knoll Planning Unit as interior designers) and Gerald Luss and Designs for Business's office for Time, Inc., as examples both outstanding and typical.

American Plan Offices

The curious term of "American plan office" has sometimes been used in Europe to describe offices in which the majority of workers sit in open pool spaces. Prior to World War II, when European offices followed the conventional multiroom pattern described above, European visitors observed with some surprise that many American offices were quite different. Large organizations such as the major mail-order houses, insurance companies, and certain governmental agencies would seat hundreds of clerical workers at desks arranged in neat rows in vast, unpartitioned spaces. Work handled under these circumstances was usually of a highly repetitive and routinized nature and the workers were considered as easily replaceable cogs in the organizational machine. It was this kind of open office that the visitor considered uniquely American, while also viewing it with alarm rather than admiration. Such offices, while quite literally open, are not examples of open planning in the sense in which the term is now used. They are, in fact, quite conventional, in that managerial personnel are given private spaces and executives are usually located in special areas remote from the vast, open pools. Layout of work places is based on formal organization and hierarchy as in any other conventional planning. The observed openness is only a reflection of a kind of work process in which the pool is dominant because of the high ratio of clerical to managerial workers.

Such offices are now diminishing in number as the kind of work which generated them becomes increasingly automated. An insurance company headquarters is now primarily a computer center where it was formerly a hive of clerical workers. The related service and managerial staff, when housed in conventional offices, occupies a high proportion of private or semiprivate spaces and the largest pools are likely to house only 10 or 12 workers, in contrast with the hundreds of the American plan spaces of the 1920s or 1930s.

The open planning under discussion in this book is an entirely different matter. It does indeed move away from the private office as the basic module of office space, but it is very different from the vast general office of the American plan. Aside from how it may appear, it is characterized by a somewhat different line of reasoning about what is expected of office space and by some new insights into what present and future office work really is. Clear understanding requires a review of how this new approach emerged, the ideas and aims of its originators, and how these ideas have developed over the last 20 years.

The American plan office of the 1920s—a vast, open space with desks in regular rows.

History

2

Origins in Germany

Many modern inventions and most new concepts that hardly qualify as inventions have origins lost in obscurity and confusion. Although open planning is more a concept than an invention, it has a clear and specific time and place of origin. In Germany around 1958 the Quickborner Team für Planung und Organisation, a management consulting group having its headquarters near Hamburg in the suburb of Quickborn (the source of the name), was led to pay some attention to the realities of office work space. The leaders of the group, brothers Eberhard and Wolfgang Schnelle, working to improve functional performance in offices, became aware that existing office layout often has a harmful effect on work performance and rarely does what it should to improve it. Although the Schnelles claimed no knowledge of planning principles, they made an alliance with Kurd Alsleben, a planning professional, and proceeded to develop and put into practice some drastically new ways of designing offices.

Shocking First Cases

Awareness of what the Schnelles were doing came to England and then to America through the publication of plans and photographs of projects that were completed in Germany in 1960-1962. The published plans departed from the concepts of conventional planning so drastically as to cause shock, laughter, outrage, and curiosity. Although the gradual spread of awareness has decreased the shock impact of these early open plans, anyone not familiar with the approach may still feel some of the amazement that these early plans generated. They seemed to violate every sensible rule of accepted planning practice. There were no private offices, no rooms at all, in fact, and desks and other equipment seemed to be strewn about totally without pattern or with patterns so erratic and varied as to be almost more disturbing than total randomness.

The familiar grid of geometric pattern and module which controlled most conventional planning was gone. Instead of elements lining up in logical order, every effort was made to avoid straight lines and consistently repeating patterns. It is not surprising that such an approach had its origins outside the architectural and planning professions. The traditions of order, pattern, and geometry are so strong in these professions even now (with origins extending back thousands of years) that this approach continues to seem threatening to many professionals. The Quickborner Team had no obligations to those traditions; its members were hardly aware that what they were doing would be so upsetting. They were solely concerned with their findings about how office organizations work and the ways in which physical setting influences office process. Their basic observation was simply that existing offices exerted strongly negative influences on office work processes.

Critique of the Conventional Office

It was the insistent presence of partitioning in office space that the Quickborner Team members focused on as the key to the physical inadequacies of the office. It is possible that European practice was more strikingly objectionable than the American norm. Examples cited in Quickborner Team publications show situa-

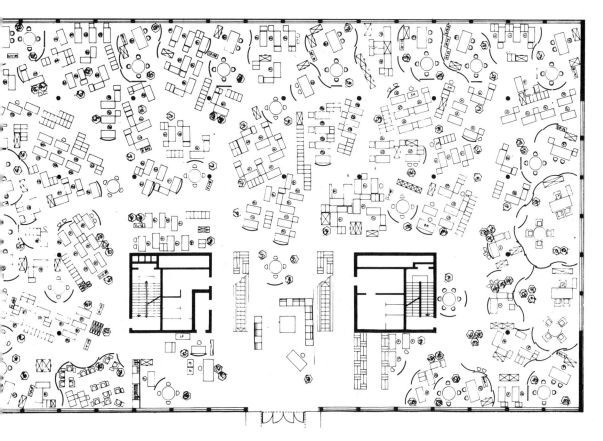

Plans such as this (Orenstein-Koppel, Dortmund-Dorsfeld, Quickborner Team, 1963) represent the first shocking glimpse of office landscape to come from Germany.

tions in which all offices are small, fixed rooms lined up along halls in small buildings. Departments are thus broken up in illogical ways with staff often distributed on various floors and even into several different buildings. Several people sharing a small office are in excessive contact, contact that may have no basis in work needs and that may well be a source of distraction and irritation. In other situations where work contact might be helpful, a wall or a distant separation may hamper communication.

Individual offices have, as a result of their sizes and locations, an ability to express rank and status. In many older office situations, events have brought about organizational change that makes it impossible to assign spaces in a way that expresses rank realistically and still places people in logical positions. Thus, one often finds a junior manager occupying a large and luxurious office or several people sharing such an office simply because it is impractical to use the space any other way. Even when office assignments are more logically related to rank, the visible expression of status may easily be excessive. Overawareness of ranking may interfere with work processes and focus attention on political office issues; striving for a larger office may become more significant than good work performance.

Even in a carefully planned conventional office in use as its planners intended, the fact that the planning has been based on the patterns defined by an organization chart will tend to make the plan unresponsive to real, everyday needs. The classic Christmas-tree-shaped organization chart suggests that each

A plan diagram from the Quickborner
Team illustrating the illogical circulation
patterns in a conventional European office layout.

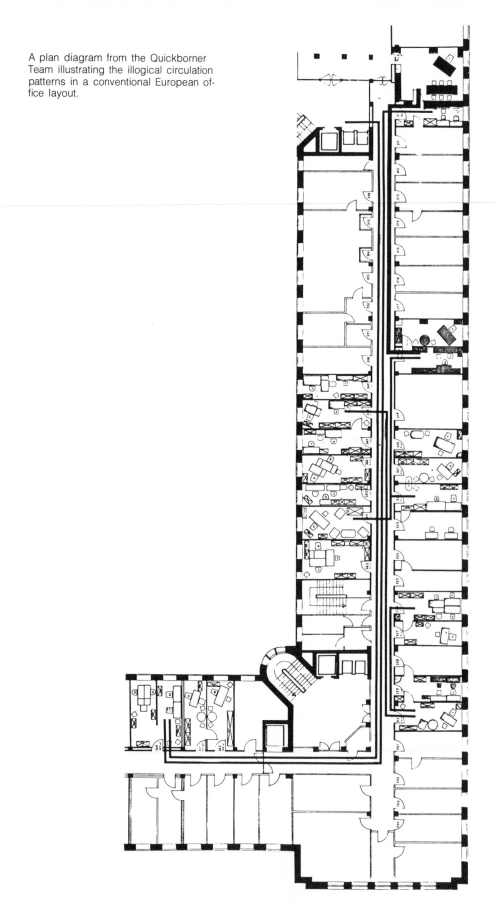

work group is an isolated (in a box) unit with connections (a thin line) only upward to superiors and downward to lower levels. It seems to define all communication as vertical, downward from boss to worker, upward to the executive level. Horizontal lines appear only near the top of the chart where they suggest links between department heads. Using this kind of chart as a guide, the planner is likely to group top executives together (in recognition of the few horizontal lines on the chart and because it is then easy to create a restricted high status environment for these people) and to group working departments together in areas that make each into a self-contained unit. Such planning isolates executives from the working groups that they are supposed to lead and makes of each department a separate and seemingly independent organization.

Logical and efficient work patterns usually do not and should not follow the rigidities of the organization chart. Sales may need direct contact with production or with accounting. Engineering may need information from sales and may have information for production. Advertising might benefit from contact with all these groups. Top management needs contact with every work group, but can easily become an isolated elite viewed by the majority of staff as a hostile and repressive officer class. In such a setting needed communication becomes slow and cumbersome, competition and rivalry thrive, and all the kinds of wastefulness and stupidity one associates with bureaucracy become commonplace.

The Quickborner Team was advocating development of horizontal communication as needed along functional lines and found that the built office environment tended to block or discourage such communication.

Their next major observation had to do with the modern need for rapid organizational change. Economic and technical developments occur at a frantic pace in modern life, and an organization's success is closely related to its ability to take account of such changes. Departmental reorganization can and should take place constantly if an organization is to avoid obsolescence. The conventional office tends to hamper such changes. Offices are built as if the pattern existing at the time of planning was expected to last forever, or at least for 10 to 20 years before a move or major remodeling is to be expected. It is common knowledge that the time from planning to completed construction is long enough to have produced significant change even before new office space is occupied. If it is already obsolescent by the time it is first occupied, it must surely become obsolete within a few years.

In most offices people are to be found occupying oddly inappropriate space because it is all that is available. Overflow space is found in odd and often remote locations to take care of unexpected expansion; half empty spaces elsewhere reflect unexpected staff reductions. People with unrelated jobs will share a space while a close-knit work group will be in dispersed locations simply because better suited spaces cannot be found. It is simply too difficult and too costly to constantly remodel in order to adjust to change. Instead, the staff must adjust as best it can to the existing conditions.

Movable partitioning has been in use for offices for many years. In practice, the partitions called movable could better be called "reusable" or even "salvageable." Moving a movable partition means relocating work staff elsewhere on a temporary basis, employing skilled workers to dismantle the installation and reassemble it in its new location, and in most cases, it also means ordering (and waiting for) extra parts and tolerating a leftover supply of unneeded ones since the new layout will not ordinarily be an exact duplicate of the old. Floors and ceiling will show scars where the partitions were; lighting and air conditioning will require readjustment. In the end, this means a fairly major construction project, almost as disruptive as total reconstruction. Also, movable partitions are often not used in the spaces they are most intended for;

there conventional construction is preferred for its look of permanence. In practice, movable partitions are rarely or never moved; since they are more costly than fixed construction, their value comes into serious question.

Still another Quickborner criticism of the conventional office has to do with its approach to storage problems. Everyone is assigned a massive desk plus, in many cases, a storage credenza providing many drawers and other storage spaces. File cabinets are everywhere. Some investigation of the use of this storage turns up drawers containing old overshoes and collections of dried-up ink bottles. Files are packed with copies of copies of notes confirming lunch appointments of bygone years. Everyone files a copy of every incoming paper and of every outgoing response and, in addition (especially with the help of the modern copying machine), sends copies of each paper to other staff who might be interested. These copies are also filed. To find a needed document becomes increasingly difficult as the mass of filed paper increases, while reduction of filed material becomes a hopeless task because of the sheer volume to be sorted through. Expensive file cabinets bulge and papers are heaped on top as space runs out. Too much storage space encourages the growth of personal agglomerations of material, most of it worthless and all of it difficult to retrieve.

To these functional criticisms, one can add the cramped and depressing atmosphere of the typical office, with its many cluttered spaces, its poor lighting and noise, its pretenses of status privacy, combined with conditions that make it all too easy to overhear undesired or inappropriate conversations. From the viewpoint of Quickborner consultants, improvement in organizational performance required a new attack on these problems leading to some kind of sweeping reform.

The average office, a scene of horrendous clutter.

A New Approach

It may well have been the absence of training and involvement with the interior design and architectural professions that made it possible for the Quickborner Team to make proposals that design professionals would never have suggested. Historic and modern professionally developed esthetic preferences have their bases in a desire for order—mathematical and geometric order of a kind that implies the exercise of authority based on logic. The order of the organization chart translates quite readily into this kind of designed order. The realities of life are often somewhat at odds with this order.

In any case, the Quickborner Team chose to undertake office planning in a way that had no preconceived expectations that any particular result would be most desirable. "Let us plan in a green field," they said, that is, in unrestricted open space with no known boundaries or limitations. Personnel would be placed at work stations grouped strictly according to working needs for easy communication. Needs for space and for privacy would be realistically evaluated and only what was really required for a particular kind of work would be provided. All furniture and privacy barriers would be made easily movable (not in the limited sense of the movable partition, but instantly movable by anyone). Storage would be reduced to the absolute minimum that daily work equipment really requires. Files would be consolidated in a truly efficient central file and only the papers needed on a given day would be out in light, open file carts or racks. Environmental conditions—lighting, air temperature and humidity, and acoustical conditions—would be made ideal throughout the office space so that rearrangement of equipment in any pattern anywhere would be unrestricted.

Translating this program into reality involved development of new methods in two different areas that might be called "environmental" and "organizational." The first has to do with specific building conditions—architectural realities that proved to be essential to making this new kind of office work. The second involved the development of a new basis for planning.

Environmental Requirements. The Quickborner Team developed a short list of specifics that characterize space to be used for office occupancy. These included:

Openness. The largest possible unrestricted office floors were desired. Columns, service cores, and other obstructions were to be eliminated or minimized.

Lighting. It would be uniformly excellent throughout the space.

Acoustics. Conditions would be made ideal by the provision of sufficient sound-absorbing materials to reduce noise to a low level, but one still well above the extreme quiet that makes every "pin drop" sound stand out. In practice this meant acoustic treatment of ceilings and the carpeting of all floors. Solid furniture masses and any surfaces that might reflect sound were to be minimized or eliminated.

Organizational Method. Having challenged the validity of conventional organizational charts and hierarchical rank as bases for planning, the Quickborner Team had to create an alternative approach. Their system was based on the following:

Communication survey. The *actual* patterns of communication within the real organization would be studied through the use of accurate records of the real communications that took place during a short but representative period of time. A log of all communications would be kept by every worker during this research period.

Interaction charts. The data elicited by this survey is used by the planners to generate charts which show as numerical values the density of contacts between every possible combination of individuals. People can be thus identified as parts of working groups whose composition may be quite different from anything that departmental organization would suggest.* The numerical charts can be converted to graphic charts which show sizes of empirically discovered work groups and the extent of their need for interaction.

Planning. It can now proceed with the placement in a central location of the work group with most communication with others. Surrounding it are the groups with which it has most contact. And then around that are placed additional groups with which *they* have contact, continuing in this way outward until the entire organization has been distributed in a way that makes the most active lines of communication shortest in physical length.

Participation. As diagrammatic plans are translated into real patterns of work stations, the expected users, or at least some representation of the users, are asked to discuss and criticize the proposed plans. Models can be used to show how work groups will be set up, and these models are made available for study and experimentation with alternatives.

Rules. So that this process will not become chaotic, certain planning principles are set down as rules, and it is understood that alternate proposals must take account of these rules. Consultants from the planning firm work with participating representatives of the user organization in explaining the rules and their application.

Revision. Once the space is occupied, it is the very essence of this approach that revision to take account of changing realities must be easy and possible. Free, ad hoc change is not to be encouraged, however. Instead, an established and organized system is set up through which needed change is identified, new plan layouts are generated, and the actual changes put into effect.

Early Landscapes
By 1961, 250 office personnel of Buch und Ton, a mail-order firm, were working in an office landscape at Gütersloh in Germany. By 1962 the offices of Krupp at Essen housing about 1,000 workers were in a new five-story building planned specifically to accommodate an office landscape installation. As these and then more and more projects settled into use and were photographed and published, the originally shocking and now familiar characteristics of the office landscape as developed by the Quickborner Team became clear. A large open space is carpeted throughout and equipped with a consistent ceiling system incorporating lighting, acoustical treatment, and air conditioning distribution. Across the open floor are arranged (seemingly strewn) the light table desks of office workers in clusters that relate to the daily work patterns of various groups. There are no partitions. Managers and executives occupy larger areas, close to the staff with which they are involved. Light, movable screens offer them some limited privacy and are also used to break up long vistas that might be unattractive. There are no file cabinets, only light, open file carts. Small lounge areas with kitchenettes are located so they are easily accessible to all the staff at any time. There are many live green plants in pots.

The aspects of this kind of office that generated the shock reactions had to do with two factors: the seeming random scramble nature of plan layout and the

*Planners and designers can easily visualize how, for example, an organization chart of a planning group might identify such units as partners, designers, draftspeople, interior designers, clerical and accounting while actual work process would usually involve a project team made up of people from each of these groups. Analagous situations exist in most office work.

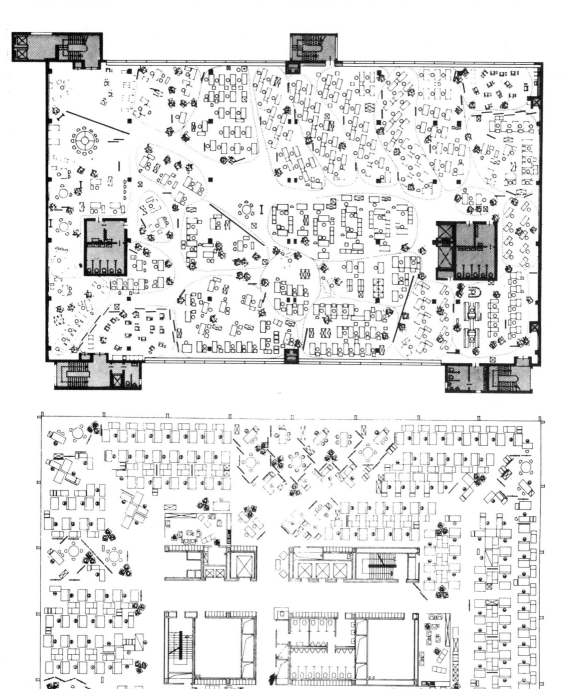

Top: Buch und Ton, Gütersloh, 1961. Above: Krupp, Essen, 1962.

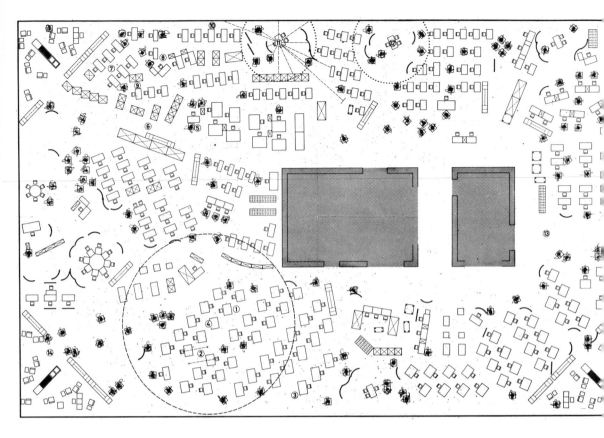

A Quickborner Team plan illustrating:

1. Keypunch machines staggered to permit easy service.
2. Desks staggered to avoid eye-to-eye confrontation.
3. Desks angled in relation to window wall.
4. (Circled) A subjective space that will be perceived as a unit.
5. Plants screening desks from circulation route.
6. A main circulation route.
7. A grouping of desks suggesting a working relationship.
8. Desks placed to avoid a sense of being watched.
9. File access space is shared by an aisle.
10. Desks placed to avoid shadows cast by window light.
11. Manager screened by plants, files, and screens.
12. Manager assigned extra space to symbolize status and increase sense of privacy.
13. Space for future expansion.
14. Rest area—one of three at corners.

After Frank Duffy in *Office Landscaping*, Anbar, 1966; with a plan from an Alsleben article in *Kommunikation*.

absence of partitioned private offices, even for top executives. The first issue caused shock among design professionals; the second among office personnel (especially on the management levels) who heard of office landscape as a possibility being considered for their own organization. The members of the Quickborner Team and the handful of others who respected what they were doing offered explanations of these matters as follows:

1. The seemingly random arrangements were not, in fact, random at all but resulted from the application of logical principles. Work groups (or subgroups) are clustered to help suggest their relationship. Different groups are deliberately oriented at shifted angles to help visually suggest their differentiation. Application of the rules (some of which are listed below) having to do with lines of sight and the possibilities of distraction often dictates work station positions and angles. Besides, the vast, unbroken areas need the irregularity to avoid the monotonous and dehumanizing effect of the endless rows of orderly desks in the American plan offices of the U.S.

2. The absence of private offices results from the desire to avoid the inflexibility that arises when fixed rooms are created, from the desire to make contact between manager and staff easy and informal, and from the need to reduce emphasis on rank and status. If private offices were introduced for managers or executives, this symbol of class distinction would make other workers dissatisfied with open situations and would reintroduce a struggle to gain a private cubicle as an outward sign of importance. It was clear (and continues to be repeatedly demonstrated) that landscape offices are best received by their users when the top people present share open space.

Practical objections to the effect that some people *require* privacy because of their need for quiet or because of the sensitive and confidential nature of their conversations are refuted on several grounds. It is easy to observe that most private offices are not truly private; it is possible to hear through walls and doors are almost always left open. In fact, privacy comes about, where it exists, as a result of location and the nature of adjacent uses. An open work place can be screened by wise choices of adjacent spaces, just as easily as a walled one. Conversations cannot be clearly heard over any great distance in a space where there is a hum of background noise, as is easily demonstrated in restaurants where highly sensitive private conversations take place in the open. In the end, most demands for privacy really cover a desire to hide from contacts and from work. An effective manager finds that his performance is enhanced, not hampered, when he moves into well-planned open space.

Visitors to the landscape offices in Europe brought back reports that varied from enthusiastic to mildly skeptical. No reports were heard of blatant failures; no organization gave up an open installation to rebuild it with conventional partitioning. Inevitably there was a desire for experimentation with the new approach in the United States.

First American Landscapes

In 1967, a department of DuPont moved into an office landscape floor in an office building in Wilmington, Delaware. This was frankly treated as an experiment or test. It was an admirable test in some ways, but a flawed one in others. Identical floors in the same building were laid out in conventional fashion so that direct comparisons of costs, acceptance, and long-term flexibility were possible. The Quickborner Team itself was employed so that the planning process was in full compliance with the originators' ideas. However, several basic rules were violated. The space was smaller than the planners considered an ideal minimum; it housed only a particular department so that it was quite evident that higher

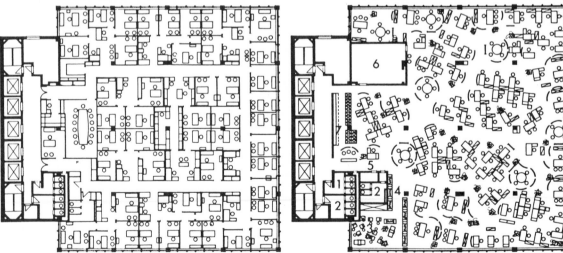

Top: The famous DuPont test space in Wilmington by the Quickborner Team in 1967.
Above: The plan of the DuPont test space compared with the plan of another floor in the same building that had conventional planning with partitions.

rank executives were not sharing in the test but watching it from their remote, conventional offices. In fact, the plan layout adopted placed the top-ranking manager on the floor in a location surrounded by fixed walls on three sides and so well screened on the fourth as to be, for all practical purposes, a disguised private office. Nevertheless, the test was widely observed, much visited, and published and discussed in any number of conferences and symposiums. The hoped-for dramatic yes or no conclusion never, however, emerged. Certainly the space worked in the sense that 76 people worked in it without protest or difficulty. Managers reported that, on balance, it was all right, although they might have preferred a bit more privacy! Other DuPont managers observed the space in use, but none opted to adopt the approach for their own divisions. Since DuPont gives its managers considerable autonomy in such matters, the space remained an isolated anomaly in the otherwise undistinguished hives of cubicles that house the corporation's vast number of office personnel.

A test space for Eastman Kodak housing 195 employees went into use in 1968. That example involved fewer departures from the Team's ideals and has, apparently, been more successful since the approach has been used in a number of other Kodak offices built since. Gradually more and more experimenters and accepters surfaced: Corning Glass, Ford Motor Company, John Hancock, the Port of New York Authority (the last so convinced on the basis of early trials as to adopt the approach for its own offices in the vast New York World Trade Center). Debate continued about the success of each project and about the merits of the (it was said) excessively rigid approach of the Quickborner Team. The famous rules were said to be "Germanic" and too restrictive.

Rules

A landscape project *had* to, according to the original doctrines of its developers, be planned in accordance with strict principles set forth, at one point, in a list of no less than 68 rules! The thought of even reading, let alone memorizing and following, 68 rules is clearly repellant to most planners and it is this rather authoritarian view of planning that has probably been the focus of much criticism of office landscape method even when the criticism is stated in other terms. Too many rules are called "Germanic" or even "fascist" in private, if not in public. Actually, the famous rules can be boiled down to a much shorter list of principles that still define what a true or pure example of office landscape is. These may be stated as follows:

1.   Office planning is not an exercise in esthetic or visual design. It is rather a problem in making realistic and practical provision for *actual* (as distinguished from supposed) work patterns. Any kind of visual design regarded as pleasant may be used in working out visible details.

2.   An office is a center for communication and information processing. Work relationships are not to be understood in terms of administrative departmental organization nor in terms of rank and status, but only as matters of communication flow.

3.   The real patterns of work communication should be the basis for physical planning. Those who need frequent communication must be placed close together. Groups that work as teams need to be placed in a way that makes the group a visibly identifiable unit.

4.   Discovering the real patterns of communication and the functioning work groups requires a survey of communications that can be converted into numerical values displayed on charts.

5.   Diagrams are developed from these charts (perhaps with the aid of compu-

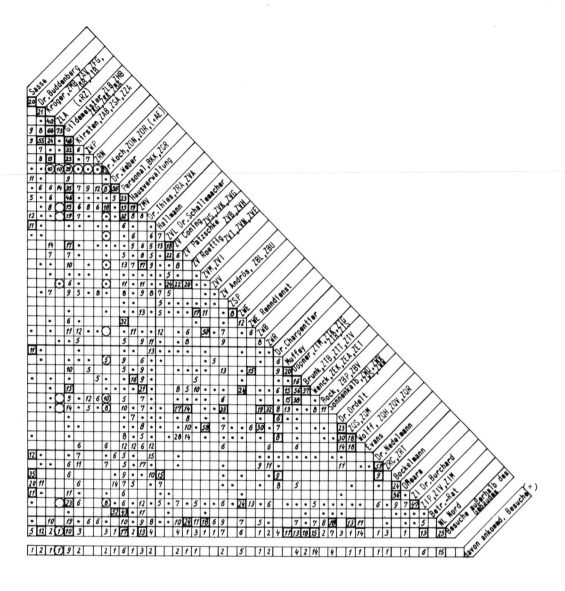

Above: A matrix chart from a Quickborner Team project. Opposite page: An interaction diagram based on the matrix. Boxes indicate working groups; lines show extent of interaction by varied weights.

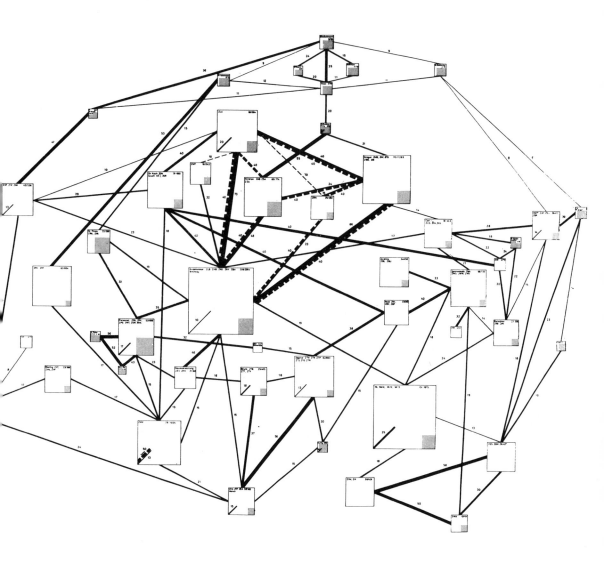

ter-based techniques) and the diagrams are manipulated to become idealized space plans. These are then fitted to actual available space to become proposed plan layouts.

6. The spaces best suited for this planning are large, open, and unencumbered. A minimum of 100 workers in one space is considered desirable.

7. Work stations are to be equipped with only the furniture actually required for work. Partitions are not to be used under any circumstances. Managers and executives may occupy larger spaces, possibly with more and more luxurious furniture, but their space must be part of the open area.

8. There should be a developed system of central filing so that an absolute minimum of paper and other stored material will remain in the work area. Only light, open file carts are used.

9. Noisy equipment is to be relocated in special areas isolated from the general space.

10.   Work stations are to be carefully arranged with consideration of sightlines from each workplace. Direct eye-to-eye confrontations is to be avoided, but possibility for some visual contact within each work group is to be maintained. Movable screens and green plants are used to cut off undesirable sight lines and to give visual privacy where it may be needed.

11.   Carpeting must be used throughout to aid noise control and general amenity.

12.   Acoustical conditions (with an ideal noise level) must be developed through the use of ceiling treatment, movable screens with acoustic surfaces, and the use of electronic background sound systems to provide a background sound level sufficient to mask intelligibility of conversations at a distance of about 18 ft (5.5 m) or more.

13.   Rigidly geometric patterns are to be avoided in all cases since their maintenance interferes with the flexibility in planning and replanning that is particularly desired. Clear circulation patterns are to be developed, but these should not be straight avenues. The presence of many plants and the irregularity of patterns are, of course, the basis for the term "landscape"—the pattern of parks, woods, or forests rather than those of a grid-iron street layout.

14.   Rest areas must be available in convenient locations for use by all staff members at their discretion.

As the number of office landscape installations in the United States (as well as in England, Holland, the Scandinavian countries, and other European locations) began to increase—although success was regularly reported—certain criticisms also surfaced. It was the very idea of so many rules that made planners without connection to the Quickborner Team resistant. It is not surprising, then, that various alternate approaches to the original *Bürolandschaft* began to surface and gain supporters.

An American Approach
Robert Propst, a researcher and inventor who had previously worked with such projects as a plastic heart valve and a mechanical timber harvesting machine, was led to an interest in furniture when he took up a post as a researcher for Herman Miller, Inc., in 1960. His own needs for practical office accommodations led him to probe the needs of the typical office worker and to develop some original approaches to office furniture problems. In 1964, Herman Miller introduced Propst's proposals under the name of "Action Office." The orientation was towards a highly individualized analysis of each office worker's needs. Standard desks, chairs, and files were replaced by units that combined work surfaces, storage, and seating (or standing) in components endlessly adjustable into differing configurations. Panels, standing free on feet, carried storage boxes, shelves, and work tops. Files were imbedded in work tables or hung on panels. Users could sit in chairs, but they could also stand or perch on a specially developed high stool.

The original Action Office was to be used in whatever office spaces the user might choose—probably most often in conventional partitioned private spaces. The timing of this system was, by chance, closely synchronized with the appearance of office landscape concepts in the U.S. Questions about suitable furniture for a landscape installation had been raised from the beginning of that concept; the Quickborner Team insisted that any ordinary, standard furniture would do as long as it was light and open—almost a contradictory set of requirements. Action Office furniture was light and open and the panels on which storage units were hung recalled the movable acoustic screens of landscape. In

Top: An Action Office work station. Courtesy Herman Miller, Inc. Above: Action Office in use in the Chicago offices of JFN Associates, space planners.

the minds of American planners, the two concepts were linked up. An open office, equipped with Action Office furniture, might be somewhat at odds with the theoretical bases of each, but it seemed to solve a number of problems that had been previously troublesome. Action Office was clearly more tolerant of the desire to provide storage at the individual workplace, and it tended to generate a more closed and private set of spaces because of its ubiquitous use of panels to support that storage. Although this might be contrary to landscape theory, it tended to please users who enjoyed the possibility of assembling highly personalized workplaces that seemed, in many cases, as private and as attractive as any private office of a conventional type.

Certain planning firms (notably, J.F.N., Inc., in New York and Chicago; now no longer in business) adopted Action Office and its principles with great enthusiasm, and open plan projects based more on this system than on the Quickborner Team concepts began to appear. Inevitably, imitations, more or less accurate, of the Action Office product group began to appear. Propst and Herman Miller have carried on a continuing developmental process in which the furniture system is improved and adjusted as user experience accumulates. Imitators follow along with imitations of each improvement as it appears. As a result, just as conventional office furniture has developed a certain degree of standardization among many manufacturers, there has come to be a new family of panel-attached furniture intended for use in open planning. It has its origins in Action Office, but includes a range of variants—some with certain unique features, some merely less expensive while basically imitative.

Use of Action Office and its followers has generated certain criticisms along with certain satisfactions. In American practice, the availability of more storage space, of unique, personalized work stations, and of a generally greater level of privacy seems to be well received. However, the complexity of such systems and the need to synthesize each work station on an individual basis can become a burden. The use of panels to support components often leads to more subdivision than is really desirable and can also be costly.

Further Alternatives

A number of furniture manufacturers not content to simply imitate have developed alternate approaches to open office furniture. In many cases these systems have been originated by office planners working on specific projects who have been dissatisfied with available products and have therefore designed or encouraged the design of new equipment systems. Typical examples would be the system called T.R.M., by its manufacturer, J. M. Eppinger, or the Stephens system developed by Knoll International. The former was developed by William Pulgram for use in a corporate headquarters for McDonalds Corp., the latter by Stephens on the request of designers at Skidmore, Owings, & Merrill for use in a corporate headquarters for the Weyerhaeuser Corp. in Seattle, Washington. In each case the direction taken has involved the development of work station units more massive and enclosed than Quickborner theory would encourage and less flexible and varied than Action Office would suggest. Openness is encouraged in each case, to the extent of omitting all conventional partitioning, but the spaces equipped with such furniture often seem quite similar to conventional private offices in spite of that fact.

Work station systems are proliferating, based on three primary directions:

1. Quickborner landscape concepts

2. Action Office related systems

3. Work stations based on enclosed furniture modules

Various combinations of these concepts are also being developed.

Top: TRM (for task response module) furniture as produced by Eppinger Furniture, Inc. Courtesy of the manufacturer. Above: Stephens System furniture from Knoll International as used at Weyerhaeuser headquarters. Photograph by Ezra Stoller/ESTO; courtesy Skidmore, Owings, & Merrill, architects.

Planners' Decisions

It is now necessary for the office planner, together with the client, to make several choices of a sort that would have seemed inexplicable only a few years ago. Diagrammed in a decision tree, these run as follows:

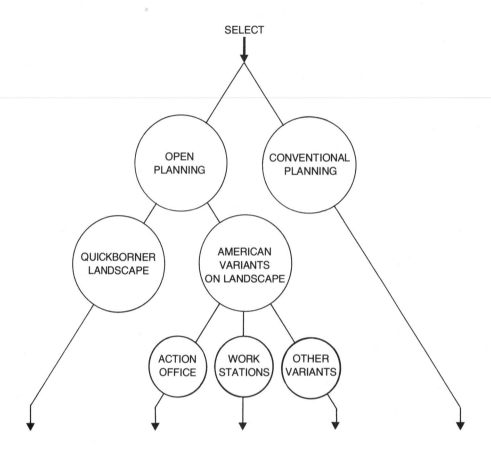

The need to make decisions about basic philosophy of planning at an early point in a project and about choice of equipment systems almost before planning has begun, is an unfamiliar and upsetting circumstance. There is still no escape from it. Once a project has proceeded to any extensive planning on either a conventional or an open plan basis, turning back and starting over becomes too time wasting and costly to consider. Planning in both modes simultaneously so that results can be compared has been tried in a few cases, as a kind of test, but it is unreasonably costly and is not certain to generate any clear-cut basis for decision even after both approaches have been extensively developed. Similarly, choosing furniture and equipment systems before planning has progressed to a detail level seems illogical, yet detailed planning can only be realistic if it is undertaken on the basis of a particular system. One can not change from an Action Office-based plan, for example, to adoption of a Stephens system installation without drastic replanning, almost equivalent to a fresh start. In contrast with the former process of planning according to a universally accepted approach (that we now call conventional) and then making furniture choices on the basis of competitive purchasing of one or more products chosen from well-standardized, almost identical product lines, the current situation is confusing and disturbing. There is no escape from these realities, however. In the era of the open plan, the planning process is different, more complex, but also more interesting than ever before.

How Projects Begin

3

Office planning projects may begin in a number of ways and the nature of the beginning can influence the success of a project. An illogical beginning *can* lead to a successful end result, but it may saddle the project with illogicality through to its conclusion.

Planning *should* start before any decisions about space acquisition are made. The preliminary part of the planning process will establish criteria for space selection or construction. All too often the planner is only introduced to the project after space has been rented or a building contract signed, with the result that the project is burdened from the start with limitations that are unnecessary and may be very troublesome.

Planning Beginnings

Projects usually originate one of the following ways, each with its own special set of advantages and problems.

Expansion.   The typical beginning of an office plan project involves the need to select or to construct new space. Expansion of an organization leads to overcrowding and/or illogical layout in its present space. A move to a new space offers a chance for better planning and may offer other advantages—for example, better location, consolidation with other parts of the organization—at the same time.

Working Relationships.   Another type of beginning involves organizational change that alters work relationships. This is a logical time for an all new planning approach and a move to a new location. It differs from a move predicated by expansion only in the fact that existing conditions are a less helpful guide to what will be best in the new situation. Even if the changes have been put into effect in an old facility on a makeshift basis, there will be a need for more imaginative thinking about how things could and should be.

Work Process.   A variant of the above which is very characteristic of current office operation is a drastic change, not in organization as such but in work process. Organizations that were based on "paper flow," the processing of forms passed from hand to hand, can change drastically almost overnight when such functions are taken over by computer processing. Kinds and numbers of workers and their relationships change drastically and the physical needs of the equipment itself can make an existing office obsolete.

New Organization.   The creation of a new organization sets up a different and magnified planning project. In this case it is not possible to rely on experience as a guide for planning the work process and staff. In the past, most organizations had tiny, ad hoc beginnings and only thought of office planning needs after substantial experience had been developed under informal circumstances. This is probably the best developmental process. But large modern organizations (corporate or governmental) do not hesitate to create a new department or agency, a branch in a new geographical location, on a large scale from the very beginning. Planning for such a future organization is made easier by the absence of habits and quirks that characterize existing work groups, but is made more difficult by the lack of information about real needs. Inevitably, such projects include the great possibility of error and so put a premium on planning that permits easy change to adjust to realities as they develop.

Making Use of the Concept. The very concept of open planning has given rise to new planning projects. Where open planning has been tried successfully in part of an organization, other departments or units will in many cases initiate replanning to make use of the concept. It is probably unusual for this to be the *sole* basis for a new office installation, but combined with other pressures (for example, crowding, poor or obsolete layout), it can be a strong pressure. By its nature it will establish the direction that planning will take.

Change of Plan in a Fixed Location. A variant on any of the above beginnings will arise when the same originating forces are present, but when for one reason or another, the facility is to remain in its present location. If a long lease has been taken on a certain space or a special building has been constructed for an organization, the existing space may saddle the project with less than ideal conditions. There is, however, at least some sense that the existing space has worked in the past to some degree and therefore some assurance that it will still work, probably even better after replanning. Renovation of existing space also involves the temporary but often upsetting problem of trying to carry on normal operations while it is in progress. This usually requires some complex plan for multiple relocations, doing construction work in phases, and making other adjustments that can involve extra cost, delay, and some loss of work efficiency.

One Thing Leads to Another. Any of the above beginnings can be reasonable and logical. A very common beginning, however, might be called the process of "one thing leads to another." Some little thing must be done—a door relocated, a partition put up or taken down. Preparing to do this leads to a realization that it will only create a new problem unless something further is done—several partitions moved about, perhaps. This leads to changes in lighting and air conditioning and a realization that the whole department or the whole floor really requires a new approach. Soon, an entire facility is being totally replanned. There is nothing inherently wrong with this way of backing into a major planning effort project unless the modest start is allowed to limit the scope of the major planning necessary. This sometimes happens when control of the project remains in the hands of the originators who are not prepared to deal with the major project that their small beginning has spawned.

Planning Project Manager

However it may get under way, any planning project comes up, almost at once, against the key decisions that will in the end control the success or failure of the effort. These are the decisions about who will do the planning and how it will be done. Modern practice has generated a confusing variety of possibilities so that the making of sound decisions in this area has become quite complex, especially to organizational executives who may supervise a planning project only once in a business career. Since the various professionals who are available to handle office planning projects are consultants who work for a fee, each has self-interest motives in presenting himself or his organization as best qualified to do the job. Finding the ideal planner for a particular project is never easy. Two approaches often surface, neither of which has much prospect for success. It is probably worthwhile to explore the reasons for dismissing them.

Organizational Managers. The first involves the thought that often comes to managerial executives and even more often to proprietors of small businesses: "I'll do the planning myself." The manager who knows every detail of his needs and who may have had some experience in arranging minor renovations often is tempted to get out a pad and ruler and try planning. Unfortunately, do-it-yourself office planning like do-it-yourself medical treatment or legal advice is usually only effective when the problem is so minor that it could well be ignored. A modern office is a complex of systems that are difficult enough for professional planners to cope with. An amateur, dealing with the matter in addition to a normal work load, cannot realistically expect to handle anything more than the relocation of some furniture or, possibly, a partition or two. Even making a few suggestions in the form of sketched plans is often more of a handicap than a help to the professional who must process them. The energy would be better directed in listing the problems that need to be dealt with than in trying to find hasty solutions.

In-House Staff. The second possibility involves an existing department or individual who functions as the in-house facilities planner. Many organizations of substantial size have enough activity in the field of renovation and construction to make it logical and economical to employ a full-time person or group to carry on this kind of work. Such people have some or all of the qualifications to undertake a major office planning project. Why shouldn't they do the job? The most obvious answer is that the work they are now doing is occupying their time. If they are given a major project in addition, who will do their daily work?

A more subtle issue is that the in-house planner is too close to the project. He knows too much about what *cannot* be done, has too much involvement in organizational politics, and does not usually have high enough organizational rank to resist pressure from within the organization that may have to be resisted. In some large organizations, a facilities planning unit may develop sufficient professionalism to become, for all intents, an outside consulting firm. In that case, these reservations need not apply. Still, even when such a planning unit can handle projects of some size successfully, there remains some question about whether major projects—replanning the organizational headquarters, for instance—are not best dealt with by independent consultants.

Independent Consultants. The kinds of independent consultants prepared to deal with office planning have become quite varied. Many projects will require more than one of these professionals and the idea of team planning has some logic. If a team is to emerge, it is usually best to build it up one step at a time. As the first consultant involved tends to take on the role of leader, it is best to begin by carefully selecting the first individual or firm and to build whatever team is required with its consent and help.

Before a discussion of the kinds of professionals available, let us consider the phrase "individual or firm." Modern business tends to think in terms of organizations or firms and most office planning professionals have, in response, set up some kind of organization—in many cases a large organization for the design fields. Firms of 20 or 30 professionals are common and firms of hundreds are not unknown. Large projects often require many hands to process the mass of work involved and even a small project may require several, varied skills. Nevertheless, planning involves creativity in a way that demands individual leadership if a project is to be more than routine. Whatever the size of a planning firm, the key question is always who will be the effective leader, the developer of the problem solutions, the responsible chief? The assumption that the head of a design or planning organization will be that person is very much open to question, the more so the larger the organization involved. The head of a large design or planning firm may have been its chief designer at one time, but as the firm has grown, he or she usually becomes an executive administrator. There are exceptions, but only probing will discover the situation in any particular case. A project chief in a larger firm who is not its head may well be the ideal leader for a project, but it is important that such a person be identified and that his or her role be made a matter of clear understanding. Individuals can quit, be fired, or be transferred to other assignments, in some cases to the detriment of a particular project. In the end, it may be wiser to search for a suitable individual than for an ideal firm. That individual may be part of a firm (or its leader), but he or she may also be an independent practitioner. Can an individual handle a large project? As the size of a project increases, the need for support staff increases proportionally, but staffing is always available through association with a firm or on a free-lance basis. From the viewpoint of the client organization, it is best to locate the appropriate creative individual person, whether a member of a firm or an independent consultant, first, and then assemble the support staff or team that the total project will require as needs develop. If the total staff or team is available as part of one firm, that may be a convenience, but it may also limit freedom of choice to select other consultants.

Consulting Team Members

Whether firm or individual, the primary planning responsibility can be placed in the hands of several different types of professionals.

Architects. The training of an architect includes planning skills and full knowledge of all aspects of construction work. Many architects welcome assignments in office planning, particularly if new building or major building renovation is involved. Some architects prefer to concentrate on the aspects of projects that involve construction, and will suggest that office planning at the detailed levels be turned over to another specialist. In this case, it is important that the office planner be involved in the project from the beginning—possibly even before a final selection of an architect is made in order to avoid any chance of drifting into the troublesome error of planning a building (or space within a building) in advance of adequate study of the nature of the offices that are to be housed. In many cases where offices are to be housed in existing space (including newly rented space) the portion of the project that actually requires the skills of an architect may be minor. In such cases, although an architect may become the primary planner, it is also possible to retain an architect in a secondary, consulting role only to deal with the aspects of the project that specifically require those services either to meet legal requirements for the filing of plans or to deal with constructional problems that are beyond the scope of the other types of professionals discussed below.

Office Planners. The profession of office planner (also often called "space planner") developed from the need to deal with the problems posed by the modern office. The nature of this specialization makes an office planner the most obvious and logical choice as the key professional in charge of any office project; and an individual or firm with this orientation is usually needed at least as a consultant where the primary responsibility is with a different profession.

Interior Designers. The old profession or trade of "interior decoration" has, at least insofar as business projects are concerned, largely disappeared, and its place has been taken by interior designers who have developed a professional approach analogous to that of architects and engineers. These professionals (who in Europe are usually called "interior architects") provide the same planning and technical services that an architect provides in relation to total buildings, but restrict their work only to interiors. Office interiors are a logical part of such a practice. Space planning and interior design are often viewed as overlapping fields, handled in combination by one individual or firm.

Other Consultants. Regardless of which of these professions provides the key project planner, most projects will require in addition several (or possibly all) of the following specialists, either as members of a firm or as consultants:

1. Structural engineer (only when major construction is involved)

2. Mechanical engineer (to deal with plumbing, electrical and HVAC aspects of the project)

3. Lighting expert

4. Acoustical expert

5. Landscape architect (only when major landscaping is involved)

6. Art expert (only when a major art collection program is involved)

In many cases a planning team will also include one or more of the following, not in a creative role, but as a source of information and representation of their respective points of view:

7. Management expert

8. Employee (user) representative(s)

9. Staff facilities planner (to establish communication for continuing change as well as a maintenance program)

10. Client purchasing manager (where direct purchasing of furniture, etc., is contemplated)

11. Construction expert (to aid in placement of contracts and project supervision)

Many projects will involve only a few of these specialists, and only some are involved at any given stage in a project. There is no need for all team members to be present at every project meeting. Management representation is the final key element in decision making, and will be discussed subsequently.

Selecting the Head of the Planning Team
The process of selecting the individual or firm that will have primary planning responsibility requires consideration. Who will make this selection and on what basis? The client organization must designate an individual or a committee to consider possibilities and make a wise decision.

The controversial nature of open planning concepts further complicates the matter. Planners have been inclined after first exposure to the idea to take positions for or against this approach. Some with extensive involvement in conventional planning rejected the idea and made public statements to this effect so strongly that it made it almost impossible for them to retreat from their negative views. In contrast, some planners have been so closely associated with the development of the concept as to make it certain that they will approach any assignment in this way. Since at the beginning of a project, the appropriateness of the open plan is often in question, planners committed to a position pro or con confront the client organization with a difficult problem: the selection of a planner with such a commitment has the effect of making a key decision, perhaps the most important of decisions, before the first step of problem study has been taken.

Where a client organization is certain that open planning is *not* appropriate for it, selection of a planner with no enthusiasm for this approach may be reasonable. Where the project originates with a certainty that open planning is desired, specialists in this kind of layout alone may be the possible choice. In either case, however, and in all cases where no advance decision has been made, a planner who is willing to examine the individual circumstances of the particular project and to compare the merits of conventional and open planning with respect to that project is probably the most sensible choice.

Compatibility. The most satisfactory basis for the selection of a planner is returning to one with whom successful projects have been developed in the past. If such an on-going relationship does not exist, locating work done for other clients that is of the desired quality standard offers the most promise. This does not necessarily mean a similar project. A planner who has never dealt with an office project or an open planning project might still be an ideal choice if previous clients testify to a good relationship and if earlier projects are of high quality. Discovery of work of high quality can lead to conversations about the new project; such conversations will usually indicate the level of compatibility between client and planner. A high level of compatibility is probably the most important aspect of client-planner relationships. A newly established firm with little past work may still be an excellent choice if the necessary skills are present and if the compatibility of attitudes between client and planner suggest that a sound relationship can be developed as the project proceeds. Even outstanding projects for other clients are no guarantee of a satisfactory relationship (in fact, many outstanding projects mask a history of friction and dissatisfaction in the client-planner relationship).

Candidates. It is common practice for a client organization first to make up a list of three to five candidates for a planning assignment, choosing these on the basis of nominations by any interested or influential parties within the organization and then to conduct interviews with each in an effort to evaluate which might be best suited to the assignment. This method of proceeding has an air of orderliness and impartiality, and may lead to a good choice. It should be noted, however, that it tends to favor firms that present a good front and that have developed salesmanship skills to a high degree. Expertise in signing up clients is not always an index to expertise in executing a project. Finding the right planner for the job and going ahead without competitive interviews has a record of success at least as great as the multiple-interview approach.

Asking for written proposals from a number of firms or even for some rough ideas or approaches is usually both a waste of time and, at least in the latter case, a means of eliminating most ethical and competent planners. Comparing proposals is a confusing process that tells nothing about the quality of work to be anticipated. Rough ideas or free sketches are not available from ethical professionals, and would be meaningless in any case in advance of a full study of the project's requirements. Selection on the basis of social contacts, old school connections, and similar non-professional criteria are also, of course, not likely to lead to good results, although there may be some exceptions to this rule. In the end, the best route is to find someone who has done other good work and to explore the kind of relationship that could be developed in reference to the new project in question.

Other Team Members. Having made a choice of the key planner to lead and coordinate a project, it is best to add the other participants in the team as the need arises. A responsible coordinator will suggest what is needed at the proper time and will usually have some suggestions about whom to retain (but, if professional, will be ready to accept any competent alternatives).

It is necessary to note that two possible sources for planning help that are widely available have been omitted here for reasons that need explanation. These are office furniture dealers who provide a planning service and manufacturers of office furniture (and other office products such as partitioning). Good work has been done from time to time by planning services in either of these categories. The Knoll Planning Unit under Florence Knoll's direction was, for example, one of the best office planning services in practice for many years. But the fact that in each case the planner has a financial interest in the products that will be selected means that real professionalism is inhibited by the potential conflicts of interest that can arise. An office furniture manufacturer can hardly be expected to specify a competitor's products, even if they might be the best or the most economical. A dealer will be aware of what products offer the most profit. In many cases a manufacturer can supply valuable planning assistance in the use of a particular product line *after* it has been selected by an independent planner, and a dealer can be similarly helpful in supervising delivery and installation. Decision making must remain in the hands of an independent professional (and client) if the best purchasing decisions are to be assured.

Payment

A written proposal from the planner is the best way to work out the details of fees, schedules, and areas of responsibility that the project will involve. There is no single fee basis that the design professions have standardized, but several alternatives have become commonplace.

Time-Based Fee.   An agreed figure per hour or per day can be billed on the basis of timecard records. When working with an individual, a simple dollar figure can be arrived at. In the case of a firm, various staff members will probably require differing hourly rates. Usually a standard rate for each category of staff is established that is made up of the average salary cost for this category (averaging out differences based on seniority, etc.) plus a share of organizational overhead costs and a factor for anticipated profit. Different rates, for example, will usually be established for:

Principal or partner

Chief designer or planner

Senior designer or planner

Junior designer or planner

Draftsperson

and possibly several other such categories. A monthly bill shows the hours expended by each staff member and the resulting charge. This is probably the most logical and most professional basis for planning fees, but it often leads to some worry because it is open ended and gives no hint as to what the total fee might be.

Time-Based Fee with Fixed Maximum.   Once the scope of the project is established, the planner estimates the hours that will be required and converts this to a not-to-be-exceeded figure. Where all proceeds as expected, this works well, but in cases where a project changes or expands as it progresses or where many revisions are required, this basis often leads to disputes. A fixed maximum is only fair and workable when the work has been accurately defined in advance and remains unchanged. Otherwise, there must be provision for extras whenever the scope of the project increases.

Percentage of Cost of Work.   This has been the basis for most architects' fees for many years. In the case of office planning, this basis presents problems. Some aspects of the work (partitions, ceilings, lighting) may be provided in whole or in part by a building landlord. Existing furniture may be reused and so represent no cost. An economy approach may involve extra work for the planner, and yet will lead to a reduced fee. As a result, this basis is rarely used as a primary basis for fees. It survives, however, as a component in the following, not uncommon, compromise arrangement.

Area-Based Fee Plus Service Charge for Contracts and Purchases. This is an arrangement that attempts to solve the problems of the alternatives listed above. The planner receives a set dollar fee per square foot of space dealt with. In addition, there is a percentage fee (or commission) on all purchases or contracts that the planning firm handles. If existing furniture is used, for example, or if the client firm arranges for contracting and supervision or purchasing and expediting, no service fee accrues for these parts of the work. It should be noted that this arrangement often seems appealing to a client at the beginning of a project when the square foot planning fee seems modest and it is anticipated that the service fees will be minor. In practice, the service fees can become very large and result in a total larger than would result under a simple time-based arrangement.

Additional Costs. In all these arrangements out-of-pocket expenses (travel, prints, long-distance telephone calls, shipping costs, model-making) are billed at cost in addition to fees. The idea of travel expenses sometimes makes the choice of a local planner seem more attractive both to save travel costs and to encourage easy day-by-day contact. In practice, it is far more important to find an ideal planner for a project, wherever located, than to consider this limitation seriously. Small projects admittedly may be heavily burdened if there are large travel costs, but in projects of any substantial size, this becomes a trivial factor and close proximity is only significant for on-site supervision, an aspect of a project that can usually be provided by a local construction consultant or design firm.

Communication

As soon as a planner has been selected, the client organization must have some orderly structure for communication of needs and for decision making as questions arise and proposals are developed. The design of a new office creates a forum for the kind of maneuvering usually called "office politics": who will be located near whom, what will be the most prestigious locations and who will occupy them, what departments will expand and which will contract? All such issues raise possibilities for conflict of a kind that can generate delay and possibly lead to destructive results. The client organization needs to think about its pattern of information transfer and decision making at the earliest possible time, even before a planner is retained. Planners will usually have some suggestions about how these matters can best be handled, and the way of working finally selected is usually the result of consultation between the planner and the client organization.

Decision Making. Decision making by the client organization can be structured in the spectrum between two extremes: authoritarian and democratic. Most businesses and many nonbusiness organizations have in the past been primarily authoritarian in their structure and many remain so. Management is organized by rank, and decisions made at lower levels are subject to review, approval, or rejection at higher levels. In its most extreme form, this means that the top executive makes all decisions—a situation that makes work easy for the planner if he has access to that person. However, modern business management has become increasingly conscious of the limitations of the purely authoritarian way of working. The head of the company may not know the details of every situation, he may lack time and interest to explore them, and he may for political reasons be kept unaware of realities in a way that will handicap his judgment. Even his wise decisions may have less than total acceptance when those affected by them are excluded from any involvement in the processes of decision making.

The opposite extreme—totally democratic decision making—is attempted occasionally in community projects and in organizations with many equally ranking top executives (a law firm or group medical practice might be examples of the latter). This situation presents great difficulties to the planner since he or she is then confronted with too many decision makers, all with power of veto. Some plan which falls between those extremes is usually most workable. An example might involve a structure something like the following:

1.   A project coordinator for the client is selected. Someone with fairly high rank (not too easily overruled) but with enough time to handle the project is required. An Assistant to the President might be appropriate or a specially designated executive. In any case, this person should have authority to make all day-by-day decisions and should have access to top decision makers when needed to obtain approvals at major decision points or to resolve differences that may arise.

2.   A committee is developed (or possibly several committees in the case of complex projects) with members selected in some quasidemocratic fashion to represent the points of view of various functions and ranks present in the organization. In addition, certain specialists may be added to this group at appropriate times (such as maintenance or purchasing management and in-house planning personnel if they exist in the client organization). This committee helps to develop needed information and offers advice and suggestions as proposals are developed. It serves to establish communication between staff and planning functions and also carries information back to all staff members in a way that helps to build acceptance for the proposals that are finally put into effect.

3.   The professional planning staff is encouraged to collect information directly from management and staff, and managers should be consulted directly about proposals for their own areas of concern. Information collected in this way is subject to editing and review by the project coordinator.

4.   The highest level at which approval (or veto) will be given should be established in advance, and specific points at which such approvals are to be given need to be set. Will the project be approved by a department chief, a president, a chairman of the board, or the entire board of directors? Will there be just one such OK before proceeding with construction, or will there be several checkpoints along the way? A typical plan is as follows:

Approval of	To be given by
Selection of planner and each major consultant	President
Preliminary plans	President
Final detailed plans and budgets	President and Chairman of Board
Major contracts and appropriations for all purchases	Board of Directors

Small projects or even large projects in giant organizations may not need the attention of those top levels, but a comparable plan for reviews and approvals at appropriate levels is still needed. Organizations with different kinds of control structures will need to devise some similar way to structure decision making.

Poorly structured and disorderly decision making is one of the prime causes for unsatisfactory end results and for major cost overruns. All too often decisions are made and then reversed. Authority is moved from one individual or group to another, with the planner confronted with constantly changing or contradictory information and instructions. Such situations are usually symptoms of major managerial problems within an organization, and they are surprisingly common. A clearly ordered relationship with planner and consultants and a methodical way of progressing through a project are generally characteristic of a client organization with sound management.

Choosing the Planning System

With a planner selected and with a sound structure established for decision making and planner-client communication, the choice of whether to adopt open planning or not must be faced. Because for so many years all offices had been planned according to one well-established point of view (that we now call "conventional"), it often comes as a surprise and an irritation as well to find two fundamentally different approaches in direct competition. In some cases the decision may be easy. Perhaps the organization is already sold on open planning on the basis of good experience with previous installations or on the basis of a successful example in another organization. Perhaps a planner has been chosen who has elected to specialize in open planning. In most cases, however, it seems reasonable to make a study of the two kinds of planning in relation to the particular problem and arrive at a considered decision about which will really serve the best. If the planner involved is open minded and ready to admit that each type of planning can be useful in the situations to which it is best adapted, he or she can be expected to undertake some preliminary study of the situation in question. Special consulting skills from the fields of psychology and/or sociology may be helpful, but at least as yet there are no clear and well-validated tests that can be relied upon to generate certain answers.

Study Procedure.   A reasonable outline for study of an organization and for a resultant report on its character is as follows:

1. Considerations influencing a decision in favor of open planning:
   a. Is the nature of the office work strongly interactive; does it involve groups or teams in constant intercommunication? Ease of communication, visual and spoken, has been one of the prime virtues of the open plan concept. Conversely, if work done is mostly independent and solitary, if interruption is a major threat, this will argue in favor of a conventional approach.
   b. Is the organization subject to frequent change, growth, contraction, organizational change, and regrouping? Ease of change is a major open plan advantage. A static and changeless organization will not benefit from this characteristic of the open approach (although it will not necessarily find it disadvantageous). A study of how much change has taken place in the recent past and of how much change should have taken place (but did not because of practical considerations) is an index of how significant a factor this may be.
   c. What *realistic* needs for privacy, confidentiality, and even secrecy does the work involve? It should be noted that such needs are habitually overestimated in most situations. Private conversations can take place in a public restaurant, and the platform of a bank where delicate financial matters are discussed is traditionally open. Still, a doctor's consulting room may require a sense of privacy, if only for the comfort of the patient. Obviously, open planning is most serviceable where privacy is of minor importance.

2. Attitudinal considerations which influence the probable success of an open plan approach may be harder to identify because of a natural inclination to conceal or deny factors which are, in current managerial thinking, considered negative. Still, skillful probing can usually find:

a. Is the organization progressive, in the sense of welcoming new ideas and searching for changes that will be favorable? Or is it conservative in the sense of preferring to stay with established routines? The former direction is, obviously, far more likely to find open planning congenial.

b. Is the organization authoritarian and bureaucratic in its operations or is it inclined to be democratic, open, and flexible? Management may be inclined to deny bureaucratic inclinations even when they exist, but they can usually be discovered quite readily by an outside consultant. A high level of bureaucracy is not in itself a negative indicator of acceptability of open planning if the functions involved do not include wide ranges of rank and status. Where a wide range of rank and a bureaucratic structure are both present, there will be a tendency to reject and, in the end, to defeat the concepts of open planning even if they would be advantageous in a practical sense.

c. Is organizational style formal and rigid or informal, free, and open? This issue is closely linked with b above, but somewhat different. Open planning is not by its nature supportive of formality.

d. Are there existing attitudes, especially at high executive levels, overt or hidden, that oppose open planning? In spite of protestations of open-mindedness, many upper-rank managers harbor a deep distrust of a new concept that they suspect may undermine their position or expose hidden weaknesses. If a top executive in a decision-making role is, in fact, opposed to the concept, it has poor chances of success even if accepted and put into use. Most histories of failure of open plan installations involve upper levels of management that have open or secret objections to the concept and that permit its use only with a hidden intention to prove that "this will never work here." Where such attitudes exist and seem unshakable, open plan approaches are almost certain to be rejected or to prove unsatisfactory.

It should also be noted that open planning is, in some cases, regarded by management as advantageous for primarily economic reasons. It may be seen as a bargain approach. This attitude is a poor basis for acceptance, even though it may prove to be realistic. Open plan installations do not, in most cases, turn out to be less expensive than conventional approaches. Certainly the two ways of planning overlap in cost terms to such an extent that a given cost level can usually be achieved in either way. Savings accrue to open planning most strikingly when over a period of time many changes take place, but since such changes might simply not be possible with conventional planning, and therefore go unmade, it is hard to present this economy as a clear and certain saving. Moving toward open planning in an effort to save also has a tendency to create an atmosphere of skimping that can hurt the project's success and limit its acceptance as well. A realistic point of view about the economics of a project should be faced quite independently of any selection of open versus conventional plan approach.

Mixing Planning Systems.   Balanced consideration of the merits of open planning for any project will lead to the possibility of a compromise approach—a mixture of open and conventional planning, each used where it will serve best. Reasonable as this idea may sound, it involves great difficulties and has not worked out well in situations where it has been tried. It is certainly possible for a large organization with many office facilities in various locations to use open planning for some and conventional planning for others. As soon as offices are part of one organizational unit, however, splitting the planning approach becomes problematic, even when separate departments or divisions are involved. For example, in Avon Products Headquarters in New York, three floors of the International Division are housed in open plan space while the balance of the offices are conventional. The occupants of the open space consider themselves disadvantaged, in spite of the fact that there is no objective reason for this attitude.

The difficulties arise from several sources. Office staff is so strongly conditioned by the conventional use of private offices as an indication of rank and status as to find it difficult to escape from this interpretation. As a result, offering privacy on a basis of functional need sets up tensions between departments and between individuals and tends to create dissatisfaction among all those housed in open space. It might be supposed that this was indicative of real problems in the use of open planning were it not for the fact that comparable or identical groups feel no such dissatisfaction when all occupants of a facility are housed in open areas.

It is often proposed that top managers or an executive floor be given conventional privacy when open planning is used elsewhere, since the status line recognized in this way is a real one. This is, however, merely a reversion to a kind of conventional planning that has been used for many years in which managers occupy private offices while others work in a pool or bull-pen. In this situation rank and status are emphasized, leading to a conviction that upward movement in the organization requires capturing a private office, whether needed or not, while functional need for privacy is ignored. A manager working closely with a group may well be hampered because of occupying a private office, while a writer or researcher at a lower rank level will be denied the privacy that might have some functional value.

It develops then that a split plan almost certainly faces difficulties. If privacy is granted on a functional basis, this will be misinterpreted as indicating rank. If privacy is granted on a rank basis, many functional needs will be ignored, and the basic merits of open planning will be defeated—in fact conventional planning will simply have been reestablished. Practical experience has shown that open planning is most successful when *all* users of a space are assigned open work stations, especially those of the top rank present in a facility. A president, chairman, or director who occupies an open office himself asserts in a visible way his acceptance of the concept and support for it. This tends to generate support in the entire organization and eliminates any hint that high rank can only be sustained in a closed space. Real needs for enclosure are far less than usually supposed and in most cases are restricted to the isolation of noise-making machinery—a usage that cannot be easily interpreted as symbolizing status. Spaces for confidential conversations and sensitive conferences can be set aside (as discussed in Chapter 8), providing that these are not assigned to any individual but are available to all on the basis of need. Such spaces are in actuality needed far less than is usually supposed, and will show up as only very minor elements in an open installation.

It should also be noted that in cases where open and enclosed spaces have been mixed in one facility difficult visual problems result. Boxlike enclosures here and there in an open space, with corners cut off to provide executive offices or a wall with a single opening forming a barrier between open and closed territories become very prominent visually and are disturbing esthetically at the same time that they raise disturbing organizational questions. If open planning is good, why do *they* not want to use it? Why does he or she need to sit in a box while *we* are all out here? Why is a consistent approach being interrupted or limited in an arbitrary way? The visual equivalencies of these questions are as disturbing to the appearance of an office space as the questions themselves are to operational acceptance. In the end, it is best to accept the reality that if open planning will not be accepted by some part of an organization, it is best to revert to conventional planning throughout and forego whatever advantages the open approach has to offer.

Tests. Deprived of the attractive possibility of a compromise with each part of an organization or even (alarming thought) each individual making an independent decision in favor of open or conventional planning, it is natural to cast about for a test, an objective measure of some sort that will deliver an impersonal and reliable answer to the question of whether the open approach will really work for a particular installation. The idea of a paper test—a series of questions about an organization's staff, style, and work processes filled out by staff members or by impartial researchers which after some kind of statistical processing would deliver a clear answer of yes or no—is an attractive one. However, as yet no one seems to have even attempted the development of such a test, and it is obvious that development and validation would be an extremely difficult process that could take years—with its validation still probably a matter for debate.

What then of another kind of test, the actual construction of a sample space, a portion of a real working office laid out exactly as proposed for the project under development? Actual staff can move in and use the space for a period of time, and researchers can, through interviews and similar tests discover the level of satisfaction reached. This is an appealing idea and it has been tried in a number of cases. [The history of several such tests is reviewed in John Pile, *Interiors 3rd Book of Offices* (New York: Whitney Library of Design, 1976), pp. 46-52.] It is also, unfortunately, subject to many difficulties and usually either generates results that were obvious without the test or results that are ambiguous and that leave more questions unanswered than not.

Valid results in any comparison test depend on what researchers call "a double-blind, A-B test." This means that both subjects and testers must be unaware of which test material is A and which B, obviously an inherent impossibility in the case of testing office environments. Lacking this kind of objectivity, testers and subjects become involved in the desired results. Managers may have, even if they deny it, a preconceived desire to either prove the new concept valid or proee it worthless. Workers in the test space sense these intentions and tend to have their own leanings, often in favor of more private offices on the theory that they will lead to status elevation for all. In any case, the group assigned to work in the test space is, in the nature of things, unique and takes on special qualities as a result of that special assignment. The so-called Hawthorne effect, in which the very fact of being tested tends to generate special positive reactions, may apply, while the human tendency to resist whatever is new and unfamiliar generates a counterveiling negative reaction.

Time is needed to filter out any effects of shock that may result from relocation into new space, conventional or otherwise. How long can a test last while waiting for this to happen? How do the test space users integrate the attitudes of managers, who are still not committed to the concept being tested? What are they asked to react to: do they *like* the new space? Is their work performance improved? How is the latter value to be measured?

In the end, test space reactions seem most often to reflect the desires of management. When a test is undertaken in a spirit of "we doubt that this will work, but we will give it a try to prove that it will not," negative results are almost assured. If, however, the test takes place in a climate of "we believe that this is a good idea, and we want to have some supporting evidence," the desired positive reactions are usually forthcoming. In the latter case, a test space has a secondary usefulness in bringing out various detailed matters relating to equipment and planning which may suggest ways to improve the final installation. A rather small mock-up test of a few work stations will usually do as well in this respect as a major test involving dozens of participants.

In the end, it must be concluded that testing in a limited reality situation turns out to be a poor basis for decisions about the suitability of open planning for a particular organization or installation. Intelligent study by a disinterested management in cooperation with planners who have made no commitment to one or another planning approach is more likely to yield solid conclusions than elaborate tests based on questionable assumptions and necessarily imperfect research techniques. What open planning has to offer is no secret, and the possible problems it may present are fully visible. Confronting these realities will give a better basis for a sound decision in respect to any particular case than will a series of slow, costly, and in the end indecisive tests.

There is one more aid to decision making about the merits of open planning that has more usefulness. This is a comparison, on paper only, of plans developed in parallel in the open and conventional modes. Such a comparison is, unfortunately, easily rigged in favor of one or the other approach, but, if conducted in fairness, it makes it possible to look at comparative plans and comparative budgets. It offers no way to evaluate the level of satisfaction that will develop on a day-to-day basis, except insofar as this can be projected in the imagination by inspecting plans. Such a comparison may still make the decision between alternatives a difficult one where the merits of the two approaches are close to a balance, but in many cases it will make one approach so clearly superior as to make a decision almost inescapable.

Conclusion

However complex these issues may appear when discussed in detail, every project must pass through certain simple steps which must be clearly defined and dealt with at the outset and throughout the project.

1. Define the need for the project. Why should it be undertaken at all, and what is it to achieve?

2. Define the scope of the project. What will it include and exclude?

3. Establish a structure for project management. How will information be developed, and how will decisions be arrived at within the client's organization?

4. Select a planner or planning organization and establish a format for communication between the client organization and the planner.

5. Make a decision for or against open planning on the basis of a study of client needs and the known characteristics of open plan approaches.

6. Proceed with the project at the levels of detail discussed subsequently.

Preliminary Work

Time Schedules

Since every office project is developed and executed in real time, the logical first step is to plan the way in which the necessary steps will be fitted to the calendar. Specific dates set by external circumstances often establish a skeleton for schedule planning. A lease on existing space may expire at a known date or newly rented space may become available at a known (or, at least, predicted) time. New work groups may be scheduled to begin operation at a specific time or an organizational change may have been preprogrammed. All such situations place certain key target dates on a schedule which influences all planning.

Some situations may simply demand that certain things happen as soon as possible. It is usually best to translate this amorphous situation, with its pressure for haste, on the one hand, and its seeming tolerance for indefinite delay, on the other, into a set of sharply identified target dates. Whether established by external realities or by administrative decisions, target dates must be tested at once to determine if they are realistic. Setting an impossibly early completion date may seem to be a way to encourage speed, but it is more likely to be recognized as unrealistic and so be set aside as meaningless, leaving the project without a realizable time program. In most cases a schedule must begin with identification of known specifics (the current date is always available as the earliest possible start, even if no other times can be fixed) and can then proceed to desired targets against realistic estimates of time needed for each of the steps along the way from start to completion.

What the steps will be varies according to whether the project involves new building construction, a move into rental space in a new building, a move into an existing building, or renovation of existing space while it is occupied or temporarily vacated while work is in progress. Each kind of project will require a certain minimum, irreducible time, while extra time above the minimum will reduce stress and possible extra costs resulting from a crash program approach. It is also a fact, however, that too much time is not an asset. Circumstances change as time passes and planning done too far in advance will often have to be redone later to take account of changed circumstances.

Unfortunately, it is not possible to list the *right* timings for each kind of project; circumstances vary too widely and make it necessary to study specifics before a reasonable timetable can be established. Still, it is possible to note that certain minima are established by the fact that furniture and equipment usually require between 12 and 24 weeks for delivery from date of order. Allowing equal time for the planning process sets a minimum of 24 to 48 weeks for any project of substance. If construction work is involved for even modest renovation projects, 12 to 16 weeks is a reasonable minimum. If complete building construction is to be undertaken, something in the range of 1 to 2 years must be anticipated, with planning time allowed in advance. The long periods involved in building construction present special problems since the rapid pace of organizational change makes it impossible to plan in detail in advance with any hope that the completed space will be appropriate for the occupants at the time of move-in. Instead, construction must be planned on the basis of rather loose generalities and must allow flexibility for more precisely detailed planning closer to the time of actual occupancy.

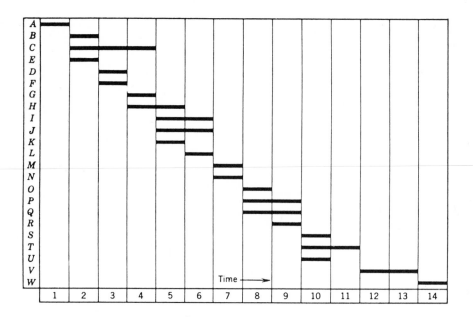

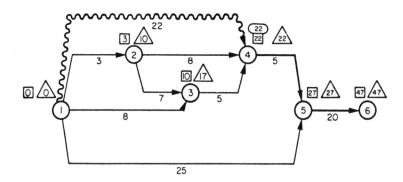

Top: Bar chart showing sequential steps of a typical project in relation to a time base. Dependencies between steps are not indicated in such a chart. Above: CPM (critical path method) chart. The network shows the relationship of steps; time is only indicated by numbers at start and finish points and in a separate, related schedule.

In all cases it is necessary to draw up a list of all the steps to be taken from project beginning to move-in, to assign realistic durations to each step, and to organize the steps in sequential relationships. Simple sequencing (first this, then that, etc., etc.) is not adequate since steps will in most cases overlap. Nevertheless, there will be relationships in which certain steps can only begin when preceding steps have reached key points. Light fixtures cannot be ordered until the required types and quantities are known; furniture cannot be selected until the general type of plan layout has been determined. The complexities of scheduling are best dealt with through the use of the technique called "critical path method" (CPM), a well-established, sophisticated system for charting time overlaps and step interdependencies in a way that relates desired target dates and key intermediate deadlines and deals with the possible usefulness of managed delays or accelerations in certain phases of a project. The critical path through a process chart that gives the method its name is simply the sequence of interdependent events and processes which establishes the shortest possible time in which a project can be completed. Other processes which can go on concurrently must fall into their proper places but are not "critical." It is not appropriate to review the details of CPM here,* and it is not always necessary to make use of its sophistication when simple projects are being scheduled, but some knowledge of its principles will be helpful in any effort to make up a realistic project schedule.

A standard or typical schedule is difficult to develop because projects differ so drastically in extent and character. In particular, projects that involve new building construction involve longer times, more steps, and more complex scheduling relationships than do projects using rental space or renovated existing space. The following listing of both events and processes suggests the items that might appear on a typical project schedule, although any particular actual project might involve other steps and might bypass some of those listed.

1. Retain planner or planning organization.

2. Establish project goals in general terms.

3. Develop characterization of organization on basis of observations and interviews.

4. Study comparison (as applicable) of newly built, rented, and renovated existing space.

5. Make census of personnel and special purpose space requirements with estimates of expansion needs.

6. Prepare general program of requirements.

7. Decide in favor of rental, renovated, or newly built space.

8. Select architectural and engineering professionals.

9. Establish building systems requirements (lighting, HVAC, floor loadings, acoustical requirements, etc.).

10. Prepare construction drawings and specifications.

11. Take bids and let construction contracts.

12. Survey user requirements and make communication interaction survey.

13. Prepare matrix charts and diagrammatic space utilization charts.

14. Prepare detailed layout plans.

* A. T. Armstrong-Wright, *Critical Path Method* (Longman, 1969) is an excellent brief introduction.

15. Obtain user reactions and revise layout plans as necessary.

16. Develop typical work station types incorporating individual user requirements to appropriate extent.

17. Select furniture and other equipment systems and individual furniture components. Develop decorative schemes.

18. Specify, take bids, and order furniture and equipment.

19. Lay out and order telephone and other communications equipment.

20. Supervise construction and installation. Organize move-in.

21. Organize needed revisions and adjustments.

These steps will inevitably overlap, and in many cases, certain ones may have to be repeated (with revision and adjustment) several times. The exact order of steps is in some cases optional, with different opinions current as to the best sequence. For example, selection of architectural and engineering professionals (step 8) could be step 1. Preparation of detailed layout plans (step 14) can be moved to follow step 7. Exact sequence is less important than scheduling that establishes the relationship of steps to be adhered to on a particular project. Administrative decisions to take steps out of logical sequence, to repeat steps unnecessarily, or to act without regard to an agreed-upon schedule tend to cause confusion and are wasteful of both time and money.

Some of the steps listed above are self-explanatory while others require detailed discussion.

Characterization of User Organization

In much conventional design work this step is carried out through a process of tacit understanding. The designers simply sense what is appropriate and generate proposals accordingly. But when dealing with the complexities of modern corporate and governmental organizations, it is usually best to attack this issue in a more explicit and open way. In addition to fulfilling a technical function, user organizations expect an office facility to express the character of the organization. This character can be an elusive matter made up of current realities, future plans and aspirations, and, quite possibly, contradictory elements representing differing aspects of a complex organization. "Characterization" is a process by which consultants outside the organization study all these issues through observations, interviews, survey of published materials, etc., and make an effort to generate a verbal statement of what the existing and intended character of the organization is and the general way in which this should be interpreted in the realities of the built facility.

Successful characterization is an extremely useful guide to design work and can greatly expedite development of proposals that are readily approved. Drafts of such a statement need to be reviewed with key managers and administrators until some agreement is reached between client and planners about the basiˉ for decision making that will govern the innumerable, small decisions that are to follow. It is, of course, easiest to characterize, in terms that a client organization can accept, an organization in which positive qualities are dominant. Is a firm progressive, lively, flexible, optimistic, and growing? If so, it is easy to say so and to find expression of those qualities through design. Actually, many organizations are narrow, stingy, paranoid, disorganized, and drifting toward decline and collapse. Designing for an organization in which all those ills are prominent would be a difficult (and unpleasant) task in any case, and expression of such negative qualities would hardly be desirable. Still, any experienced designer or planner will confirm that designing for ideals that are too far from existing realities will result in a poor match between a user organization and a built facility.

While avoiding characterization in terms so negative that they would be unacceptable, it is still possible to place an organization along a scale between opposites such as:

Conservative	Experimental
Formal	Relaxed
Reserved	Open
Bureaucratic	Democratic
Serious	Cheerful

Such pairings tend to suggest implications of "good" versus "bad"; few managers want to call their organizations "bureaucratic" even when that is the reality. It takes some assurance to agree that "conservative, formal, and reserved" might be a favorable description of a certain kind of organization—a Swiss bank, for example. If managers insist on characterization in terms seen as good, even when these are inaccurate, it is probably best to avoid presenting dichotomies in an obvious way. Instead, an alphabetical list of terms might be used with a rating scale for how well these apply (not at all, slightly, moderately, quite, very). One planning organization uses such a list that begins:

Aggressive
Adaptable
Calm
Cheerful
Cold
Colorful
Conventional
Dependent
Economical
Efficient . . .

Using such a checklist leads to a scoring that suggests an organization's character profile quite clearly. It is particularly revealing when scores are developed separately for upper management, other staff, and outsider observers. Such a study of perceived reality taken together with discussion of desired reality can form the basis for a characterization that will be a realistic and useful guide to those working on the planning project. It is far easier to work toward explicit and clearly stated goals than to grope toward vague and ill-defined objectives.

Space Requirements

In contrast with the rather general nature of characterization, this step is concerned with assembling more precise information about what the new space is to contain. This process will usually proceed through several steps involved with increasingly complete detail.

Early on, there will be a need for a numerical estimate of total space requirements, possibly even before the project is defined as such. Is there enough space for needs in the reasonably foreseeable future in the present space? If not, how much space will be required in a newly rented or built facility? Several ways of estimating space needs are available, and it is generally wise to use each in turn. If similar results are generated, these can then be accepted with some confidence. Here are the three methods:

1. Existing space with adjustment factor. This is a somewhat crude approach

suitable to a preliminary consideration of needs. The space currently occupied is totaled and a simple percentage adjustment is made to allow for expected expansion (or contraction) and relief of any existing overcrowding. Upper level managers can usually make such an estimate with fair accuracy and the rough square footage figure generated will serve for feasibility studies dealing with the merits of renovation, new rental, or new construction.

2. Existing space modified by detailed adjustments estimated at departmental levels. The rough figure generated by the first method (present space plus 30 percent, for example) can be checked and made more precise by breaking down space requirements into departmental or work group needs. Each administrative unit is asked to review its present situation and develop specifics as to needs for additional space (or reduced space) at present and in the near future. Needed or desired additional facilities (more storage, more conference space,for example) are also tallied as are space estimates for any new work units that are expected to appear during the life of the new facility. The resulting totals may be somewhat inflated because of the tendency for middle managers to overestimate needs and to present hopes or wishes as requirements. Still, if carefully edited by upper level managers, such figures are likely to be more precise and therefore more reliable than the very general estimates of method 1.

3. Space requirements at levels of both the individual work group and summary totals. A listing is made of every individual who will work in the new space. Each is then identified with a space need based on the nature of work and factors of rank or status. This is usually done through the use of a table of standard area requirements regarded as appropriate for the kind of organization in question. Such a table might read:

Type	Function	Area in sq ft (Sq m in parenthesis)
A	Top executive	500 (47)
B	Executive	400 (37)
C	Junior executive	250 (24)
D	Middle management	150 (14)
E	Secretarial/clerical	100 (9.5)
F	Minimum work station	50 (4.7)

The areas used above are typical, but larger or smaller figures may be selected for each category according to the individual organization's needs, desire for luxury, economy, etc.

In addition, functions not assigned to any person—conference areas, rest areas, files and storage spaces—are added department by department as are other general needs such as reception or display areas or dining facilities. Finally, an allowance for circulation space (usually 10 to 25 percent) is added to generate totals, broken down by department or work group. If the grand total is similar to that generated by methods 1 and 2, the results can be put to use with some confidence.

Preliminary Cost Estimates
Space requirement data are essential for development of the preliminary cost estimates generally needed for feasibility studies. Rental figures are readily available, and construction costs or costs of renovation, although varying greatly with location and from year to year, are usually available for a given time and place. Figures can thus be developed for comparison of costs among renovation, new

rental, and new construction. In making cost comparisons, it is important to be aware of two factors:

1. There is a tendency to underestimate new construction and renovation costs. These costs have a long history of rapid increase. Figures remembered from recent experience are likely to be obsolete, and present costs are likely to rise during the time when planning is in process. Estimators working for contractors and planning organizations are often overly optimistic out of a desire to encourage management to undertake the project under discussion.

2. There is a tendency to overemphasize the significance of first cost. The real cost of any facility over its life is an amortized first cost plus the continuing costs of operation and maintenance plus costs for changes and revisions. Recent and anticipated rises in energy costs have made many existing facilities built in the days of cheap energy surprisingly costly to operate.*

Anticipated costs must be studied in comparison with the more elusive factors, such as costs that result from inefficiencies, burdens from changes that are needed but are not made, morale factors resulting from an outmoded facility and similar values.

Although more precise cost estimates will become available as planning progresses, figures generated in the ways suggested usually form an adequate basis for deciding to proceed with a particular project.

Data Collection

The simple census of personnel and rough estimates of area needs that suffice for early decision making are too general for use as a basis for detailed planning. Much more specific data is required, but it must be determined exactly *how* detailed and specific data collection should be. In the past it was customary to ask each department head or manager to prepare a listing of the needs of his staff. Often an office manager would assemble all such information, edit it as he thought best, and pass it on to planners as an authoritative program. It has become obvious that this approach tends to perpetuate shortcomings and il-logicalities of existing situations. The alternative that has been developed by the pioneers of office landscape and by the developers of Action Office (working quite independently) has been survey techniques that go to the individual office worker and survey his or her needs on a person-by-person basis. The surveys of the Quickborner Team focus on communication patterns and ask each worker to compile a detailed log of every communication, written, telephoned, or face to face, which takes place during a typical, sample period of time. Action Office planners are more focused on physical equipment needs. They ask a detailed account of work process habits (sitting, standing, reading, talking) and of storage and display needs. Both kinds of data can be collected to develop an inclusive picture of the needs of each individual staff member.

Data collection at this level of detail generates a surprising quantity of information for an organization of any size. It is essential to use standardized forms of some kind that elicit the desired data and can be organized into some kind of standard format. Various survey forms have been developed (see illustrations on pages 59-63), but it often seems best to devise new forms for a particular project that are especially adapted to the unique qualities and needs of the organization in question.

In practice, person-by-person surveys often turn out to be excessively time consuming and generate masses of overdetailed data that are, in the end, impos-

* In a recent project involving an older building in a cold climate, air conditioning had been required throughout the year in a computer room while oil heat was used in other offices. In the course of renovation it was possible to rearrange HVAC so that computer heat is used in other offices and outside air cools the computer. Such savings will pay for the entire renovation in a short time.

sible to use in any fully constructive way. In a small organization where each person is a significant, individual factor, person-by-person data may be valuable. In larger organizations, particularly at clerical and other junior levels, individual workers are in fact (however unpleasant it may be to admit) interchangeable units whose personal requirements do not differ in any important way from person to person. Turnover among employees is often rapid and changes of work assignments mandated by management often move individual workers from place to place. In such situations, efforts to identify personal needs and work patterns are often pointless; even if such data might be significant, they change so rapidly that they become obsolete before they can be put to use. Recognition of these realities means that it is rarely practical to conduct data collection surveys on a fully individual basis in organizations of any size.

The individual workplace is still a unit of significance, but the aim is generally to study its requirements on an individual, personal basis only at personnel levels where such individualization is significant. At more junior levels, it is more practical to study needs of an average or typical workplace. This can usually be done effectively by observing existing facilities, discussing needs with the group manager, and then taking detailed requirements data from two or three selected typical members of the work group. Where there are a large number (anywhere from six or eight to hundreds) of clerks, typists, draftspeople, or bookkeepers all doing similar work, information collected from a small sample will serve to identify the requirements of all members of the group. Minor variations to suit special, personal requirements can usually be provided through flexible elements that are available as part of many modern office furniture systems.

In addition to workplace requirements, data must be collected on needed spaces for conferences and meetings, special equipment, storage, and files. Group managers are the usual sources for this information, but extensive editing may be necessary to avoid over- or underestimated needs. Existing facilities are usually regarded as a minimum even when it appears that some are underutilized. Estimates of future needs are often excessive, with demands for special spaces and equipment based more on wishes than on real requirements. The planners' own observations, tempered by the views of the next higher level of management, are usually used to adjust such lists of requirements.

Filing and storage requirements particularly need a careful review. There is a tendency in most organizations to file many copies of everything forever, and the resulting space and equipment needs tend to grow beyond all reason. A planned move to new space creates a natural time for a general review of filing practices. The Quickborner Team's insistence on central filing has already been discussed. Other possibilities include adoption of an increased use of microfilm and related techniques, removal of archival records to remote storage locations, and at the very minimum a sweeping clean-out of existing files. It is an unusual organization that cannot reduce its existing files by 50 percent by simply cleaning out obsolete and trivial material and that filed in duplicate. Specialized consultants are available to assist in the aspects of office systems that generate paper and lead to its retention, and their services are often very useful in dealing with this problem.

At the same time that other equipment needs are being surveyed, it is convenient to collect data on needed communications equipment and business machines. In these areas also, existing equipment is the usual starting point, but it is extremely worthwhile to use the projected move as a stimulus for study of possible changes and improvements. Telephone and intercommunication systems are constantly being improved, and study of them, possibly through another specialized consultant, will often reveal better ways of dealing with communication equipment. Similarly, existing office machines are often outmoded and may

ACTION OFFICE
INTERVIEW FORM #1   PRESENT OFFICE PATTERNS

NAME:_____ TITLE:_____ DATE:_____
COMPANY OR ORGANIZATION: _____
JOB DESCRIPTION:_____AGE:_____

A. PHYSICAL PATTERNS: **B.   TASK PATTERNS:**
Hours per week spent in own   Of actual time in office, what   Do you desire
office   _____   % of 100 is spent: more or less
Of actual time in office, what   1.   Reading   _____   _____
% of 100 is spent: 2.   Conference   _____   _____
1. Seated   _____   3.   Telephone   _____   _____
2. Standing   _____   4.   Writing   _____   _____
3. Walking   _____   5.   Dictating   _____   _____
4. Resting   _____   6.   Come and Go   _____   _____
                                 7.   Personal   _____   _____
                                 8.   Other   _____   _____

C. ACTIVITY BREAKDOWN:
1. Travel: Times per day in and out of office_____
             Total number of trips per year_____
             -one day or less_____   2-5 days_____   1-3 weeks_____
             -on regular basis_____   on irregular basis_____
             -carry more than 1 lb per trip_____Dictaphone_____

2. Paper work: Number of letters, memos, copies received per day_____
                 Number letters, memos, copies sent per day_____
                 Do individual paper tasks take longer than 4 hours_____;
                 longer than 1 day_____; longer than 1 week_____
                 Have you more than one paper project underway at once_____
                 Total estimated pages per week scanned_____; read_____
                 Time per day writing_____; dictating_____

3. Conference: No. meetings per day less than 5 min._____; over 5 min_____
                 Number planned meetings per day in own office_____
                 Number of associates in office per day_____
                 Number outside visitors per day_____
                 Number of sessions per day with secretary_____; total time_____

4. Telephone: Number of calls per day received_____; placed by you_____
                Do you refer to papers or drwgs_____; take notes_____; record_____

5. Information Retrieval and Filing: Time per day spent retrieving information_____;
                 with others involved_____; proportion of success_____%; time per day
                 spent classifying information_____; number of active folders in own
                 office_____; number of active files out of own office_____

First of three pages of an interview form developed by Herman Miller, Inc. for use in
Action Office planning projects.

2.0

Of time spent in office per week, how many hours are normally spent reading?

O 1-2   O 2-5   O 5-10   O 10-15   O 15-20   O Over 20

Your reading consists mainly of:

O Letters O Forms O Orders O Editing O Periodicals O Technical Material
O Reports O Memos O Drawings O Proposals O Sorting-Collating O Other:_____

What percent of time, when reading, are you:

_____% Sitting   _____% Standing

3.0

Of time spent in office per week, how many hours are normally spent writing?

O 1-2   O 2-5   O 5-10   O 10-15   O 15-20   O Over 20

Your writing consists mainly of:

O Reports O Letters O Proposals O Forms O Drafting O Specifications
O Memos O Orders O Charting O Letters O Creative Material O Other:_____

What percent of time, when writing, are you:

_____% Sitting   _____% Standing

4.0

Of time spent in office per week, how many hours are normally spent:

	2-5	5-10	10-15	15-20
Dictating	O	O	O	O
Intercom	O	O	O	O
Phone Calls				
Received	O	O	O	O
Placed	O	O	O	O

What percent of the time, doing the above tasks, are you:

_____% Sitting   _____% Standing   _____% Walking

Do you place your own calls?   Reasons for refusing calls —

YES   NO   O Meetings
O   O Local   O Lack of Information
O   O Long Distance   O Involved in conference
O   O Do you refer to large papers or drawings? O Involved in task — not to be disturbed
O   O Do you take notes?
O   O Do you ever refuse calls?

A more detailed form for analyzing the nature of the individual office worker's task patterns (two pages from an eight-page booklet).

5.0 VISITORS FROM OWN ORGANIZATION
In own area:

No. of Visitors per Meeting	No. Meetings per Week	Length of Meeting			
		1-5 m.	5-15 m.	30 m.-1 hr.	1-3 hrs.
1	_____	O	O	O	O
2-3	_____	O	O	O	O
4-6	_____	O	O	O	O
6+	_____	O	O	O	O

In conference space:

No. of Visitors per Meeting	No. Meetings per Week	Length of Meeting			
		1-5 m.	5-15 m.	30 m.-1 hr.	1-3 hrs.
1	_____	O	O	O	O
2-3	_____	O	O	O	O
4-6	_____	O	O	O	O
6+	_____	O	O	O	O

In other individual's work area:

No. of Visitors per Meeting	No. Meetings per Week	Length of Meeting			
		1-5 m.	5-15 m	30 m.-1 hr.	1-3 hrs.
1	_____	O	O	O	O
2-3	_____	O	O	O	O
4-6	_____	O	O	O	O
6+	_____	O	O	O	O

What do you do when meeting with fellow workers:

O Work with Documents   O Work with Drawings or Charts

O General Discussion   O Other_____

What percentage of time are you meeting with:

O Superiors   _____%   O Fellow Co-Workers   _____%

O Subordinates   _____%   TOTAL   100%

Average number of times you are in and out of your work space per day:

O 1-5   O 5-10   O 10-15   O Over 15

Material taken to meetings:

O Charts   O Drawings

O Reports   O Project Folders

O Others   _____

This survey is designed to help us determine the working relationships between all individuals and their best physical locations. Please describe all personal contacts with individuals, other than those which take place by telephone or mail.

INSTRUCTIONS:

1. Print the first initial and last name in the space provided on the answer sheet for each individual with whom you have contact.

2. Read each question and indicate your choice by making a solid black mark in the appropriate box opposite each individual that you contact. Use pencil only and completely erase all mistakes.

QUESTIONS:

I. For those individuals you have personal contact with, is the majority of the contact:

    A. Originated by you
    or
    B. Received by you

II. How do you rate the importance of the contact between you and this individual?

    A. Very Great
    B. Great

III. How do you rate the frequency of the contact between you and this individual?

    A. Several Times Daily
    B. Once Daily

IV. Which of the following best describes the reason for the contact between you and this individual?

    A. Required by me to perform my function or activity.
    B. Required by another to perform his function or activity.
    C. Because we are part of the same Group or Department.
    D. A result of physical proximity irrespective of any of the above.

A form for recording intercommunication as a basis for analysis of adjacency requirements.
Courtesy JFN Associates.

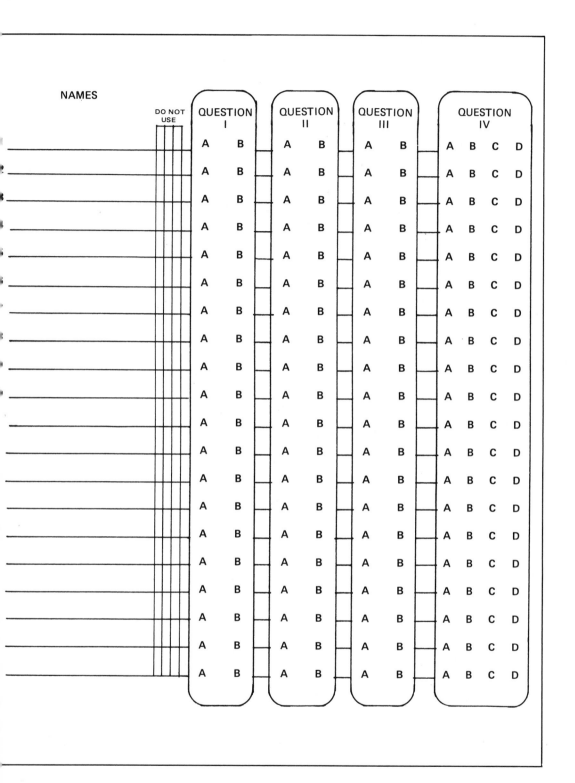

NAMES

well be replaced by newly developed alternatives. In particular, computer-related equipment will often be suitable for making basic changes in many office processes—if not at once, then possibly in the near future. Records now on paper may be suited to storage in a computer memory, while access which is now a matter of shuffling papers can become available through a data terminal (a typewriter-type printout unit) or CRT unit (cathode ray tube, a televisionlike screen).

All such data on detailed requirements need to be assembled into well-organized forms comprising a total index of requirements. This material needs to be reviewed, edited, and approved at appropriate levels of management so that it can become a basis for detailed planning without risk of frequent or unexpected revision. In addition to the hard data which can be organized into forms descriptive of specific workplaces and facilities, soft data is also needed about the less formal realities of management style, the needs and desires for particular atmospheres, and similar intangible but nonetheless real matters. Interviews of a loosely structured sort in which managers and representative staff members describe their perception of needs to the planning staff and answer questions as they come up seem to be the most useful methods for developing this information. It is inevitable that managers' views should carry weight in rough proportion to their rank in an organization, but every effort should be made to cross-check these views against those of other staff members at both lower and higher rank levels. Managers are often less aware than they realize of events in the areas they supervise, and their personal notions and prejudices are often put forth as accepted fact. A skilled data collector regards all information supplied as somewhat suspect until verified and is particularly alert to information and suggestions which might have the effect of furthering individual and private interests, such as status elevation.

Interaction Studies

Once reliable data are available on staff to be accommodated and space and equipment needs, the remaining key information concerns who (or what) should be placed where—what needs to be close together and what can be far apart. New ways of dealing with these issues are at the heart of the theory of open planning, and although they also have application to conventional planning, they must be regarded as essential if open planning is to deliver the advantages it promises. The basic, vital principle is the idea that physical nearness between staff members should be made proportional, insofar as possible, to the amount of communication that takes place between them. On the face of it this seems such a reasonable, common-sense notion that conventional planners often insist that this has always been done in all good planning. However, observation of most existing offices shows that this is only erratically the case. Other values—such as the desire to place higher ranks near windows, to group staff in accordance with formal departmental lines of command, to offer privacy to a maximum possible degree—often outweigh logical patterns of placement on the basis of working need.

It was the insistence of the Quickborner Team that these habits could only be broken through the use of surveys of *actual* patterns that could be expressed in coldly statistical terms that led to the use of the typical interaction or communication survey. When conducted as its originators suggest, it means that a form is provided to each member of an organization on which a tally can be made of each communication (or interaction) that takes place during a stated period of time; two weeks is a suggested period. Written communications, telephone calls, and face-to-face conversations are noted by type and name of the corresponding communicator. People from outside the facility are noted separately. The content, duration, and importance of the communication are ignored, on the theory that only the simple fact that the communication took place is significant. In

OFFICE LANDSCAPE PLANNING TEAM	TALLY SHEET	NAME:		GROUP NO.	
Internal Tally Group	GRP NO.	Telephone · Calls Received	TTL	VISITS RECEIVED	TTL
Kohl and Secretary	1				
Cohen and Secretary	2				
Bushman and Secretary	3				
Saxe	4				
Thorpe	5				
Alton	6				
Owen	7				
Porter and Secretary	8				
Raynor	9				
Ullman	10				
Verney and Secretary	11				
Ward	12				

External Tally Group	GRP NO.	Telephone Calls Made & Received	TTL	Visits Made	TTL	RECEIVED	TTL
Other Statistical Personnel Located in Baltimore	31						
Other Statistical Personnel Located Outside Baltimore	32						
Other Departments Located at King Street	33						
Other Departments NOT at King Street	34						
Outside Contacts (Vendors, Customers, etc)	35						

A tally form for logging communications. Each person keeps such a tally to record communications with every other person (or unit) in the total organization.

practice, even the Quickborner Team seems to have found it unnecessary to extract this level of detail from *all* members of a staff. Clearly known groups are treated as individuals and their communications are tallied as a unit sum. Collection of data by every individual helps in recognizing and forming work groups, but once recognized the individual totals are simply added. This mass of data is the basis for the charts and diagrams used in planning that will be discussed in the following chapter. Before discussing these steps, however, some review of this type of communication survey is called for.

The process just described and the uses made of the accumulated data are subject to several criticisms which lead to modified approaches. Every planner must work out his own view about how such material should be developed and used—a view that may change from one project to another according to its scope and the character of the organization in question. Typical criticisms of communications studies and their use, with related comments, run as follows:

1. Inclusion of written and telephone communications in interaction surveys since these types of contact do not require physical closeness. The obvious comment is that these are only substitutes, more or less cumbersome, for direct, spoken contact that would be used instead if it were convenient. The inconveniences of telephone communication are well known (busy signal, no answer, interruption of on-going conversation or task, lack of visual signaling, etc.) and written communication tends to be slow and formal, and can easily be ignored by the recipient. Therefore, these kinds of contact are assumed to be inferior alternatives substituting for preferable direct contact.

2. Failure to evaluate importance of communication makes the survey data of questionable value. Since the only value sought is the fact of the contact, its importance is immaterial. The office must facilitate all communication that takes place there. To make trivial contacts cumbersome would make them more objectionable than they are—especially since they tend to be so frequent.

3. Physical closeness is not needed for good communication since telephone and writing are so widely used. The comments listed under 1 above apply to this criticism as well. Why should not direct communication be substituted if it can be made easily available?

4. Not all office work involves communication; some is solitary and independent. It is true researchers or writers may work alone at times, or even most of the time. These are unusual cases, however, and a communication survey will show these people to have little need to be close to anyone in particular and will lead to their being placed accordingly. Offices exist because of the need for most staff to be in touch; otherwise, office work could all be done at home with great savings in rent, commuting costs, etc.

5. While communication is a factor, other values are also important and are not adequately taken account of in communication studies. One must first ask what these other values are. Status display, impression made on visitors, esthetics? Even if given major importance, none of these values run counter to the desire to position workplaces in a way that makes needed communication easy.

6. Proximity is being overvalued in this approach. Face-to-face communication is available at the cost of a short (and possibly pleasant) walk even within a fairly large office facility. The logical extension of this view would call for a random plan that would assure the constant need for short (and long) walks. Nothing about a logical plan prevents taking walks, and occasional needs to visit a distant workplace will occur in any case. The aim is to avoid the necessity of too many such walks or, worse, skipping needed contacts because they are inconvenient.

As a practical matter, none of the issues discussed above invalidate the use of communications surveys. Many planners have found it practical to modify and simplify survey practice with no significant loss of usefulness in the following way:

Simplified Interaction Survey
Two simplifications can make an interaction survey much more rapid and can reduce the data generated to a quantity that is more readily comprehended and managed.

First, it is possible to make the unit studied in the survey any person or group known to act as a unit. The large number of individual people making up an organization is thus reduced to a much smaller number of units. In most organizations it quickly becomes clear that many groups, departments, sub-departments, or work teams are already correctly identified. Totaling the communications of members of such groups only reveals what is already known: that the level of communication within the group is so high that it should remain together. If certain individuals within groups are known to have extensive reasons for contact outside the group, those people should be made separate units for the purposes of the interaction study. It does not take research to discover that an executive and secretary form a unit which can be treated as one item rather than two. Similarly, a person working closely with several assistants may be treated as a group unit. A group or team manager will surely need to be part of the group he manages and can usually identify subgroups and their needs for interaction without anyone resorting to survey techniques. Some care must be taken to avoid making unfounded assumptions. An accounting department may seem to be one unit, but it may turn out to include subunits that have more contacts outside the department than within it. Only explicit inquiry will locate such situations if a complete, person-by-person survey is not undertaken.

The second available shortcut is to replace the numerical count of communications with a simple estimate of actual or needed communication. Each person or group considered as a unit in the survey is simply asked to indicate communication (or interaction) need on a scale such as:

0-None, 1-Rare, 2-Occasional, 3-Frequent, 4-Very Frequent, 5-Constant

There is always some possiblility of false information being generated either deliberately or through inaccurate recollection of events. And there are two checks on this possibility. The first is that each interaction is evaluated separately by two different sources: A estimates communication with B, B with A. In most cases these separate estimates will match or be within one step of matching. Where there is a serious discrepancy, both parties should be reinterviewed to shake out a realistic estimate. A second check is a review of the information the survey generates by appropriate management. Improbable values can be checked and corrected if necessary.

The form used in a simplified survey is illustrated on page 68. Each work group of the organization is listed, but top level executives are listed as individuals. "SWIFT" is one department (computer services), but five subgroups within it are shown separately. The last eight items listed are not work groups but facilities used by all (or a number of) groups. An item that might be added (regarded as not significant in this example) is "outside visitors." When used, this item relates to the need to be convenient to visitors' reception areas. The information generated in a survey of this modest scale is not difficult to deal with through pencil-and-paper records and handdrawn (or typed) reports and charts. Very large projects, especially when detailed surveys are made on an individual basis, may present problems in dealing with the mass of data accumulated.

Information Management

Information collected in informal ways is often recorded in scribbled notes on lined pads. As time passes, it becomes hard to retrieve and interpret it. Planning projects can have long durations, and it is important that records be kept in a way that does not depend on human memory to aid interpretation. A basic step is adoption of data recording forms of some standardized kind, together with routines for recording changes (updating information) that may develop. In large projects it is worthwhile to consider computer techniques for storing and managing this data. Information hand-entered into suitable forms can be converted to punch-card or other computer-readable forms. This makes it possible to store the

Dial Financial Corporation

from: M. Mazie:hn

date: July 12, 1973

to: T. Kelsay - 1-285
Business Development

subject:

Please indicate below on a scale of from 0 - 5 the frequency of interaction between your department and the other HO departments:

	0	1	2	3	4	5
Accounting				X		
Accounting Reports Department			X			
Administrative Services		?	X			
Branch Facilities/Purchasing				X		
Business Development						
Central Management	X					
Communications				X		
Executive						
E. Glazer		X				
L. Halsey				X		
E. Levitt		X				
R. Levitt			X			
M. Mazie				X+		
J. Peterson			X+			
D. Rawls			X			
T. Wahrer			X			
Financial			X			
Legal					X	
Personnel			X			
SWIFT – Branch Applications			X			
SWIFT – Customer Services		X				
SWIFT – HO Applications			X			
SWIFT – Operations Support		?	X			
SWIFT – Technical Support		X				
Auditorium			X			
Board Room			X			
Computer			X			
Library (Law)			X			
Lounges				X		
Mail Room				X		
MDI Room			X			
MT/ST					X	

0 – None
1 – Rarely
2 – Occasionally
3 – Frequently
4 – Very frequently
5 – Constantly

Simplified interaction survey form. Each unit simply rates its level of interaction with each other unit on a 0 to 5 scale. Units, in this case, are departments or facilities (such as auditorium), except for individual executives who are listed by name in order to obtain an evaluation of each one's need for communication with each other and with each departmental unit or facility.

information in computer memories. It is then easy to retrieve information in any desired form—for example, a list of spaces or equipment requirements, totals of units of equipment, or areas for certain groups or purposes. It also makes the entry of revised information simple and easy. It is not necessary to have complex computer equipment at hand to use such techniques. Services are widely available on a time basis that will process data as needed using highly sophisticated equipment that the individual planner could not expect to own or lease. A leased data terminal with phone wire access to a remote computer can make access to data quick and convenient with only modest cost. Standard programs are available that deal with the data-handling needs of typical planning projects, and the modest amount of information involved in even large projects means that the costs of computer use (charged on a time basis) are usually small.

Designers and planners tend to be hesitant to consider involvement with computer techniques, fearing, perhaps, some loss of control or understanding. Experimentation with a small project (where computer capacities may well not be required) is often a good way to develop familiarity with methods which, with a large project, can be extremely helpful and almost necessary if the information is to be used effectively to generate desired results.

Interviews

In addition to data collection of the systematic kinds already described, it is good practice to conduct fact-seeking interviews with appropriate representatives of the organization who will occupy the newly planned space. The aim of interviews is to establish a less formal type of two-way communication between planner and user organization. It is customary to interview each top executive or manager who will occupy the new space and each work group head, whatever rank designation these people have. Top executives are usually able to describe general goals and objectives and long-range intentions, but are often less knowledgable than they realize about day-to-day operational realities. Middle managers and group chiefs may know almost too much about day-to-day problems, but be unaware of larger issues.

It is also good practice to conduct interviews with typical employees in each job category as a cross check on the information supplied by bosses. An individual worker is often aware of needs or problems in workplace situations that may never have been communicated to a department head or may have been brushed aside when communicated. Good interviewing requires experience and skill in recognizing what information is trivial and incidental while searching out important facts that may not surface in systematic surveys.

It is useful to have an interview form that establishes some structure for the procedure even if it is not always strictly followed. It helps to assure that important questions are not forgotten and provides a place for recording notes in an orderly way.

Such interviews also give a good opportunity to explain the planning methods that are being used, to open channels for future communication, and to answer questions that staff members often have about a project that cannot readily be presented under other circumstances. A new office project tends to arouse anxieties in many staff members who fear that results will be disadvantageous in some way (hurtful to their own or their group's interests) or who are just vaguely nervous about undefined future events. Airing of such concerns and discussion of the issues can lead to reassurance that may ease the planning process and aid in the acceptance of final results.

Expansion Needs

Since an office facility is usually expected to be serviceable for at least 10 years—or perhaps for a much longer time—there must be some consideration of changes that may occur over that period. The normally optimistic views of most organizations interpret this to mean expansion possibilities, although contraction is also an ever-present alternative. It is general practice to provide for expansion by building or renting excess space to match estimates of anticipated growth. Near-term (1- to 5-year) prospects can often be estimated with some precision. New products or activities are planned; new methods will lead to growth in one area, contraction in another; operations to be phased out will disappear. Longer term predictions are more difficult and will tend to be more general. It is common practice to project recent past experience forward, modifying the projection by expected specific events, and then to plan to accommodate certainties or near certainties for the next 2 years, projected probabilities for the next 5 years, and then to let events beyond that take care of themselves—perhaps through toleration of overcrowding, renting of extra space, or even making a move to new space sooner than might otherwise be expected.

In developing such estimates it is good practice to ask for predictions from each department or unit head as well as from his supervisor. The prediction might be on the basis of short (2-year), medium (5-year), and long (10-year) periods and on the basis of a three-level estimate of maximum, most probable, and minimum levels. This generates nine figures as follows:

	2 years	5 years	10 years
Maximum anticipated growth	_____	_____	_____
Most probable anticipated growth	_____	_____	_____
Minimum anticipated growth or possible reduction	_____	_____	_____

Students of the technique called "PERT" (Program Evaluation and Review Technique) will recognize the vertical dimension of this grid as the "three time estimate" shifted to this issue. The idea here is simply that natural inclinations toward optimism or pessimism can be sources of misleading estimates if they are not subjected to some self-evaluation and review. When a person is asked to give a maximum and a minimum prediction, most estimates of "most probable" given at the same time will become more realistic than if only one estimate had been requested. When these estimates are then reviewed and edited by the next level of management, it becomes reasonable to assume that a satisfactory level of accuracy—at least as high as the unpredictabilities of future events make possible—has been achieved. Random future events are likely to make some estimates turn out to be high or low in ways that often cancel out so that predictions are often more reliable than might be anticipated, at least in their total impact. The greater the flexibility of the planning approach used, the easier it is to adjust future use of space to actual needs as they appear.

Formal Reporting

As the preliminary work of characterization and data collection comes to completion, it is good practice to assemble the information collected into a written document—usually a report booklet that can be distributed to all interested parties. The contents of such a report might include:

1. Scope and purpose of the project

2. Time schedule

3. Statement of general character of the organization to be housed and of the particular facility to be planned

4. Survey of personnel to be accommodated

5. Space standards for categories of personnel

6. Listing of all other equipment and facilities to be included

7. Tabulation of complete space requirements with allowances for future expansion

8. Discussion of renovation, rental, and/or new construction with recommendations for an approach to take

9. Discussion of planning approach (conventional or open) and outline of detailed planning steps required to proceed with and complete the project

Such a report might include diagrams of typical workplace layouts (to aid in understanding area assignments) and diagrammatic plans of the space suggested for rental or construction. It should *not* include any actual plan proposals; these are part of a later step that should not be undertaken until this preliminary report has been distributed and accepted. Whether or not diagrams and illustrations of typical conventional and open plan schemes should be included depends on when and how decisions about this issue are to be made. If the decision is a foregone conclusion, there is no need to do more than refer to it. If the issue is likely to be a matter for discussion, debate, or even struggle, it may be desirable to give as much basic information about the alternatives as possible at this point. Those who will make or at least ratify the final decision need to be informed in good time so that they can become acquainted with the possible approaches, have their questions answered, and develop conclusions without excessive time pressure.

A formal report of this kind has a number of values. It forces the collection of data and estimates by a particular deadline, it makes this information available for review and correction, and once needed corrections have been made, it establishes a single reference that is approved and accepted as a basis for further steps. Managers often find decision making difficult and can delay and confuse a project by withholding decisions or making contradictory decisions on a piecemeal basis. Generating a single document that is either to be approved or corrected by a specific date is an effective technique for overcoming vacillation and hesitancy. Changes and revisions can still take place, but each must be made in some formal way with consequences in costs and delays taken into account.

Finally, within the planning organization, an accepted report can become an established reference for use by whatever number of people will ultimately be working on the project. Newly assigned planners can become acquainted with the project at any time during its production. Data that might otherwise be scattered in various notebooks and on note pads mislaid in various desk drawers is kept together in one visible and accessible place.

The Planning Process

5

Let us now assume that the decision in favor of open planning has been made. This may actually occur before the selection of a planner, before the preliminary steps described in the preceding chapter, or at the end of the preliminary work. If the decision is deferred further, however, while actual planning is in process, either there will be wasteful duplication of work as planning proceeds in parallel according to open plan *and* conventional practice, or there is the risk that work done will become obsolete and will have to be redone after the key decision is reached. If undertaken on a limited basis as an aid in otherwise difficult decision making, parallel planning in the two modes may have some usefulness, but every effort should be made to arrive at an early decision so that the duplication of process can be eliminated. In any case, the process described here applies to the open planning aspect of such a comparison as well as to the total planning of a project undertaken after a firm decision to pursue the open approach has been made.

Using Interaction Data

The data on communications and interaction that were collected as part of the preliminary process described in the preceding chapter is stored awaiting approval of the preliminary report and a go-ahead to proceed with open planning. The point of collecting this information in advance is simply that one survey dealing with both personnel and area requirements and interaction data is more efficient and rapid than two separate surveys, provided there is no long time lapse between survey and processing. If a long delay has made the data stale, a new interaction study should be undertaken. The time period from planning to realization is inevitably long enough to introduce some degree of obsolescence in the executed plans. It is important, however, to keep such time lapses to a minimum.

The aim of the planning process is now to use the interaction data as a tool in generating plans that will position all workplaces so as to minimize physical distances where communication is most frequent and assign more remote locations to those who have least contact. Doing this in situations where the number of units to be placed is very large can become so complex that computer techniques are required. Where the number of units is modest, pencil-and-paper manipulation may serve quite well. Many large projects can be simplified (by grouping work stations with known and obvious similarity of function) so that the number of units to be treated is greatly reduced. In any case, study of a project involving a small number of units demonstrates the principles involved and makes clear what the aims are in projects that may require computer techniques.

The first step in this process is to bring all the data on intercommunication to a common numerical basis which can be set out in chart form. The numbers which appear in the chart can be raw data, that is, the actual count of communications which occurred during the survey period, or it can be figures based on a simplified classification scale (such as never, seldom, occasionally, frequently, very frequently, constantly, which can be reduced to a 0 to 5 scale). The latter is usually preferred. The choice of the steps in the scale can be made by the survey participants, or if they provide raw data only, the assignment of scale value can be made as part of the planning process according to a systematic method of evaluating the raw data. If the raw data show communication frequencies for the survey period ranging from 0 to 400, for example, this can be reduced to a scale as follows:

Actual Frequency	Designated as	Numerical Scale Value
0-10	Never	0
11-80	Seldom	1
81-160	Occasional	2
161-240	Frequent	3
241-320	Very Frequent	4
321-400	Constant	5

For any pair of units surveyed (A's estimate of interaction with B, B's estimate of interaction with A), there are then two figures which represent each unit's report of its frequency (density) of communication with each other unit. If reporting was perfect, the two figures would always match. In practice there are often discrepancies which, when they are extreme, must be resolved through discussion as outlined in the preceding chapter. Where the discrepancy is small, it is usually satisfactory to simply average the two figures. If a scale of 0 to 5 has been used, adding the two figures reported places all interaction estimates on a scale from 0 to 10. These data can then be charted.

The Matrix Chart

The matrix chart has become widely used in any number of situations where it is desirable to display a large number of relationships between two sets of factors. For example, a small portion of the multiplication tables could be displayed in a matrix as follows:

		Multiplicand		
		6	7	8
Multiplier	3	18	21	24
	4	24	28	32
	5	30	35	40

This is a nonsymmetrical matrix in which each of the figures (quotients, in this case) displayed is the unique product of two factors which are not repeated in the horizontal and vertical factor lists.

A symmetrical matrix occurs when the same factors appear in the horizontal and vertical lists; each relationship is displayed twice except for the relations of identical factors which occur along a diagonal of the chart:

		Multiplicand		
		3	4	5
Multiplier	3	9	12	15
	4	12	16	20
	5	15	20	25

Since 3×4 is no different from 4×3, the redundant figures can be omitted and the same chart written:

	3	4	5
3	9	12	15
4		16	20
5			25

This is the format of the familiar road map chart which displays all the distances between any possible combination of towns shown in a triangular grid. In this case the diagonal line of symmetry can also be omitted since the distance from any town to itself will always be zero.

Mileages between:

	New York	Chicago	Los Angeles
Los Angeles	2,454	1,746	
Chicago	719		
New York			

The development of this kind of chart for use in planning can be demonstrated by a small-scale, very simple example.

A Simple Matrix. Assume a tiny organization consisting of

> Senior partner
>
> Junior partner
>
> Secretary
>
> Receptionist
>
> Conference room

The last item is, of course, not a person, but it can still be called a unit for the sake of an interaction survey. Each person is now asked to fill in a form indicating the level of interaction with each other unit on a 0 to 5 scale representing a range from "never" to "constant". The results are

Senior partner	Junior partner	4
	Secretary	3
	Receptionist	1
	Conference room	4
Junior partner	Senior partner	3
	Secretary	3
	Receptionist	2
	Conference room	3

	Secretary	Senior partner	4
		Junior partner	3
		Receptionist	3
		Conference room	1
	Receptionist	Senior partner	2
		Junior partner	2
		Secretary	3
		Conference room	0

Since the conference room cannot be asked to estimate its interaction with the four people, the resulting matrix will not be completely symmetrical. If we arrange the informants in a vertical list and the unit interacted with in a horizontal row, this matrix will result:

	Conference room	Receptionist	Secretary	Junior partner	Senior partner
Senior partner	4	1	3	4	
Junior partner	3	2	3		3
Secretary	1	3		3	4
Receptionist	0		3	2	2

The discrepancies in the parties' estimates of interaction do not exceed one step on the 0 to 5 scale in any case, so it is sufficiently precise to average the values given in each direction by adding the two figures together. This converts the matrix to an asymmetrical pattern with a scale of 0 to 10. The values for the conference room must be doubled so that they will be converted to the 0 to 10 scale also. The matrix is thus reduced to:

	Conference room	Receptionist	Secretary	Junior partner
Senior partner	8	3	7	7
Junior partner	6	5	6	
Secretary	2	6		
Receptionist	0			

This will become even more compact if code letters are used for the items:

	CR	RE	SE	JP
SP	8	3	7	7
JP	6	5	6	
SE	2	6		
RE	0			

The same information can be arranged in a slightly different format so that the items need only be listed once:

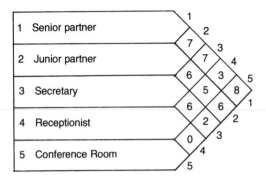

Some users find this format confusing, at least when first encountered, and it is more difficult to produce on a typewriter or as a computer printout. But when encountered in project reports, it should be recognized as an alternate form of matrix presentation.

With a small matrix chart, the most significant relationships can be located easily and all others can be identified in order of importance. It is then possible to make a list of these relationships in rank order:

8	Senior partner - Conference room
7	Senior partner - Junior partner
	Senior partner - Secretary
6	Junior partner - Secretary
	Junior partner - Conference room
	Secretary - Receptionist
5	Junior partner - Receptionist
3	Senior partner - Receptionist
2	Secretary - Conference room
0	Receptionist - Conference room

For a large organization, such a list will be long and can be broken into arbitrary categories such as "very important," "important," etc., down to "no relationship." Even if no further use of matrix-based techniques were to be made, such a list is a useful planning tool.

There is another interesting possibility for generating significant listings. All the numbers referring to each unit (usually called "link values") can be added up to give an "index of interaction" for that unit. This means adding both the horizontal and vertical (or in the diagonal format the upward and downward diagonal) columns relating to each unit. In this example we would get:

Senior partner	8 + 3 + 7 + 7 = 25
Junior partner	6 + 5 + 6 + 7 = 24
Secretary	2 + 6 + 6 + 7 = 21
Receptionist	0 + 6 + 5 + 3 = 14
Conference room	0 + 2 + 6 + 8 = 16

The units can now be listed in rank order on the basis of this interaction index:

Senior partner	25
Junior partner	24
Secretary	21
Conference room	16
Receptionist	14

Both logic and experience suggest that units with a high index of interaction belong in central locations and units with a low index in peripheral locations. In this example, custom might lead a planner to assign the senior partner a secluded corner space while the interaction data suggest a central location based on real working needs.

A strictly theoretical approach would now suggest drawing in diagram every possible arrangement of the five spaces and trying every possible assignment of occupant units in every arrangement. For each plan diagram, it is then possible to generate a "figure of merit," that is, a number or score which represents an evaluation of the plan as to its success in achieving ideal or optimal spatial relationships. Such a figure of merit has no meaning by itself, but when compared with a figure relating to another plan layout, it serves to show which layout is better and by what margin. To compute a figure of merit, give a value to the degree of adjacency of or separation between each possible pairing of spaces and multiply this value by the link value that corresponds to the relationship between the units assumed to be occupying the spaces. The sum of these products is the figure of merit for the particular plan.

If this is confusing, it will become clearer by working an example. Suppose this plan is diagrammed:

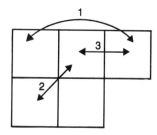

In it, the only relationships available are

Adjacent   3

Diagonal   2

Removed   1

Two slightly different cases of removed are present, but they are sufficiently similar to be given the same adjacency value number. The five units of the sample organization are now placed (using the letter abbreviations) in the following example:

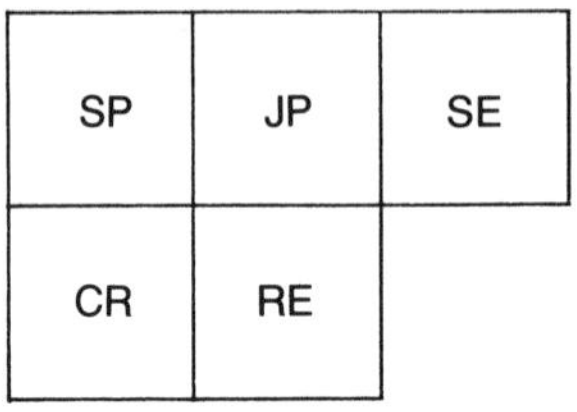

SP	JP	SE
CR	RE	

Evaluation of the plan proceeds as follows:

Relationship	Link value (from matrix)	Adjacency value in this plan	Product
SP - JP	7	3	21
SP - SE	7	1	7
SP - RE	3	2	6
SP - CR	8	3	24
JP - SE	6	3	18
JP - RE	5	3	15
JP - CR	6	2	12
SE - RE	6	2	12
SE - CR	2	1	2
RE - CR	0	3	0

Figure of merit for this plan   117

This figure has no particular meaning until an alternate plan is proposed and evaluated. For example:

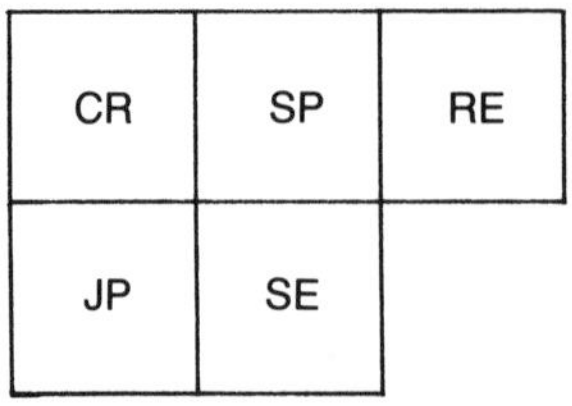

CR	SP	RE
JP	SE	

Evaluation is as follows:

Relationship	Link value	Adjacency value	Product
SP - JP	7	2	14
SP - SE	7	3	21
SP - RE	3	3	9
SP - CR	8	3	24
JP - SE	6	3	18
JP - RE	5	1	5
JP - CR	6	3	18
SE - RE	6	2	12
SE - CR	2	2	4
RE - CR	0	1	0
		Figure of merit	125

This plan is, therefore, superior to the one evaluated first, but only by a narrow margin. Any proposed plan can be given a rating in this way, and the best proposal selected for final development.

Every possible plan can be evaluated in this way and the best proposal then selected with some confidence that it is truly best among all possibilities. But this turns out to be a larger assignment than one might anticipate. If we ask how many arrangements of the five units are possible, we are surprised to find that the answer is a number called "factorial 5" (written 5!) arrived at by multiplying $5 \times 4 \times 3 \times 2 \times 1$, which equals 120 possible arrangements. If we then note how many physical arrangements of these five units are possible, we have:

```
                    00000

                    0000
                    0

                    000
                    00        (used in the examples above)

                    000
                    0
                    0

                    000
                      0
                      0

                      0
                    000
                    0

                    0  0                      0
                      0     (and its variant   000)
                    0  0                      0
```

Each of these has inversions and mirror images which can be omitted from consideration, but there are still seven configurations which each offer 120 possible arrangements. This gives 7 × 120 or 840 possible layouts, each to be evaluated as shown above to derive a figure of merit. This is a clerical chore that might well take someone a day, although a computer, suitably programmed, might run through it in seconds. Yet even the computer can hardly help as problems become more complex. We have used an example with only five units. Suppose there were 10. The number of arrangements now becomes factorial 10 (10!) or, believe it or not, 3,628,800 for each possible plan diagram that might be suggested. For 100 units, its concomitant factorial 100 (100!) boggles the mind.

Although both mind and computer boggle at an approach that demands evaluation of *every* possibility, this technique for evaluating any given possibility can prove to be useful. The human mind, particularly the mind of a planner who has some special skill and experience, can do surprisingly well at finding layouts that reach high scores after only a few trials. The interested reader might like to try a few experimental plans. Assume 10 units and construct a matrix with link values as would be developed from a survey and its matrix chart. Diagram an abstract version of ten units placed in space as follows:

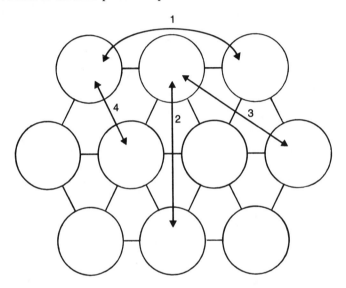

In this case the adjacency values might be taken as:

Adjacent	4
Near	3
Far	2
Very Far	1

Total up an index of interaction (the total of all link values) for each unit. Place the unit with the highest index in one of the two central spaces and that with the next highest in the other. Place the units with highest levels of interaction with these units in the surrounding spaces, noting levels of interaction with other units and selecting the spaces accordingly. Units with lowest indexes of interaction should find places in end or corner locations. Now develop a figure of merit for the proposed plan as described above. It will almost certainly be far higher than the figure of merit developed for a random plan. Several alternate plans can be tried and the one with the highest figure of merit will prove to be closest to the maximum value that can be arrived at as a result of all three million plus trials. A computer can be quite useful in calculating each figure of merit, but it hardly seems to be needed to find a plan with a high score.

Larger Problems

Examples with only 5 or 10 units serve to demonstrate the theory of matrix and diagram planning, but what happens with complex problems involving hundreds or thousands of units? It is not practical to deal with such large numbers directly, even with computer aid. Instead, the large number of units need to be reduced through the process of making "clusters," each one of which can be viewed as a superunit. For example, if the original survey unit was an individual person, groupings can be determined of individuals who work closely together (in teams or work groups) which can be treated as units. If the clusters are large, each can be treated as a unit in general planning, but then dealt with as an organization of many units as more detailed planning is undertaken. Identification of clusters to be treated as units can be dealt with in several ways. In many organizations, these are already identified in clear and realistic ways. They show up as a leader and several assistants, a group of specialists all doing the same work, or a group cooperating to perform a single function. Where such groups are truly units, they can be treated as such without further concern.

One of the key insights of the Quickborner Team, however, is that designated organizational groups are sometimes not truly operational groups. Accounting may, in fact, be a number of small teams, each closely associated with some other function and having almost no interaction within the accounting department. An interaction survey, if it has been conducted at a sufficiently small level of units, will generate information on how unit grouping can be devised on a more realistic basis than organization chart values permit. Various techniques for clustering on the basis of interaction data are available, some more dependent on computer aid than others.

Assume that an interaction survey deals with 100 units (perhaps individuals). For each unit, it is then possible to draw up a list of a limited number (say, 10) of other units with which the highest levels of interaction occur—listed in declining order with the interaction value figure in each case and a sum of the 10 interaction values. The lists with highest interaction sums may be considered as possible "super units." Since units will be duplicated on many different lists, the reduction to a reasonable number of super units requires a kind of barter process. Suppose the highest 10 summed units have been accepted for consideration as super units. Any duplicated units (appearing on more than one list) must be kept on the list where their level of interaction is highest and dropped from the others. Units not appearing on any of these lists must be added where they have most interaction, or they may be considered as possible candidates for formation of additional super units. Computer programs can be set up to conduct this kind of dealing out of units into larger groups, but it is often more workable to do this on the basis of a simple visual survey of an interaction matrix with the support of some first-hand advice about the known realities of the organization's actual operations.

With the total organization reduced to a manageable number of units, matrix-based planning can quite readily help develop diagrammatic plans with good prospects for effectiveness. Each large unit can then be regarded as an organization in itself and be planned on a matrix basis in turn.

From Diagram to Reality

The units and diagrammatic plans discussed above have all been abstract in the sense that they included no consideration of realities of size and shape. Fitting real working units into an actual building with entrance points, windows, finite dimensions, and possibly such special attributes as multiple floors involves a transition from abstraction to specificity. There are a number of steps that can be taken to make this process possible and rational.

1. It is often possible to make certain external considerations into units suitable for manipulation through matrix and diagrammatic planning. A typical example is the treatment of access. Every space has an entrance-exit point which is a significant line of communication for arriving and departing occupants and visitors. Arrivals and departures of each staff member and each visitor to any staff member may be made part of the interaction survey. "Entrance point" can then be treated as a unit in the matrix. Values can then be developed for needed proximity to the entrance.

2. The abstract space diagrams used in developing diagrammatic plans can be made to conform, in some rough way, with actual space available. When new space is to be constructed to house the organization, this is, of course, not necessary. The abstract plan can govern the planning of the real space to be built. But if an existing space is to be used, a related space diagram will make the transition from abstract to real much easier. Such diagrams as

```
00000000        000000        00000
00000000        0000          000
                000000        000
                              00000
```

each make an approximation to a particular space layout.

3. The actual, absolute physical size of units can be taken into account. Where the unit used in planning is one worker (as in the simple example discussed above), it is usually practical to ignore the differences in areas occupied by different work categories, assuming that the transition from abstract diagram to realistic plan can take care of the range of area assignments to be anticipated. In practice, it is easier than might be expected to deal with multiperson units of quite varied size as an abstract plan is pushed, pulled, and squeezed to make it a reality. An intermediate step in this process that has proved helpful is making area diagrams as outlined below.

Area Diagrams

Architects and office planners working in conventional ways have made use of area diagrams for many years. The Quickborner Team has suggestions for combining the simple area diagram with diagrammatic representation of interaction study results in ways that planners working with landscape and open plan concepts have generally found very helpful.

In a conventional area diagram, each space to be included in a plan (usually each room) is drawn as a square or rectangle whose area is proportional to the area that space is expected to require. Sometimes these rectangles or "boxes" are made into cardboard cutouts which can be shuffled about into various patterns to illustrate relationships—organizational, spatial, or both. If the rectangles are drawn at a standard architectural scale (⅛" = 1' 0", for example) and placed on or near an architectural plan, they help to visualize ways in which the space might be divided.

For use in open planning, the area boxes should correspond to the working units that have been identified as cohesive clusters in functional terms. In some cases it seems helpful to avoid the roomlike connotations of rectangles by using circles or possibly rectangles with rounded corners (hence the term "bubble diagram" often used to describe such charts). The box or bubble must be propor-

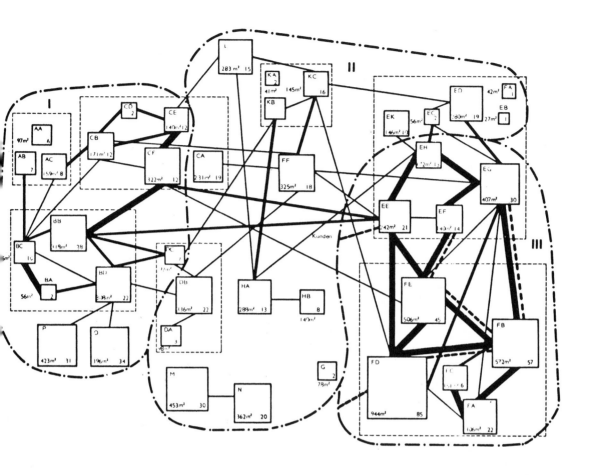

Area diagram. Each box is a working unit; closely related groups are shown within larger, dotted boxes. Varied weights of link lines symbolize different levels of interaction. Bubble shapes in dot-dash lines show three main clusterings of relationships which, in several cases, break into the boxes established by organizational patterns. Courtesy Quickborner Team.

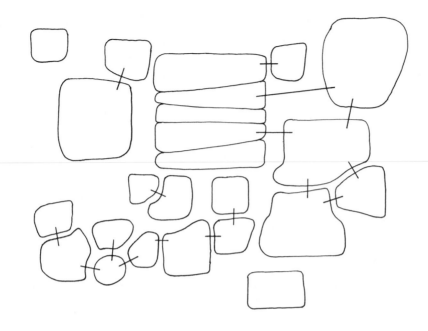

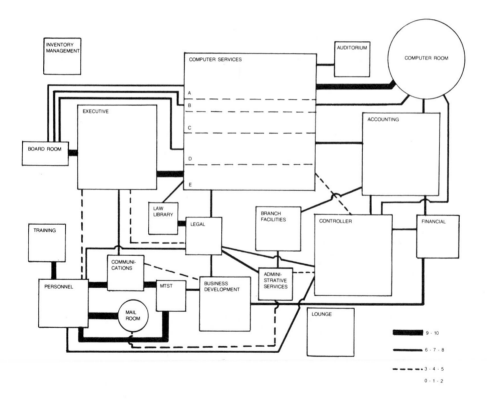

Top: Bubble diagram chart as first roughed out in freehand form. Numbers identify specific individuals or work units of several individuals. Above: Diagram with link lines added. Links vary in weight to correspond to a 1 to 10 scale of density of interaction.

tioned accurately to scale, and it is convenient to note on it such data as its area in square feet (or square meters), the number of work stations it will house, and any special notes about other items to be placed within it. The units are spread out on a work sheet and lines drawn to connect one with another to represent paths of interaction. These "link lines" are varied in thickness according to the density of communication between the units discovered through the interaction survey. A thick line represents dense traffic, a thin line less, and no line at all is drawn for links where communication falls below a certain selected minimal level.

The boxes are arranged in a pattern that approximates the pattern of the plan diagram which showed the best figure of merit among those tried, with whatever adjustments the varied areas of the units may require. When the link lines are drawn, the heaviest, thickest lines, representing most interaction, should be shortest; those progressively thinner may become increasingly long. No very thick line should need to follow a complex path or extend a great distance. Manipulation of the area boxes may be carried out to try to improve this process of minimizing the lengths of heaviest link lines. The physical form of the chart can be made roughly analogous to the shape of the space to be occupied. It thus becomes a helpful intermediate step on the route towards an actual plan layout in which units are located in appropriate spaces at accurate scale. Planners with experience in fitting together areas in conventional plans will generally find it quite easy to progress through the steps as follows:

Abstract diagrammatic plan		Bubble or area diagram		Preliminary floor layout plan
	$\rightarrow$		$\rightarrow$	

This process is most direct when the space to be occupied is a large, relatively open space of near square proportions, all on one floor. Unfortunately for simplicity of planning, most larger projects must occupy more than one floor.

Multifloor Problems

The need to occupy more than one floor can arise out of several circumstances. An existing building, currently occupied or in which space is to be rented, has floors of a particular, finite area. If the organization's space needs outrun one floor, there is no alternative but to occupy several, possibly even many, floors. Even new construction may be constrained by the size of available sites (as in cities where block size is usually limited) or by the realization that, when large areas are involved, a single level layout may become so spread out that horizontal walking distances become excessive. A walk up or down one flight may be preferable to a horizontal walk of an eighth or quarter mile. A quick elevator ride to a distant floor (even 10, 20, or more levels removed may be equally quick and easy. Therefore, even suburban and rural office buildings are often built on a multilevel plan. Arrival at an ideal number of floors, each of ideal area, for any particular occupancy is a complex problem involving building economics as well as problems of organizational subdivision. The merits of various building forms are discussed in Chapter 6. By the time planning reaches the phases discussed here, the number of floors and their areas have usually been established. When options are available, it is worthwhile to note:

1. Occupants of a floor in a multilevel facility tend to exhibit group loyalty and often feel out of touch with or even hostile to occupants of other floors.

2. This effect is often more pronounced when there are only two floors. A spirit of "us against them" surfaces, which is usually not so evident when a number of floors are involved.

3. It is particularly undesirable for any one floor to be used in a way that can be interpreted as better or worse. Conventional planning is particularly apt to generate an executive floor, viewed with hostility by those not occupying it, or a bull pen floor, seen as inferior by both those assigned to it and those on other floors. Open planning aids in avoiding such class distinctions.

After a decision has been made in favor of a multifloor facility and after the number and areas of floors have been established, it is necessary to make an assignment of occupants to each floor. This is done through the medium of a chart usually called a "stacking plan."

Stacking Plans. In conventional planning, occupants are assigned to floors on the basis of departmental organization and, in most cases, according to certain traditions as well. Executives are commonly placed on the highest available floor; divisions thought to be important are next below, down through the stack, with an effort to keep related departments on adjacent floors. Sometimes certain units used by many staff members are placed on the middle floor, with the thought that this maximizes convenience for all. In tall buildings, setbacks, area variations in core size, location of floors in relation to express/local elevator service, and similar factors may also enter into decisions about stacking. In survey- and matrix-based open planning, it is possible to make stacking somewhat more logical.

The bubble or area diagram of the complete organization is an extremely useful tool in planning stacking. Actual floors are drawn in diagrammatic plan at the same scale as the area chart and are spread out in sequence. Units from the area diagram can be compared visually with the available space, and trial space assignments made in an effort to keep links showing dense interaction as short as possible—preferably within the area of one floor or only one floor removed if this is not possible. When the stack is made up of a small number of floors (two, three, or even four), it is usually possible to assign all closely linked unit pairs to the same floor and to assign units with medium linkage to adjacent floors with locations near stairs or elevators. When the number of floors is large, the situation changes somewhat since elevator usage becomes the primary means of travel between floors. An elevator trip is not perceived as varying significantly according to the number of floors traveled; riding up or down 10 or 20 floors is not noticeably different from riding 2 or 3. Remoteness in the stack is rated as follows:

Close	= Same floor
Not far	= Adjacent floor provided stair is available and convenient
Far	= Elevator ride when elevator is convenient
Very far	= Elevator ride when elevator is far removed

The last case should not arise and will not when floors are of reasonable size and have well-located elevators. It may arise in a very extended plan with elevators at one end or at the center of a floor where a trip from one unit to another can, at worst, require a walk of 1,000 feet to an elevator, a wait and ride, and another similar walk on the arrival floor.

Logical stacking thus proceeds from floor to adjacent floor. When adjacent floor space cannot be assigned, the degree of remoteness can be considered the same in all trips involving an elevator. A unit removed by 3 floors is not, as a practical matter, any closer than one removed by 10 floors. Usual practice is to place the unit with the highest index of interaction on the center floor of the stack, group those units with which it has most interaction on the same floor until space on that floor has been consumed, place units with the next highest degree of interaction with the units already placed on the adjacent floors, above and below, and proceed both up and down the stack adding units with most interaction with the units already placed on successive floors above and below. Two-floor layouts are a somewhat special case of this situation in which it is logical to seek in the area diagram two clusters each with high internal interaction and with minimal interaction between clusters.

In cases where one floor of the stack is the ground floor of the building, entrance-exit points should be treated as units in the matrix study, so that units with heavy traffic to entrances and exits can be considered for assignment to that floor. In multistory occupancy on upper floors of a building, it is often desirable to designate a particular floor as a primary entrance floor for visitors or even to designate several entrance floors for different categories of visitors (to different divisions, perhaps, or service versus nonservice). Location of these primary entrance points must be considered in stacking. Their floor assignment can be made after the primary stack has been completed. They should be treated as units to be placed where they will be close to the units which have most traffic to the external world.

Evaluation of Stacking Plans.   Once a stacking plan has been proposed, a methodical evaluation on a mathematical basis is possible; evaluation of different alternatives makes it possible to select a best choice with confidence. Such an evaluation is made by assigning a numerical value to each case of an interfloor relationship, for example:

Same floor	3
Adjacent floor	2
Remote floor	1

Notice that such a scale makes an assumption that the step of difference in convenience is equal between each case and the next. The availability of convenient stairs (or even escalators) or the lack of such convenience might alter the difference between the cases so that values could be assigned as:

Same floor	10
Adjacent floor	3
Remote floor	1

to take account of the fact that poor stair access makes an adjacent floor only slightly different from a remote floor.

The index of interaction of each unit with each other unit in the organization is now multiplied by the interfloor relationship value. When all the products are summed, the resulting total is a figure of merit for the proposed stacking plan. In doing this, notice that the indexes of interaction must be expressed in a way that includes an indication of the number of people involved; if the raw total count of communications is used, this issue is already taken care of. If estimates on an arbitrary scale of the "Never, seldom, . . . , constant" type have been used, the numerical scale value should be multiplied by the number of people present in the two units in question.

The point of this is, of course, that the aim of stacking is to maximize convenience for a maximum number of people. An inconvenient location for a small group is less significant than the same inconvenience for a large group. An example, deliberately small to make the process clearer, is as follows:

Example. An organization made up of six units is to occupy a three-floor space. An interaction survey has been made and the results on a 0 to 5 scale (never to constant interaction) are shown in this matrix:

	F	E	D	C	B	A
A	4	3	5	2	4	
B	1	2	3	4		
C	0	1	3			
D	4	5				
E	1					
F						

Personnel in the units total:

A	12
B	5
C	3
D	10
E	8
F	6

An index of interaction for each unit is obtained by adding all link values relating to that unit. In rank order these sums are:

D	20
A	18
B	14
E	12
C	10
F	10

A proposed stacking plan is now developed. The usual approach would be to place on the middle floor the unit with highest index of interaction. This is D. On the same floor would logically be placed the unit with which D has most interaction; that is A. Since the remaining four units will inevitably be placed on adjacent floors, above and below, it is only necessary to sort these into two pairs with high levels of interaction. Looking again at the matrix, note that the only high link value remaining is that between B and C—4. This suggests that B and C should share a floor and E and F, the only remaining units, another floor. In theory, which pair is assigned to the first and which to the third floor does not matter. In practice, one pair or the other might be preferable on the ground floor either because of expected visitor traffic or because of its own occupancy population. In this example, E and F are placed on the first floor because of their larger population. This stacking diagram results:

Third floor	B	C
Second floor	A	D
First floor	E	F

Note that this stacking makes the populations of the floors very uneven: first floor, 14; second floor, 21; third floor, 8. A different stack might be proposed to make the distribution somewhat more equal:

Third floor	B	F
Second floor	D	E
First floor	A	C

An evaluation of the merit of each of the two proposed stacking plans can now be made by developing a figure of merit for each as a sum of the products of:

Link value for the pair × sum of people in both units

× adjacency value in proposed stack

Adjacency values should be calculated on the following scheme: same floor, 3; adjacent floor, 2; remote floor, 1.

Unit pair	Link value	Sum of people in both units	Scheme 1 Adjacency value	Product	Scheme 2 Adjacency value	Product
AB	4	12 + 5 = 17	2	136	1	68
AC	2	12 + 3 = 15	2	60	3	90
AD	5	12 + 10 = 22	3	330	2	220
AE	3	12 + 8 = 20	2	120	2	120
AF	4	12 + 6 = 18	2	144	1	72
BC	4	5 + 3 = 8	3	96	1	32
BD	3	5 + 10 = 15	2	90	2	90
BE	2	5 + 8 = 13	1	26	2	52
BF	1	5 + 6 = 11	1	11	3	33
CD	3	3 + 10 = 13	2	78	2	78
CE	1	3 + 8 = 11	1	11	2	22
CF	0	3 + 6 = 9	1	0	1	0
DE	5	10 + 8 = 18	2	180	3	270
DF	4	10 + 6 = 16	2	128	2	128
EF	1	8 + 6 = 14	3	42	2	28
Figure of merit for scheme:				1,452		1,303

Scheme 1 is significantly superior, but not by as great a margin as might be expected. The interested reader may wish to suggest other stackings and calculate their merit to see if an even better solution is possible.

As with area diagrams, it is theoretically possible to propose every possible stacking in a particular situation and to generate a figure of merit for each so that a mathematically proven best plan can be selected. In practice, as with area diagrams, the number of possibilities in a problem of any size becomes so great as to make this approach impractical. In the simple example above, there are 90 possible stacking plans, with two units on each of the three floors. With a larger number of units and/or floors, checking every possibility becomes a vast task, often beyond practical computer processing. Here also an experienced planner can do surprisingly well at arriving at good proposals by starting with a scale area diagram, scale plans of the floors to be occupied, and a rank order listing of link values for interaction between each pair of units. Once stacking plans are proposed, mathematical evaluation of each that is under serious consideration can be helpful; in many cases pencil and paper or calculator can deal with the figures although computer programs to speed the job can also be considered.

After stacking plans are presented, alternatives or modifications are often proposed by members of the organization for which the planning is being done. It is very helpful to the professional planner to have an objective means of evaluating any such alternatives or revisions. Acceptance and approval of a stacking plan should occur before more detailed planning of individual floors begins. Once stacking has been frozen, each floor becomes, in a certain sense, a self-contained project and the planning techniques that have applied to the total project can be reapplied at smaller scale to the individual floors.

One other issue will arise as stacking is being planned: providing for future expansion. The needs developed in the course of space requirement surveys are on record as allowances estimated for individual work groups. If this space is provided within the areas assigned to these groups, there will be an excess of area distributed more or less evenly throughout the space as a cushion to absorb expansion as it takes place. This will mean building or renting space for the estimated future expansion needs from the original occupancy date. While this is the most convenient way of providing for expansion, it may seem costly in terms of rent or construction cost. An alternate plan will provide for a future expansion of the building or for rental of additional space as needed. In a rental situation, it is not unusual for the prime tenant to rent enough space to include an allowance for expansion, but to sublet the part not immediately needed with short-term leases so that the excess space can be taken over as required. Unfortunately, this will almost certainly mean that the excess space will be in large blocks, possibly complete floors, so that it cannot be distributed through the occupied space in locations where needs can be expected to arise. In such a scheme, expansion will mean some extensive replanning and rearrangement. Open planning, with its unusual flexibility, makes such expansion easier than with conventional, partitioned layouts, but it can still be troublesome. A stacking plan which includes such sublet space will ideally place units where most expansion is anticipated adjacent to the space which can provide room for it. Units where expansion is not anticipated or where it will be minimal should be located so that they need not be disturbed when expansion takes place.

Stacking Plan Format.   A stacking plan can take the form of a simple listing which gives each floor number and a list of units assigned to that floor with their areas, or it can take the form of a graphic chart, a bar graph, in which each floor is shown by a bar representing its total area with the units occupying it marked off as parts of the bar proportional to their individual areas. Expansion allowances are shown in either format. It is often best to provide the plan in both graphic and tabular form. Different viewers will find one format easier to understand, and converting one form to the other does not involve much effort.

Detailed Floor Planning

The next step is the detailed planning of each floor, which is identical with the planning of a complete project that occupies only one floor. The portions of the interaction and area diagrams that apply to the particular floor are isolated, and

STACKING PLAN

(Tabular Form)

FLOOR	FUNCTION	PEOPLE	AREA
1.	Key Punch	3	200
	MTST	5	400
	Branch Facilities	9	875
	Central Management	6	710
	SWIFT Customer Service	8	1405
	Lounge		1000
		31	4590
2.	SWIFT Branch Applications	28	2470
	" Home Off. Applications	25	2175
	" Operations Support	29	2650
	" Technical Support	24	2400
	" Executive & Secretarial	2	500
	Communications	4	660
	Personnel	7+2PT	1130
	Training		700
	Meeting and Conference		800
		119	13485
3.	Accounting	30	3008
	Controller	18	2669
	Legal & Admin. Services	11	1265
	Law Library		400
	Financial	4	945
	Executive	13	2880
	Business Development	10	1280
	Conference		950
		86	13397

SUMMARY

FLOOR	AVAILABLE AREA	ASSIGNED AREA	CUSHION
1	4038	4590	(-452)
2	14190	13485	705
3	14690	13397	1293
	32918	31472	1546

Stacking plan in tabular form.

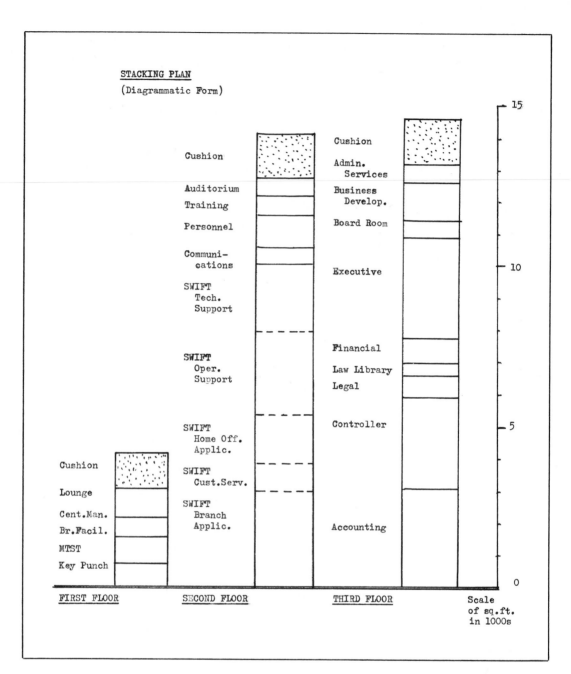

STACKING PLAN
(Diagrammatic Form)

15

Cushion

Cushion
Admin.
    Services

Auditorium

Business
    Develop.

Training

Board Room

Personnel

Communi-
    cations

Executive

10

SWIFT
    Tech.
    Support

SWIFT
    Oper.
    Support

Financial

Law Library

Legal

SWIFT
    Home Off.
    Applic.

Controller

5

Cushion

SWIFT
    Cust.Serv.

Lounge

SWIFT
    Branch
    Applic.

Cent.Man.

Br.Facil.

MTST

Accounting

Key Punch

0

FIRST FLOOR

SECOND FLOOR

THIRD FLOOR

Scale
of sq.ft.
in 1000s

The same plan in diagrammatic form.

STACKING PLAN diagram (Chubb & Son):

Floor 9:
INT. AUDIT 47·08 / PURCHASING 47·09
| PERSONNEL 47·: | MEDICAL 47·10·05 | CAFETERIA 47·12·02 | STENO POOL | 176 | 356 | LAW LIB. | OFF. SVC. | OPEN 1500 |
| 3120 | 1420 | 5900 | 1577 | | | 1200 | 684 | |
47·01·01

Floor 3:
| PROP. LOSS 47·80 | LIABILITY CLAIMS 47·83 | CONT 400 | OPEN 1650 |
| 7,212 | 6,000 | | |

Floor 7:
| CLAIMS SVCS 47·55 | MAIL | SW.BD. | CARGO 47·35 | FILES 47·54 | YACHT & HULL 47·36 | MARKETING 47·42 | OPEN 1042 |
| 1877 | 2000 | 962 | 2789 | 3,069 | 1644 | 1884 | |

Floor 3:
PERSONAL LINES 47·34 / DATA OPTNS 47·50
| TREAS. 47·03 | ACCT. 47·07 | TAX 70·01·97 | 47·30 | INTERNATIONAL 47·23 | BOARD ROOM COMPLEX | OPEN 1942 |
| 1133 | 516 | 1500 | 420 | 3677 | 216 | 5745 | |
108 — COMM'L PROP.

Floor 5:
| LEGAL 47·02 | INVESTMENT 70·03·01 | BUS. DEV. 70·00·01 | CORP. EXEC. 47·00 | 269 | OPEN 1330 |
| 1661 | 3200 | 1150 | 7,657 | | |
REINSUR. 47·11

Floor 4:
| SURETY 47·40 | PROD SVCL. 01·51 | FID. & SURETY LOSS 47·82 | SURVEY 01·33 47·33 | OPEN 870 |
| 5184 | 977 | 3821 | 3118 | |

Floor 3:
| COMM'L PROP. 01·30 | COMM'L CASUALTY 01·31 | COMM'L FID. 01·39 | INLAND MARINE 01·32 | D.F.I. 47·38 | OPEN 410 |
| 5395 | 2676 | 780 | 1320 | 1944 | |

Floor 2:
DATA 01·50 / COLL. 01·07
| PERSONAL LINES 01·34 | PROD. 01·21 | PROD. SERVICE 01·51 | 276 | EXEC 01·01 | OPEN 4334 |
| 2549 | 756 | 1577 | | 636 | |
120

Scale: 1600 | 3200 | 4800 | 6400 | 8000 | 9600 | 11,200 | 12,800 | 14,400 | 16,000

METRO

CHUBB & SON
100 WILLIAM ST. N.Y.C.
STACKING PLAN
EXHIBIT III
SCALE: 1"=1600 USABLE SQ. FT.
REVISION: #8   DATE: 7·15·71

A more complex stacking plan. Shaded areas (marked "open") indicates space reserved for future expansion.

units are sorted into proposed locations on the basis of interaction needs as discussed earlier. In this process, several points may be noted:

1. A cluster, or work unit group, has a certain optimum size. One, two, or three people tend to use space in a way similar to that of the conventional private or semiprivate office—to become isolated. Such units may be unavoidable (in the case of managers or executives, for example), but they are not ideal. At the other extreme, large clusters for 10, 12, or more begin to suggest the bull pen and will in practice tend to break into subgroups. An ideal cluster is a number close to seven, say, five to nine. These are numbers in which individual relationships can be maintained and a group or team spirit developed. Where larger work groups are a functioning reality, it may be best to break them into smaller clusters.

2. Each cluster should occupy space that has some visible definition. This may be a matter of the geometry of layout, the positioning of circulation aisles, or the introduction of screens, plants, or other visual barriers. Barriers so definite as to suggest partitioning defeat the objectives of open planning, but the sense of cluster identity should be felt at each work station of a cluster.

3. Circulation needs to be planned just as carefully as in conventional planning although it need not adhere to conventional rectilinear geometry. Starting from access points, main traffic routes should flow out, leading to secondary and tertiary routes visible to the occupant or visitors. Work clusters should not be cut

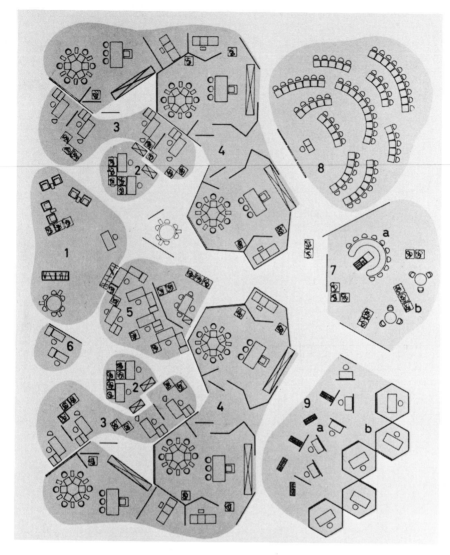

Workplace clusters, including in this case a large meeting area (8) and multipurpose meeting spaces (7). From Schnelle and Wankum, *Architekt und Organisator*.

by planned or unplanned circulation lines or short-cuts. Routes to any point on a floor should be sufficiently direct to avoid any sense of labyrinth. In planning, a circulation plan or plan overlay should be drawn indicating traffic lines with line widths proportional to anticipated traffic density. A clear and reasonable plan suggests a workable traffic flow. A tangled plan layout needs to be reworked.

4. A very difficult issue involves the degree of detailed plan appropriate to the point reached on the project time schedule. There is a tendency to desire a totally detailed plan, with every work station in place and assigned to a particular person and every piece of equipment specified in advance of approval to proceed with the project. Since projects are of long duration, such a detailed plan will certainly be obsolete before occupancy. It may in fact have to be done over and over, with confusing and wasteful revisions to deal with organizational changes, which may in turn become obsolete before move-in. Efficient planning should be kept somewhat general in early stages and only become detailed as

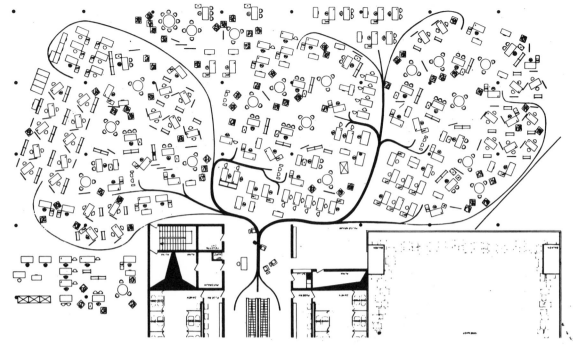

Circulation plan with major and minor traffic routes designated by varied line weights. Courtesy Quickborner Team.

move-in time comes close. Equipment can be ordered on the basis of total personnel needs with some small overage of each component to allow for detailed adjustments close to or after move-in time. Although this way of working is contrary to custom and may be disturbing to some planners and some managers, it is actually more efficient then spuriously exact planning which will simply require endless revision.

Client Participation

The management of the client organization will expect to be in constant touch with planning activities through designated contact personnel and through formal meetings from time to time to receive reports and grant approvals at designated decision points in the project's progress.

In addition, more informal contact with representatives of the user organization at all levels should be considered. It is a key principle of the Quickborner Team's methods that this kind of multilevel contact take place. Meetings are set up in which user groups (or their representatives) see proposed plans before they are fixed and have an opportunity to ask questions, make suggestions, and offer criticism. In an extreme form, a model of the planned space is offered to each user group with encouragement to experiment with alternate arrangements. The planning principles are explained in advance, and users are asked to revise with these in mind. Occasionally this process elicits genuinely helpful proposals, but in most cases it simply provides a sense of participation in planning which tends to defuse negative reactions that can occur when users are confronted with a new plan as a fait accompli. This is probably particularly important when the proposed plan is as unusual in character as open or landscape plans often are. The user group will, in the end, have the power to make the plan a success or failure. User understanding, acceptance, and, even if possible, enthusiasm are basic to the ultimate success of the project.

The Building Shell and Support Systems

6

Planner/Building Relationships

The relationship of the office planner to the realities of office building structure will vary according to the pattern that a particular project is to follow. The range of possibilities can be outlined:

1. The client organization plans to build a new building and has selected a planner in advance of any commitments on the total project. This is an ideal circumstance if the planner is involved as an equal team member along with client, architect, developer, and any other key parties involved in the project. Office planning considerations can be taken into account before any firm decisions are made about building form and structure.

2. The client organization expects to become a prime tenant in a building project being developed by an outside real estate developer or speculator. While the planner has less leverage in influencing planning decisions in this situation, it is still possible to avoid errors and urge preferred decisions before actual construction is under way.

3. The client organization plans to rent space and has involved the planner as a consultant in space selection. While this situation limits possibilities to whatever is available in the rental market, it makes it possible to avoid spaces that may present special difficulties and to arrive at selection of the most suitable spaces available at a particular time.

4. Space has already been rented, constructed, or contracted for and planning must adapt to use of the space selected. When existing space is to be replanned, a similar situation exists. The planner must adapt to the realities of the given space with only minimal possibilities for modification of building plan and structure. Whether this is or is not a handicap depends, of course, on what the given realities are. At worst, open planning may be virtually unusable; more often there are some limitations present that make planning more difficult or that saddle the finished project with limitations that might have been avoided if the realities of open planning had been a factor in building planning or in rental selection.

When compared with space for conventional planning, open planning space must be evaluated on the basis of certain different criteria.

Office Building Architecture

The complete design of office buildings lies outside the scope of this book. It involves matters of structure, economics, recognition of legal restrictions, relationship to site, and other complex interrelated values that building architect, engineer, and owner (or developer) must struggle with. The office planner is concerned with the way in which these issues affect the built space into which the user organization must fit. Such issues as the choice of many small floors in a tall building (typically on a city site) versus a few spread-out floors in a low building (probably on a suburban or rural site) are usually determined by considerations outside the planner's field of concern. Still, the issues discussed in the last chapter under Stacking have some bearing on such decisions. Once general decisions have been made about building location and character, it is timely to note that open planning is easiest when certain architectural qualities are present.

Open Planning Criteria

In a general sense, open planning is easiest in large, open spaces with a minimum of obstructions and irregularities. Building forms that provide long ribbons of space (often desirable for providing windows in private offices) are difficult to deal with, and building concepts that tend toward many defined cellular units work against the freedom of planning that the open planner desires. The original

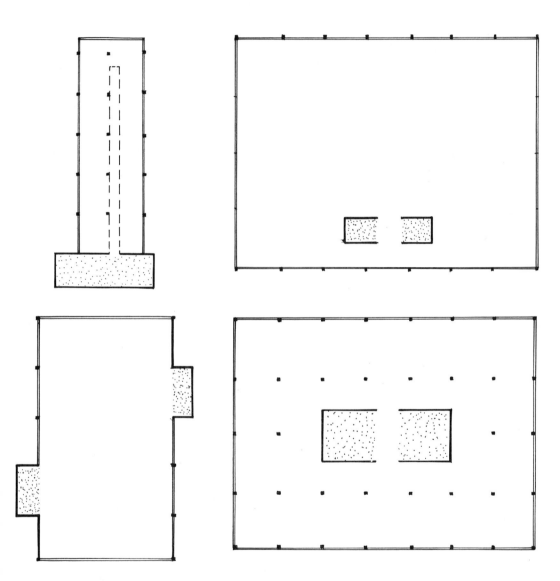

Top left: Narrow ribbon plan best suited to conventional planning where a maximum number of windowed private offices are desired. Top right: Deep space plan with minimal obstructions, usually regarded as most suitable for open planning. Above left: Open space with services in edge (perimeter) locations. Best for areas of medium size where distances from edge to center remain reasonable. Above right: Plan with service core at center. Suitable for very large floors where space from core to perimeter is large enough to provide ample, unrestricted space for free open planning.

theories of the Quickborner Team urged large, open floors totally without columns or other obstructions. In practice, columns with reasonably wide spacing [24 ft (7.5 m) on center or more] do not seem to present much problem to the planner. Although column-free space may be preferable by some small margin, the extra construction costs may not be justified by any practical gain. Obstructions in the form of cores of circulation spaces (elevators, stairs) and services present more of a problem if they insert an immovable block into a center of open space, turning it from a free area into a doughnut form.

Placing circulation and service spaces at the edges or corners of open office space is generally preferable to central cores, at least in the case of floors of small-to-medium total area [say, up to 40,000 sq ft (3,800 sq m)]. When floors are very large, the long distances from circulation and service points to workplaces may make central locations more suitable. Size of floor, shape, and core location have a complex relationship which can be outlined:

Small floor [4,000 to 20,000 sq ft (380 to 1,900 sq m)]: At the lower limits open planning may not be ideal. Narrow, ribbon space is particularly troublesome, while nearly square proportions are ideal. Core and other obstructions should be kept to edge locations.

Medium area spaces [20,000 to 40,000 sq ft (1,900 to 3,800 sq m)]: Suitable to open planning, especially if area proportions are in a range from square to 1:3 width-to-length ratio. Edge locations for core and services are ideal, and central locations are acceptable in nearly square space.

Large areas (over 40,000 sq ft): Rectangular proportions or more complex building configurations desirable to limit unbroken distance to limiting walls to about 125 ft (38 m) or less in at least one direction. Longer distances of unbroken space tend to create depressing, seemingly endless vistas. Circulation and service cores in internal locations can help to break such vistas and also keep circulation routes in cores to a reasonable distance.

Exterior Walls

Modern architecture has tended to favor the contrary extremes of the glass-walled building and the windowless building—each in its own way a dramatic concept, but each presenting certain problems to both open and conventional planning. Glass walls or walls with very high proportions of window areas are visually attractive and, in the case of open planning, offer all occupants of a floor a sense of outside light and view, which are particularly desirable where the building location and/or height make the view attractive. At the same time, glass walls present problems of heat loss (particularly on the north side) and heat gain (particularly in summer), plus sun glare on south and west walls. These are matters that can be controlled with suitable air conditioning, heating, and sun control devices, but such controls can be costly. Rising energy costs have made mechanical system controls particularly suspect within the last few years. Large glass areas can also contribute to acoustical problems since they represent large areas of hard, sound-reflective surface.

The opposite, windowless extreme denies outside view to all occupants and makes the building totally dependent on artificial light, heat, and air conditioning. Most modern buildings are sealed against outside ventilation (perhaps unwisely), but at least windows or glass walls permit some use of natural light and some gain of solar heat. The deep space desirable for open planning makes it almost impossible to avoid dependence on artificial light and air conditioning, but it is still economically sensible to try to reduce the extent of this dependence. Windowless space, always questionable on esthetic or psychological grounds, has now also become economically questionable in the light of rising energy costs. Decisions about how much outside wall should be window must be made on the basis of light and view available and the relationship of orientation to energy use impact. In general, it would seem that 100 percent glazing is too much, but just how much is enough is a matter that can only be decided in relation to the individual situation. The use of external sun control devices and openable windows, long out of fashion in the United States, deserves consideration once again in view of changing energy economics.

Floors and Ceilings

The seemingly neutral elements of office space—floors and ceilings—are each potentially involved in providing services and can considerably affect the degree of flexibility of planning. The standard practice of conventional planning involves provision of floors tiled with asphalt or vinyl asbestos tiling and hung ceilings of acoustical tile, with a regular pattern of fluorescent light fixtures sufficient to give a desired foot-candle lighting level at desk tops. In most cases, the floor also incorporates a duct system that makes it possible to locate electrical outlets and telephone connections at floor locations removed from walls or columns. These standard arrangements are not ideal for open planning. Floors must all be carpeted for acoustical reasons so standard tile becomes unnecessary. Flexibility for electrical outlets and telephones is, however, extremely important. Acoustical ceilings are essential, and the standard tiles often provided may not be fully satisfactory. The practice of lighting with inexpensive fixtures chosen only to give a desired light level and without consideration of light quality is likely to provide poor lighting at excessive energy cost. The ceiling is also expected to provide for air distribution, fire protection, and sound systems. All these matters need some special consideration in open planning and can best be handled in a coordinated way. The range of possibilities will be greatest when new construction is contemplated and least when existing space is reused, but in all cases it is necessary to consider what is possible and what is appropriate for the following areas:

Electrical (AC) service requires either floor or ceiling delivery. Ceiling service requires poles or hanging wires to connect to work stations; neither is very attractive visually if used in quantity. Floor delivery is logical if a duct system is present, but relocation of outlets is not easy unless an excessive (costly) number of outlet plates is provided in advance. Outlets on walls and columns only (common in conventional planning) are not adequate in open planning. A raised flooring system of the type used in computer rooms is a highly flexible approach (which also relates to the next item), but it is too costly for consideration except in areas where an extraordinary density of wired equipment is anticipated. A simple system of minimally elevated flooring [about 1 in. (2.5 cm)] would be a logical compromise, but it is not as yet in production.

Telephone (and other low-voltage services such as intercoms) present the same problems as AC except that wires and connectors can be smaller. Whatever solution is selected for AC distribution is usually also used for phone wires, although the two types of wiring must be isolated in separate ducts or conduits. To provide full flexibility for work station layout with a floor duct system, ducts need to be on centers that do not exceed one desk length [about 5 ft (1.5 cm)] and outlets need to be equally close. This leads to an excessive number of outlets, of which only a small proportion (20 to 25 percent) will be needed at any one time.

A possible compromise approach attempts to place outlets on a staggered grid with ducts 7 to 8 ft (2.1 to 2.4 m) apart and outlets similarly spaced but in staggered rows (see corresponding diagram). Ceiling service is more flexible but presents the visual problems already noted.

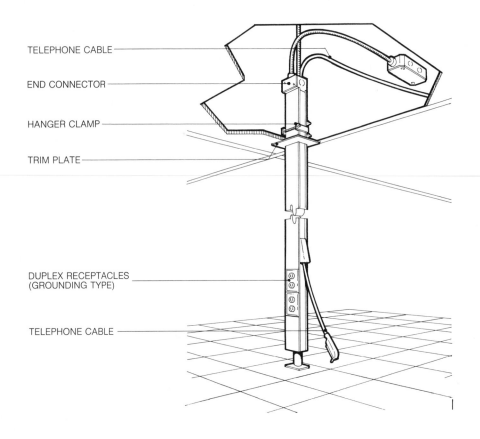

TELEPHONE CABLE

END CONNECTOR

HANGER CLAMP

TRIM PLATE

DUPLEX RECEPTACLES
(GROUNDING TYPE)

TELEPHONE CABLE

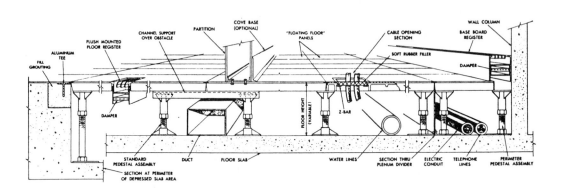

Top: Telephone and AC service from ceiling through movable pole. Courtesy Wiremold
Company. Above: Raised floor system providing generous underfloor space for wiring,
piping, ducts, etc., with access by liftable floor deck panels. Courtesy Floating Floors, Inc.

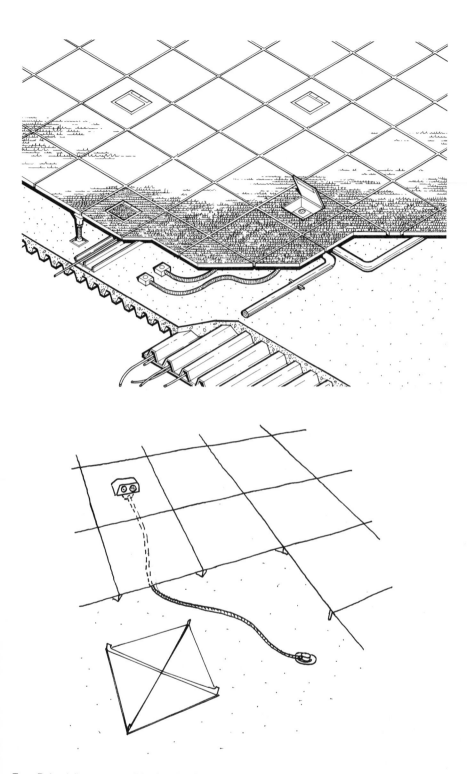

Top: Raised floor as used by Interior Facilities Associates (IFA) in New York's Citibank project. Wiring from building wiring ducts connects to access boxes in floor panels through long cables, permitting boxes to be freely located anywhere within the cable radius. Above: Mini-raised floor proposed by John Pile. Elevation of 1 in. (25.4 mm) provides space for wiring without requiring major support structure or increased ceiling height for headroom. Individual tiles can be lifted for access.

Acoustical treatment of the ceiling is a key item in the overall management of acoustical problems discussed in Chapter 8. It most often involves no more than selection of a surface material with satisfactory noise reduction characteristics and good appearance. Special approaches to acoustical baffles, possibly integrated with structure, lighting, and HVAC, are possible in the case of new construction.

Lighting is also discussed more fully in Chapter 7. It has, until recently, been thought of as a simple matter of fixture selectoon and choice of a regular spacing pattern. Energy cost issues have brought overall ceiling lighting into question so that there must now be a choice between a fixed, ceiling installation and lighting installed in furniture and serviced from the floor. The latter system will, in general, require less wattage for a given user population and type of use.

Heat and air conditioning (HVAC) requirements are closely related to decisions about lighting since light fixtures are a major source of heat gain. Some types of light fixtures (ceiling installed) permit extraction of heat before it enters the occupied space. Additional heat may be required by the windows in winter, usually supplied by convectors installed below the glass. Summer cooling and year-round ventilation require ceiling ducts and outlets, the latter possibly combined with ceiling light fixtures.

Sound systems are also part of the overall solution of acoustical problems discussed below. Ceiling location must be provided for.

Safety systems are also usually located in the ceiling. These include fire detection devices and sprinkler heads, where required.

Safety Codes
Modern office buildings are almost invariably of so-called fireproof construction, but they have proven more vulnerable to fire than might be expected. Furnishings are inflammable to some degree and modern materials (particularly certain plastics) produce dangerous smoke and fumes when burning or smoldering. Sealed outside walls, high buildings with floors above the reach of fire-fighting and rescue equipment, and the presence of fluelike ducts for air conditioning make a dangerous combination which has led to a number of destructive fires. Safety codes are in the process of being tightened in many cities, and planners should consider whether the standards set by mandatory codes are fully adequate. The safety issues requiring attention are:

1. Materials that may burn or smoulder in a way that produces flame or toxic fumes. Materials fixed in place (wall coverings, floor tiles) and materials technically classified as "removable" (carpet, furniture, curtains) deserve equal attention as potential hazards.

2. Escape routes. There should be two independent exits from every enclosed space.

3. Subdivision of space. This issue is particularly troublesome to the open planner since legal requirements that space be divided by fire walls into units of some arbitrary size can inhibit the usefulness of open planning. Under most codes the subdivision rules will not apply, however, if there is a full sprinkler system.

4. Fire detection and control systems. By far the most effective system of fire control is a full sprinkler system with automatic activation by temperature. The cost of sprinkler systems has tended to limit their use to situations where they are legally required. This probably should and may well become a universal requirement in all multistory office buildings.

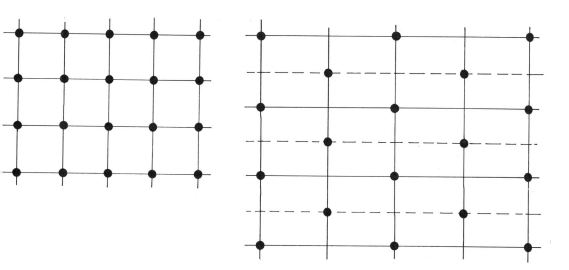

Above left: Outlets located on a 5 X 5 ft (155 X 155 cm) grid. Convenient access is assured, but the large number of outlets is uneconomical. Above right: Outlets in a staggered grid with ducts about 7½ ft (225 cm) on center and outlets on similar spaces. Many fewer ducts and outlets are required, yet access is as convenient.

Integrated ceiling at American Can Co. headquarters, Greenwich, Conn.; Skidmore, Owings, & Merrill, architects. The tubular forms are air ducts which also serve as acoustical baffles. Fluorescent tubes on top of the ducts supply diffused lighting, while the square-edged forms between are the bottom edges of structural precast concrete double-T elements.

The issue of security is closely related to that of safety. It is an unfortunate reality that office space in most cities must be protected against the possibilities of theft, vandalism, and other related problems through some carefully thought out plan for control of access and exit, although strict control by doors and locks is contrary to the concept of openness. Appropriate controls should be planned for prime access points so that internal zoning of space can be kept to a minimum.

Hard Areas

The term "hard areas" is used by planners to designate places which, for one or another functional reason, must be built in a fixed way not easily subject to the free replanning characteristic of open plan spaces. Most offices will require a few spaces with fixed walls or with special provisions for specific uses (such as computer rooms or file rooms) that must be established on a fairly permanent basis. In terms of planning schedule, these spaces must be located early, so that whatever constructional requirements they may involve can be taken into account in good time. A checklist of hard area possibilities includes:

1. Toilets, washrooms, janitors' closets, and any other units requiring water or drain connections.

2. Areas with unusually heavy floor loadings. In offices this usually means file or archive spaces.

3. Computer equipment rooms and any other facilities containing heavy equipment or equipment with special power or ventilation requirements.

4. Rooms for special group uses such as auditoriums, dining rooms, or exhibit spaces.

5. Stairways or escalators for interfloor communication that are in addition to the basic building vertical circulation systems.

6. Any spaces that require full acoustical isolation with fixed walls either to contain a source of noise (keypunch machines, for example) or to assure privacy of activity inside (a board room, perhaps). Claims for isolation for the latter reason should be viewed with suspicion since such demands for absolute privacy are usually without sufficient grounds to justify the fixed space they require.

Space Scoring

As an aid in selecting rental space or in evaluating design proposals for newly built space, it is possible to devise a score card on which each evaluative criterion is listed. Each consideration in a proposal may then be scored on a numerical scale from best to worst (10 to 0, for example). The total of the scores gives a figure of merit to the space. Such a score card must be made up for each individual project since the qualities to be evaluated will vary in different circumstances. Typical items include:

Suitability of total square foot (square meter) area available _____

Suitability of building shape _____

Suitability of distribution on different floor levels _____

Suitability of core and circulation locations _____

Provision for AC wiring flexibility _____

Provision for phone wiring flexibility _____

The score card should contain a long list including all the considerations discussed above and others that may be special to the project.

To generate a meaningful total score, the items should be weighted according to their importance. Doing this involves an exercise of judgment that cannot be mathematically precise so that the seeming scientific precision of a numerical score turns out to be somewhat misleading. If the scoring procedure is used more as a checklist of considerations to be thought about than as a route to a final evaluation, it may be quite useful.

Space Selection Decisions

Final decisions about where and what to build or rent will probably always remain matters for judgment in which intuition and management style are factors. The discussion above is only concerned with the way in which built space influences the ease of open planning, but there are additional large issues that affect the suitability of space in offices of *any* type. Geographical location in city, suburb, or rural area affect ease of access and convenience to other offices and services and influence the form of structure which can be built economically. Will a number of floors in a tall building on a constricted city site be preferable to a low, spread-out space in a country location? The nature of the organization's work, its relationship to other organizations and services, and the character of its work force all influence such questions.

In recent years there has been a drive toward exurban locations where pleasant settings, easy parking, and spread-out planning are possible. Spaces suitable to open planning can usually be achieved in such locations more easily than on constricted city sites. However, experience has shown that there are negative consequences related to such office locations that should also be considered. Isolation from urban services (shopping, banks, restaurants, etc.) is an inconvenience to employees, particularly those in clerical or other support levels (usually in the majority) who feel less mobility than managers. Visits and meetings involving outsiders become more difficult to arrange, and everyone tends to become dependent on automobile transportation. Employees must either find living accommodation close by or must accept long and possibly difficult commuting.

Given a decision on urban or rural location, spaces in existing buildings available for rental must be compared with the possibilities of a new building on available sites. Certain neighborhoods may be more or less desirable for a given user organization; and available building spaces may have positive or negative characteristics (attractive and well-managed building, suitable floors available, favorable lease terms and durations, etc., or the absence of one or more of these characteristics with a correspondingly lower rent). As in the scoring of a specific space, efforts to relate evaluations of all these considerations in a logical way have proven to be very difficult. A recent study found that the single most important factor in decisions about office location is the location of the home of the top executive! The office planner cannot hope to totally eliminate such basically illogical pressures, but involvement in the selection process will at least help to make management aware of values that will influence the ease of effective planning and the level of user satisfaction that can be anticipated when the facility is put to use.

It is an unfortunate reality that selection of office space is usually done by management without any serious effort to consider attitudes of the total work staff. Nonmanagerial staff members are usually very much in the majority, and their preferences are often quite different from those of the decision-making managers. Top managers tend to think of the office facility in terms of its cost efficiencies and prestige values connected with good location and a style that will impress their peers. Workers may be more interested in handy lunchtime shopping and dates with friends or quick and easy commuting. It should be noted that user dissatisfaction with new facilities can often be traced to an inconvenient location lacking familiar nearby conveniences. Since direct expression of this kind of dissatisfaction is discouraged, it is often displaced on the physical characteristics of the new facility; if open planning has been used, it becomes a prime target for such complaints. The obvious conclusion is that suitability of open planning is only one of a large number of criteria that must be considered in selecting office space, and when open planning is to be used, it is particularly important that the location and overall character of the space should be viewed favorably by the largest possible number of user staff members. Less-than-ideal floor size or column spacing can be accepted and dealt with if the more general characteristics of the space are favorable. Even ideal characteristics for open planning may not overcome user resistance to an unpopular location or other general aspects of a new space regarded as unpleasant by a majority of occupants.

Equipment

7

The originators of *Bürolandschaft* were emphatic that this kind of planning did *not* require any special furniture or equipment; any standard available products would serve as long as desks and storage units of massive, solid, enclosed design were avoided. While this statement may have been reasonable in Germany in the 1950s and 1960s, it presented a paradox in the United States where almost all office furniture was massive, solid, and enclosed. Even in Germany, the Quickborner Team's statement required an amendment to the effect that special "acoustic screens" would be required, which only became standard products as open plan installations began to call for them.

When the first American test was conducted by DuPont, it was necessary to persuade a manufacturer of standard office furniture to introduce a specially modified product group which would have the desired characteristics of openness and lightness.

Furniture Systems

With the passage of time, a number of approaches to furniture for use in open planning have evolved that reflect varying degrees of loyalty to the originators' theories and varied kinds of modifications of their approach. Most such furniture takes the form of systems in which a limited number of components can be combined in various ways and rearranged with ease when layout or use changes take place. Although each manufacturer's system has certain unique characteris-

Furniture in the typical Quickborner Team project in Germany was resolutely nondescript, as "transparent" as possible, and not an important focus of attention. Courtesy Quickborner Team.

tics, similarities (even clear efforts at imitation) lead one to the conclusion that there are four different approaches now available, each from several different manufacturers. These are as follows:

1. Light, conventional equipment. This is the approach originally urged by the Quickborner Team. Desks are simply tables with minimal storage provision (pencil drawers). Files are open rolling carts; other storage furniture is discouraged. Movable acoustic screens, usually slightly curved to aid stability, are provided as the only means of cutting sightlines and breaking open space. Conventional planters or pots are used to hold plants. The system called TAG (no longer in production) developed for use in the DuPont project was of this type, as is the Designcraft system designed by Hans Krieks. Many standard office furniture product lines can now provide this simple menu of units, and screens are available from innumerable sources. A particularly elegant system developed in Switzerland by Fritz Haller is distributed in Europe by Herman Miller under the name "Haller-Programm" (available in the U.S. on order).

2. The Action Office developed by Robert Propst and its various more-or-less precise imitiations have origins in study of the workplace and the activities of the individual worker in the workplace. The furniture products that result have as their key element a system of panels that offer some degree of visual and acoustical privacy and that also provide support for work surfaces and storage units. Use of these systems tends to fill the work space with panel subdivisions that create spaces somewhat similar to the spaces of conventional planning, but with more flexibility and less need to cling to a rectilinear, geometric layout. Extensive storage and other special-purpose functions are readily available. The individual workplace can be outfitted in ways that adapt to any imaginable combination of personal requirements. Since the number of screen panels is largely determined by the need to support work surfaces and storage units, there is a tendency for an excessive degree of subdivision to develop which can be costly and can also negate, to some degree, the concept of openness. It also takes careful planning to work out the complexities of system installations which involve many intricate parts and, even more problematic, to manage the technicalities of change and rearrangement. Moving units on one side of a panel may have consequences for the components on the other side. The removed units will now have no place to hang unless on a new panel or on an existing one of the right dimension in a new location. It can become a complex problem to deal with the required inventory of components and keep track of what is on hand, in use, surplus, or in short supply. The ease of providing ample storage, panels for any desired level of privacy, and a high level of personalization of the workplace make such systems popular in the United States. The required equipment can be expensive, hard to manage, and in some ways limiting to the anticipated virtues of true openness.

3. Even further from the original concepts of *Bürolandschaft* are the systems built as storage-wall-type massive cabinet units that provide barriers for privacy and extensive furniture functioning in combined units. This approach also caters to the American desire for ample storage at the workplace and for more visual privacy than the truly open office of *Bürolandschaft* can offer. It is, if anything, even less flexible than the Action Office-related systems, but gains something in simplicity in exchange. The origins of this kind of system predate open planning and can be traced back to the work stations developed by Skidmore, Owings, & Merrill for the Armstrong Cork Co. office building in Lancaster, Pennsylvania, in 1964. General Fireproofing produced the furniture and offered it as an available product thereafter. A system developed by William Pulgram for McDonald's headquarters in Chicago, marketed by Eppinger Furniture under the

name TRM (for Task Response Module), is representative of this approach in a luxurious version executed in wood.

Knoll's Stephens System, developed in cooperation with SOM for use in the Weyerhaeuser headquarters in Tacoma, Washington, also generates similar units, but because it is made up of separate panels with corner connectors, it offers more flexibility than might be expected in view of its solid, massive, external appearance.

4. A number of other systems have appeared that are based on conventional desk systems, but which generate work station units through the combination of desk and storage components plus flat panel elements. The system designated 9000 by Steelcase is of this type. Modulo 3, developed in Italy, is also of a similar kind, although it is totally new and not based on any existing furniture system. Flat panels are connected with an ingenious extruded corner connector to make up desks and complex work station units.

In a way, all these kinds of furniture except the first represent some degree of retreat from the original concept of the open office. Each offers solid elements that divide a space into closed or partly closed cells, and each offers equipment for storage at the workplace in considerable volume. Flexibility survives at a level much greater than that offered by fixed partitioning or movable partitioning, but even this degree of flexibility (with the problems of disassembling, moving, and reassembling massive furniture components) is much less than that provided with the light and minimal furniture and screens of the early landscape office type.

As they are often used, panel and work station systems seem to do no more than replace one kind of partition system supplied by a partition manufacturer with another type supplied by a furniture manufacturer. It is not surprising that furniture companies are enthusiastic about this line of development, but the planner and user organization should question whether the values of openness are not subject to erosion or elimination when the space is filled with equipment which can finally generate cubicles just as constricting as those of conventional planning. When individual user-occupants are queried in advance about needs for storage space and privacy, it seems obvious that the resultant requests will overestimate requirements by a large percentage. Almost everyone will start with present equipment, add requests for more that they may have wanted in the past, and then add on a factor of 25 to 50 percent to be on the safe side. Since every realistic survey shows that office workers store useless and obsolete material inefficiently and since privacy needs are generally greatly exaggerated, this method of estimating requirements is almost certain to result in expensive and unnecessary equipment. Both storage and screening should be provided only to the minimal level that need can clearly demonstrate. Obtaining cooperation from staff in establishing reasonable requirements and accepting reasonable facilities in the new space depends on explaining the objectives of open planning in advance and enlisting users in realistic planning for real needs.

Screens

When the furniture selected for an open plan space is of a kind that permits true openness, movable screens—usually called "acoustic screens"—are helpful in cutting off long or objectionable sightlines and in defining areas associated with particular group or individual work. To be of any use, a screen must be high enough to block vision of a seated person; 60 in. (152 cm) is a favorite height. A standing person can look over a screen of this height—perhaps on tip-toe in the case of shorter people. If this is considered undesirable in some (or all) cases, a higher screen [about 70 to 72 in. (178 to 183 cm)] is needed. Lower

Above left: American office furniture developed to suit the original *Bürolandschaft* ideals—open and light with movable screen panels. This example carries the brand name Uniline. Courtesy The Zlowe Co., Inc. Above right: Designcraft furniture developed by Hans Krieks. Tubular frames and rounded corner panels are characteristic. Courtesy Designcraft, Inc.

 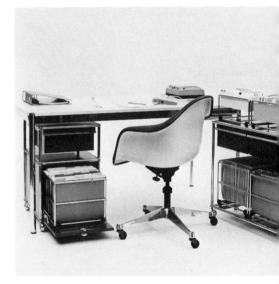

Above left: Double level interlocking file carts from the same furniture system. Courtesy Designcraft, Inc. Above right: Table desk with mobile file and general storage units from the Swiss system designated "Haller Programm" by its manufacturer. Courtesy Herman Miller, Inc.

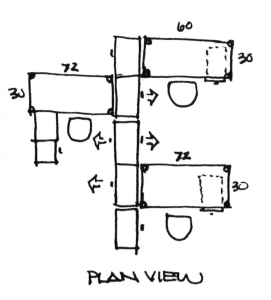

60

72

30

30

72

30

30

PLAN VIEW

Haller Programm furniture in an open work station grouping as illustrated in a planning sketchbook distributed by the manufacturer. Courtesy Herman Miller, Inc.

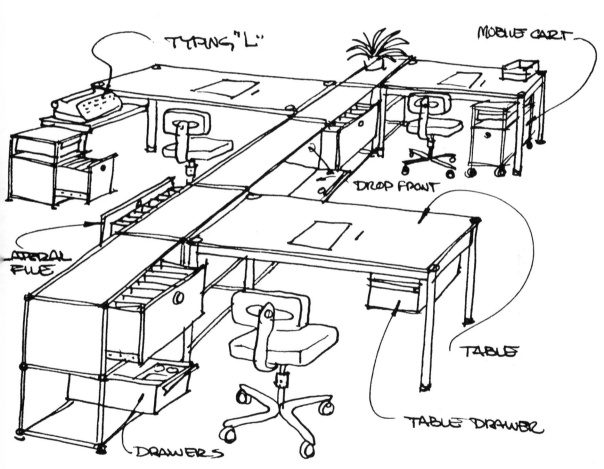

TYPING "L"

MOBILE CART

DROP FRONT

LATERAL FILE

TABLE

TABLE DRAWER

DRAWERS

Above left: Action Office work stations in use in an open plan. Courtesy Herman Miller, Inc. Above right: Chicago office of JFN Associates equipped with Action Office furniture placed on a hexagonal grid. Courtesy JFN Associates.

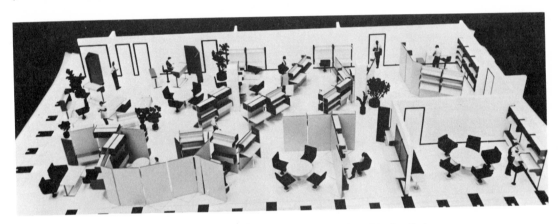

Action Office elements in scale model form for use in seminars conducted to familiarize planners with the use of the system. Courtesy Herman Miller, Inc.

Above left: A recent Action Office group. Note poles for ceiling-connected telephone and electrical service and wall-attached seating. Courtesy Herman Miller, Inc. Above right: Action Office components in a display suggesting a kind of open private office. Panels are available in two heights, curved or glazed. The round ball at lower right is an acoustic conditioner, which generates masking sound on a local basis. Courtesy Herman Miller, Inc.

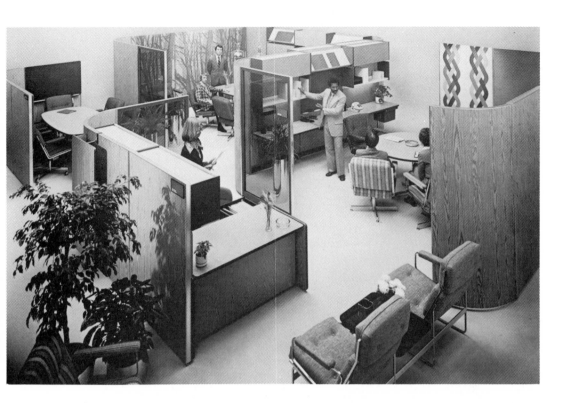

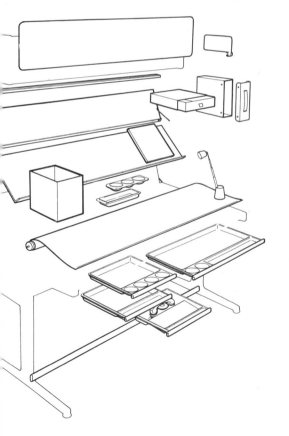

Top: Another panel-based system, Uni-Group Profile H, from Haworth ERA-1. Courtesy Haworth, Inc. Above: Offices of International Harvester Corp. with Westinghouse ASD (Architectural Systems Division) furniture in use. Courtesy Westinghouse Electric Corp.

Left: Robert Propst's Action Office provides a system of unique work stations that can be made up to individual requirements through assembly of individual components. Courtesy Herman Miller, Inc.

Top: Skidmore, Owings, & Merrill's Armstrong Cork Co. offices of 1964 with work station units manufactured by General Fireproofing. Photograph by Lawrence S. Williams, Inc.; courtesy Armstrong Cork Co. Middle: Custom-designed work stations in the offices of the Dreyfus Corp., New York. ISD, Inc., interior designers with Joseph G. Merz, architect. Photograph by John T. Hill; courtesy ISD, Inc. Above: TRM (task response module) furniture in use in offices of the Philadelphia National Bank. Note telephone locations and integral lighting. Courtesy Eppinger Furniture, Inc.

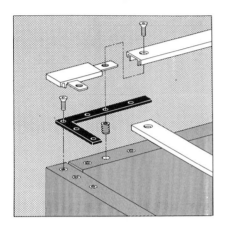

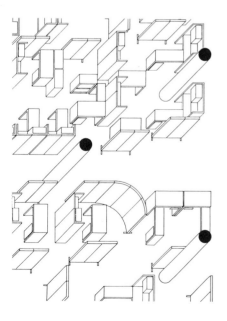

Top: Stephens System work stations in the offices of Crowley Maritime Corp., San Francisco, designed by Robinson and Mills, architects. Courtesy Knoll International, Inc. Above left: Panel connectors of the Stephens System are capped with visible trim in chrome or white. Courtesy Knoll International, Inc. Above: Stephens System components are equally adaptable for assembly into desk work stations independent of panel attachments. Courtesy Knoll International, Inc. Left: Typical arrangements of Stephens System components as illustrated in the manufacturer's application charts. Courtesy Knoll International, Inc.

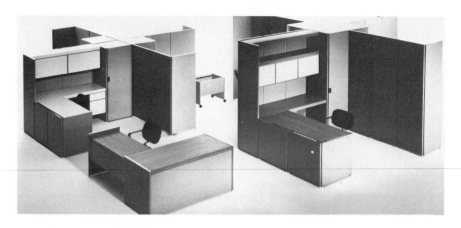

Top: Office system by Otto Zapf is conceptually related to the Stephens System but uses lighter and softer materials. Vertical panel surfaces are fabric- or vinyl-surfaced. Courtesy Knoll International, Inc. Middle: The Zapf System in use in offices for the Bussmann Corp. in St. Louis designed by the Plumb Design Group. Courtesy Knoll International, Inc. Above: A work station system designed by Warren Platner (with associates David Connell and William Smith) manufactured by CI Designs. Photograph by Ezra Stoller, ESTO; courtesy Warren Platner Associates. Above right: Arcon Furniture System R/S, designed by Richard Thompson, uses a steel cage structure to hold applied panels with wood, vinyl, or fabric surfaces. Courtesy Arcon Furniture; Group Artec.

Top, middle, and above: Steelcase 9000 series furniture in use in typical work stations, in a large work station, and in compact units for word-processing stations. Courtesy Steelcase, Inc.

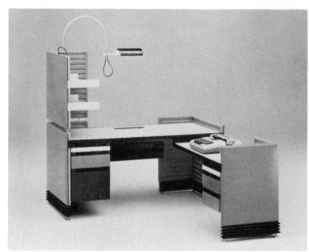

Top left: Modulo 3 System groupings shown in scale models. Courtesy Tiffany Industries, Inc. Top right: A three-station cluster of Modulo 3 units. Courtesy Tiffany Industries, Inc. Above left: Work stations by GF as installed in the Federal Reserve Bank offices in Minneapolis designed by Gunar Birkerts. Courtesy GF, Inc. Above right: A work station from the Nelson Workspaces System designed by George Nelson and Co. L-shape units support desk tops and can be added at an upper level to provide screening. Various accessories attach to edge slots. Courtesy Storwal International.

screens have the advantage of allowing a person to look across longer distances when standing in order to locate people far away, and they increase the sense of openness. High screens tend to have the same effect as regular partitioning and should not be used in any number without some very pressing reasons.

Even lower screens can, if used in numbers, begin to create areas that approach the effect of partitioned offices, and rows of screens lined up to create corridorlike spaces are particularly undesirable. Screens have relatively little usefulness in establishing acoustical privacy, and efforts to use them for this purpose result in pseudo-partitions which negate the value of open planning and still do not achieve the desired privacy. Valid ways of dealing with acoustical problems are discussed in Chapter 8. Use of screens should be limited to blocking undesirable sightlines. As a rule, any plan in which the number of screens exceeds the number of people using the space should be questioned.

The classic open plan screen developed by the Quickborner Team is slightly curved so that a foot at each end and one at the center establish a triangle sufficient to provide stability. Flat screens are also often used, but they must have feet with enough spread so that they are not easily tipped. Screens usually have a surface of cloth with a backing of sound-absorbent material so that they have some acoustical value. They may also serve as tack surface and support for some accessories (such as coat hangers or lighting devices).

The plants which are a traditional feature of the landscape office also provide a secondary element of screening. They can block lines of access or partly block vision and serve to relieve any sense of austerity that the other equipment might suggest. Selection of suitable plants and development of procedures for providing light and water needed to maintain them requires the help of a knowledgeable supplier. Contracts are available in many places that provide plants on a rotating basis so that any located where growth conditions are not right can be removed (usually to a greenhouse) and replaced on a scheduled basis. It should not be necessary to mention that artificial plants are totally unacceptable.

Lighting

The question of what constitutes adequate office lighting is subject to more debate and to more changing attitudes than any other aspect of office planning. Over the years since artificial lighting has become commonplace, any number of standards have been established, put into wide use, and then supplanted by different standards. This process is still going on, with the widely accepted standards of only a few years ago now subject to serious question.

The aspect of lighting which is easiest to measure and quantify is intensity—the value measured by a simple light meter. This is, unfortunately, only one of a number of considerations that affect seeing and the other visual qualities of a lighted space, but since it is easy to measure, it tends to become a focus for lighting standards. The unit of measure is the footcandle—that is, the illumination provided by a standard candle (an ordinary candle made to standardized specifications) at a distance of 1 ft (30 cm). Special light meters measure footcandle levels, but many photo exposure meters (which are less expensive and more commonplace) do so also with ample accuracy for anything less than research purposes.* (Interested readers should experiment with a meter to develop some sense of what various footcandle levels mean.) Sunlight out-of-doors has a level of 6,000 footcandles or more, and yet it is possible to read with an illumination level of only 1 footcandle. The reason such a great range is usable is that the eye is equipped with an iris which opens to admit light in dim conditions and closes in brightness. The light reaching the retina is thus kept within a

---

*The Sekonic model L-28 is a good choice and is widely available.

Top: Typical curved screen as developed by the Quickborner Team. The central foot establishes a base triangle large enough to discourage easy overturning. Above: Plants used as screening elements give visual relief from the blankness of acoustical screening. Montgomery Ward Headquarters in Chicago, Sydney Rodgers Associates, interior planners. Photograph by Hedrich Blessing; courtesy Rodgers Associates.

narrow range regardless of external circumstances. There are limits to what the eye can cope with at each end of the scale; one cannot read in near darkness and one must squint (or wear dark glasses) in a glare. But intensity of light will be satisfactory for most tasks in a range upward from about 50 footcandles to that of outdoor daylight.

Various studies have been made in an effort to discover ideal light levels for various tasks, usually under the sponsorship of manufacturers of lighting devices or of power companies. Suggested standards have, not surprisingly, been raised over the years until levels of 100 to 200 footcandles at work surfaces have come to be common recommendations. Office space is commonly rented with lease provisions that require installed fixtures with a uniform level of no less than _____ footcandles—the inserted figure being, perhaps, 80, 100, or 120. But in the last few years concerns over the cost of energy and its reduced availability has led to reexamination of this practice. Conventional lighting is installed in the ceiling and for it to deliver a stated footcandle level at desk top requires a certain wattage of lamps in fixtures closely spaced to make the lighting uniform. The wattage and resulting cost of fixtures, lamps, and power will be proportional to the footcandle level delivered. The cost of 120 footcandles is twice that of 60 footcandles. If it is possible to see effectively at 60 footcandles, the merit of paying for double that level is naturally questionable.

As lighting is most often installed, the fixtures are chosen on the basis of efficiency—that is, how many footcandles they can deliver per watt consumed. Unfortunately, the most efficient fixtures in these terms are lens-type units which show up as bright rectangles in an otherwise dim ceiling. Occupants of a space lighted in this way find that their field of vision includes their work area, which is fairly bright; the surrounding area including the ceiling, which is fairly bright to quite dim; and the light fixtures themselves, which are glaringly bright, by far the brightest visible areas. The iris cannot deal with this range and struggles to open for task vision and then to close to resist fixture glare. A lighting consultant will say that there is "excessive brightness contrast" and will recommend low-brightness fixtures with special lenses or louvers that direct the light straight down and make the fixture itself appear dim at normal viewing angles. It is easy to test the efficacy of this approach by going into a space with glaring fixtures and then shading the eyes with the hand, an eyeshade, or a hat brim. Vision is instantly improved. Unfortunately, low-brightness fixtures have a higher first cost than the ordinary fixture and are less efficient in terms of watts consumed for a given light level. It is only necessary to accept a reasonable footcandle level, however, to offset this difference. This leads to the most common, satisfactory lighting approach developed a few years ago: a regular pattern of low-brightness fixtures installed in the ceiling with a spacing that delivers a reasonable level (say, 50 to 80 footcandles) at desk top. The absence of fixed partitions in open planning means that a regular pattern can extend throughout the occupied space without any need to consider furniture layout.

Even this approach has certain faults. The very uniformity of the lighting establishes a monotony of character that is not totally ideal. From an economic point of view, it is wasteful to light an entire space to the level desired on desk tops since they constitute only a small proportion of the total area. Moreover, screens and equipment hung on screens (shelves or storage units) may cast shadows on desk tops so that the needed light does not always reach the surfaces where it is desired, while it floods circulation and storage areas.

In addition to the points just mentioned, the lighting engineer is aware of the physical reality expressed in the law of inverse squares, which states that light intensity varies inversely as the square of the distance of the source. That means that when a light is moved twice as far away, only one-quarter the intensity will be received; when moved half as far away, the intensity will be

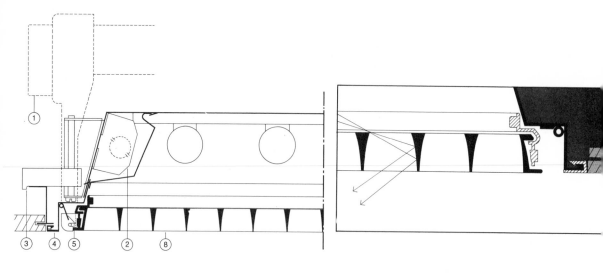

Top left: Half cross-section of a typical low-brightness light fixture with air-handling ability. (1) Connector for air conditioning duct. (2) Ballast mounted in contact with exterior to aid heat dissipation into plenum. (3) Adjustable mounting bracket. (4) Edge trim frame. (5) Adjustable vane to control air flow. (6) Grid of parabolic contoured baffles, the secret of the low-brightness idea. Top right: Detail of parabolic vanes showing how sight lines are directed away from the fluorescent tubes. Courtesy Lightolier. Above: A similar low-brightness fixture as it appears in use.

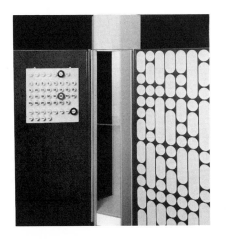

Top left: An uplighting unit which provides some incidental storage space and can be connected to screen panels. Courtesy Hauserman, Inc. Top right: Task/ambient lighting. The Stephens System work station includes light for the work surface and also directs light upward. The columnlike element in the foreground is a lighting device directing light upward to provide additional ambient light. Courtesy Knoll International Inc. Middle: Up and down lighting incorporated in work station and storage units and in one case provided by an attached light strip. TRM furniture in use in the offices of the Philadelphia National Bank. Courtesy Eppinger Furniture, Inc. Above: Task/ambient lighting in offices of Arco Chemical Co. in Houston. The chromium tube beyond the plant on the right is a movable ambient uplight. Photograph by Jeff Johnson; courtesy Morganelli-Heumann and Associates, designers.

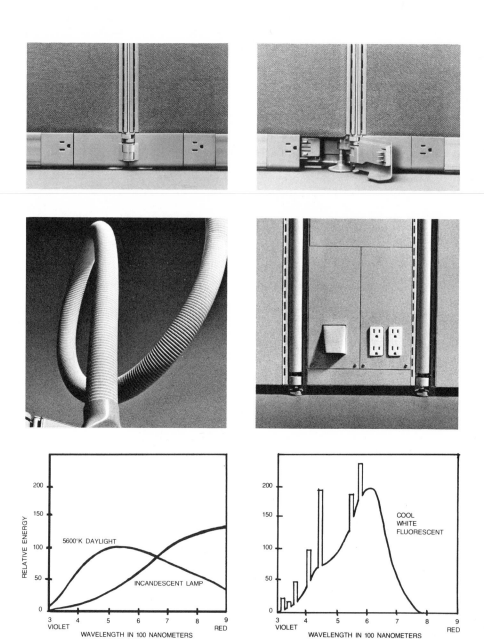

Top left: Screen panels with integral wiring in base. Top right: Electrical connection between panels is provided by swinging connector element in Haworth ERA-1 System. Courtesy Haworth, Inc. Middle left: Flexible plastic hose is offered in the Westinghouse ASD system as a visible (and possibly decorative) means of making connections to ceiling electrical and telephone service. Middle right: Wiring is led through the panels to integral base outlets. Courtesy Westinghouse Electric Co. Above left: Chart showing mix of wavelengths in average daylight and in incandescent light. Daylight varies somewhat with climate, season, time of day, and weather conditions, but always includes all wavelengths. Incandescent light, although stronger at the red-orange end of the spectrum (right) and weaker in green-blue-violet (left), also includes all wavelengths in a continuous range. Above right: Comparable chart for fluorescent light source. The curve shows the distribution of wavelengths which are continuous (all frequencies present) produced by the phosphors which coat the tube. The bars which rise from the curve represent light of specific, separate wavelengths produced by the gasses in the tube. These spectra are discontinuous. Spectra of various HID lamps show even more striking discontinuity. Charts after *IES Handbook*.

quadrupled. (The reader can test this with a lamp, yardstick, and photo light meter.) Light fixtures installed in a ceiling are about 6 ft (183 cm) above desk top. If lowered to 2 ft (61 cm) above, only $2^2/6^2$ or 4/36 or 1/9 the wattage would provide the same footcandle level! While lights hanging down over desks would be unsightly and hard to move when desks were rearranged, lights incorporated into desks and other work units can move when the units move. This line of thinking has led to task or task/ambient lighting, an entirely new approach in office illumination.

Task light is, of course, light delivered to the specific area of work from a closely placed source. Ambient lighting fills the total space, circulation, and other nontask areas with sufficient light to make it easy to move about and prevent extreme brightness contrast between task areas and surroundings. Typically, task lighting is installed in furniture units in some position close to work surfaces. Ambient lighting comes from light spilled upward towards the ceiling from task lighting, from special units added to furniture (including screen panels) to direct light upward, and, possibly, from special freestanding fixtures that direct light upward. Because sources are close to work surfaces, their number is limited and wattages can be modest; since the ambient light level can be low (as little as 5 to 10 footcandles) it also demands limited wattages. In making rough estimates of power needs for lighting, a recent common standard is provision of about 5 watts per sq ft; 2 watts per sq ft will provide satisfactory task/ambient lighting. The U.S. General Services Administration (GSA) has established a standard of 2.3 watts per sq ft for offices using this system. Energy savings are even greater than might be expected because wattage used for lighting also shows up as heat that must be removed by air conditioning. Less wattage means less HVAC, with corresponding reductions in both first and operational cost over the life of the facility.

Users' reactions to task lighting are highly favorable. The space so lit tends to have a certain quiet, soft character suggesting residential lighting (which has been task/ambient, by chance, all through history). It generates a far pleasanter ambience than the blasting glare of the usual ceiling fluorescents and is at least as pleasant as the best installations of low-brightness ceiling fixtures. Task vision is as good or better with low-brightness installations and much better than with the usual economy installation. Task/ambient lighting is particularly suited to use in open planning where the absence of fixed room divisions makes the development of overall ambient lighting easy. It does require selection of furniture that can house the necessary lighting equipment, thus ruling out the total openness of the original landscape office (unless desk-mounted Luxo or similar lamps are to be tolerated). Most panel and storage-wall furniture systems are well adapted to task lighting, and manufacturers have been quick to make the necessary equipment available in standard product lines. This method of lighting makes easy availability of AC from the floor very important and requires furniture details that provide power transmission in furniture components (through concealed wiring and connectors). When rental space is to be occupied, lease negotiations need to cover the impact of task lighting. Standard ceiling lighting is often included in rent charges, and it may be difficult to obtain credit for its omission, since the building owner will probably argue that he will have to provide it for the next tenant. As task lighting becomes a more widely accepted norm, this issue will be more easily resolved.

A final lighting issue, not yet resolved, involves the relative merits of fluorescent, HID (high intensity discharge), and incandescent light sources. Fluorescent (and, quite recently, HID) sources have been almost universally preferred for office lighting since their development because of their greater efficiency in terms of lumens per watt output, in spite of a widely felt preference for the visual qualities of incandescent light or daylight. Although the color quality of fluorescent light can be made to match daylight quite well, the energy output spectrum remains discontinuous—that is, the seeming white light is not a mixture of all frequencies (as is daylight and incandescent light), but is rather a mixture of a few specific frequencies emitted by the elements in the tube which fluoresce. When examined through a spectroscope, the light of the sun or of an incandescent bulb is the familiar rainbow. In contrast, fluorescent light is several thin, intense color lines. Recent research indicates that people have physiological needs for full-spectrum light and that dependence on fluorescent or other discontinuous spectrum lighting for more than incidental uses have long-term harmful effects on users. Research on this issue is still being conducted, but planners and lighting consultants may well consider reducing dependence on fluorescent light sources. Fortunately, willingness to accept lowered intensity levels together with the acceptance of task/ambient lighting can reduce wattage requirements so drastically that the economic impact of a retreat from all fluorescent light sources is not now as serious as might be expected.

Telephones

The problems of providing telephone wiring in flexible office space have been discussed in Chapter 6. Problems related to telephone equipment are usually considered to be minor, and good advice is generally available from local telephone companies. The number of instruments required is established by the communication needs of individual workers. There is a tendency to provide a telephone at every workplace, but phones shared by several users are often adequate in general work areas if the instruments can be located so that they are convenient to all users and so that use does not disturb the person closest to the phone. Automatic dial systems make the regular telephone convenient for internal communication to such a degree that separate intercoms have largely disappeared. Direct dial numbers for individual phones have reduced the work of the switchboard operator to a minimum so that a receptionist can also function as an operator in most small- or medium-sized facilities.

Telephone instruments are available in a variety of shapes, styles, and colors and with choices such as push-button versus conventional dialing options. Special arrangements for phone answering of one or more executive phones, provisions for conference call hookups, and other special situations are widely available with standardized telephone company equipment. Special purpose accessories such as amplifiers to make incoming calls audible to several listeners and sensitive transmitters that permit speaking at a distance from the phone are available, for whatever usefulness they may have. The much publicized picture-phone, as the service becomes available, may also have usefulness in some situations.

A problem that remains unsolved, however, involves locating people who are away from their desks so that they may receive incoming calls and limiting the irritations associated with ringing phones. Most office workers are frequently away from their desks and, in many kinds of work, for long periods. If incoming calls are dialed directly, the unattended phone will continue to ring, and the caller will have no way of knowing when to call back or how to reach the desired party at a different number. A person away from his desk, but still close by, will often have difficulty identifying the location of a ringing phone and may miss calls or answer the wrong one needlessly. Incoming callers are irritated when they receive no answer after many rings or when the person answering the phone has no knowledge of the whereabouts of the person being called. The number of tries required to reach a certain person can often be quite high, with corresponding wasted calls and resultant irritation. Several partial solutions can be suggested, but no perfect system seems to be available at present.

1. Provide a flashing light as an alternative to a bell wherever sightline patterns

make it practical. A bell which can be switched on or off can be available as an alternative, to be used when circumstances require.

2. Group several users on one line, even if separate instruments are provided, so that incoming calls can be answered, calls switched, or messages taken in a high proportion of cases.

3. Provide a system for calls unanswered after a reasonable number of rings (three to five) to be picked up by an operator who can take messages or explain how to reach the called party.

While these arrangements still do not totally eliminate problems of telephone communication, they will reduce irritations.

It should be noted that open planning, particularly if the space is truly open to vision, makes it easier to observe light signals, to locate call recipients who are away from a workplace but still nearby, and to deal with responses to calls for people who are absent. It often makes it possible to substitute a short walk and face-to-face conversation for a call or series of calls with their related frustrations of no answer, messages, etc.

The exclusive right of telephone companies to provide all phone instruments is in the process of being broken through legal actions. In the near future, the occupant organization will have the option to accept standard equipment provided by the phone company or to buy and own its own equipment. In the latter case, it is possible that equipment of unusual design or with special functional characteristics will become available that may offer new alternatives to standard telephone equipment.

Data Communication
Access to computer memory and processing is available through the typewriter-like data terminal which permits keying in data or inquiries and provides response by typed-out paper reply. An alternative is the CRT (cathode ray tube) unit which accepts inquiries and instructions through a typewriter keyboard but responds through a visual display on a television-like screen. Both types of device are rapidly moving from a highly specialized role into wide usefulness for a great variety of office tasks. The CRT unit in particular helps to reduce reliance on paper with its physical problems of sorting. locating, and filing and

CRT units in compact work stations. Courtesy Steelcase, Inc.

substitutes instantaneous access to large amounts of information in a way that is easily useful to the average office staff member without special training in computer technology. Such units may well become as common as or more common than the typewriter.

Preparation of conventionally typed communication is also tending to change through the techniques of word processing in which phrases and paragraphs held in a tape memory can be combined with data from a computer to synthesize letters that deal with many routine (and some not so routine) communications. Even unique written communications can be composed at a CRT unit, with changes and corrections easily made. The final typing then becomes a mechanical operation that happens quickly and, if desired, at a remote location where noise can be isolated. Under such circumstances the job of stenographer and the aspects of secretarial work that were primarily stenographic tend to change totally.

Other Equipment

The office planner is usually expected to select suitable incidental office gear of the kind that do not differ significantly in open or conventional planning. A typical checklist of such items includes:

Desk chairs

Visitors' chairs

Secretarial chairs

Lounge and waiting space seating

Conference and incidental tables

Letter trays

Desk pads, calendar and note pads, pen sets, trash baskets

Clocks

Ash trays and receivers

Washroom equipment and accessories

Signs and directories

Wardrobes, coat racks, and holders

Bulletin and tack boards; chalkboards and screens

Audiovisual facilities and equipment

Coffee and minor food service equipment

Fire safety and exit marker equipment

Security arrangements (locks, closed-circuit TV, etc.)

Art works and decorative graphics

It should be noted that the higher visibility of all spaces in open planning makes it particularly important that all these items be of good appearance and, to whatever extent possible, coordinated in design and color so that they do not become a source of excessive visual confusion.

Selection, Purchase, and Installation

Conventional planning routines proceed from general plans to specific layout and then after layout approval to selection of furniture and equipment with, in many cases, competitive bidding or at least comparative pricing as a basis for purchase decisions. The equipment systems useful in open planning are much more individualized than conventional furniture and therefore call this seemingly logical order of procedure into question. In conventional planning, desks may be laid out and file cabinets located using standard sizes that only vary slightly between different manufacturers. In the case of open planning, this is also possible in areas truly open in *Bürolandschaft* fashion, but where panel systems and/or work stations are to be used, it is not practical to plan in detail until after systems have been selected. A change from use of Herman Miller Action Office to the Knoll Stephens System, for example, would involve an almost total replanning of the space. Once the system or systems to be used are selected, the character and details of the system influence planning very strongly, and assistance from the system's manufacturer is often useful and even necessary if the system is to be used to greatest advantage.

This situation is upsetting to traditional purchasing approaches. So that comparison and competition are not totally obviated, it is good planning practice to proceed through planning processes up to a general layout in which all work stations are located and defined in terms of area and general type. Planning should then pause until systems selections have been made. In doing this it is helpful to select a few work station types that are roughly typical of all those that will be present in the project. For example, these might include:

1. Executive space

2. Typical middle staff work station

3. Clerical or accounting work station

Each of these work station types can then be designed in detail in terms of each of the various furniture systems that may be under consideration. Manufacturers may be asked to criticize the planned stations or to offer alternatives. Firm prices can now be requested for the anticipated number of stations of each type. While not bids, such prices give an accurate basis for cost comparison between different system approaches. It may be worthwhile to set up a prototype work station of each type in each system under serious consideration so that cost comparison can be related to direct physical comparison. Such prototypes can also be used to examine alternate lighting, seating, and other equipment options. Firm decisions can then be made about furniture and other equipment with some confidence that comparative costs and merits have been rationally evaluated. Planning can then proceed on the basis of the products to be used and full advantage can be taken of manufacturers' aid in planning without fear of unwillingly becoming a captive customer and without duplication of work in obtaining comparative pricing.

Purchasing and installation follow the same standard practices that apply to conventional planning. But note that in systems developed for open plan use, installation is a particularly important matter. Any mover or janitor can place a desk in a conventional room, but system product assembly is often complex and may require considerable knowledge and skill. The system manufacturer or dealer should be invited or even required to provide installation services and supervision.

KNOLL   Stephens System

HERMAN MILLER   Action Office

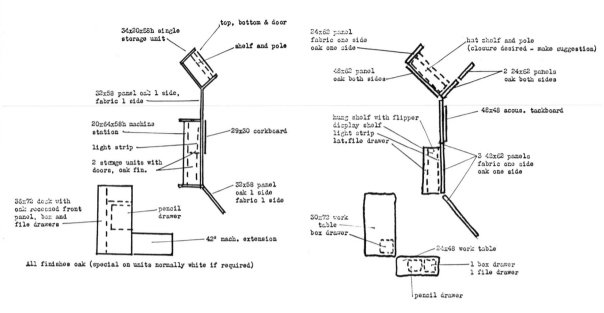

Knoll (left):
- 34x20x58h single storage unit
- top, bottom & door
- shelf and pole
- 32x58 panel oak 1 side, fabric 1 side
- 20x64x58h machine station
- 29x30 corkboard
- light strip
- 2 storage units with doors, oak fin.
- 32x58 panel oak 1 side fabric 1 side
- 36x72 desk with oak recessed front panel, box and file drawers
- pencil drawer
- 42" mach. extension

All finishes oak (special on units normally white if required)

Herman Miller (right):
- 24x62 panel fabric one side oak one side
- hat shelf and pole (closure desired – make suggestion)
- 48x62 panel oak both sides
- 2 24x62 panels oak both sides
- hung shelf with flipper display shelf light strip lat.file drawer
- 48x48 acous. tackboard
- 3 48x62 panels fabric one side oak one side
- 30x72 work table box drawer
- 24x48 work table
- 1 box drawer 1 file drawer
- pencil drawer

KNOLL   Stephens System

HERMAN MILLER   Action Office

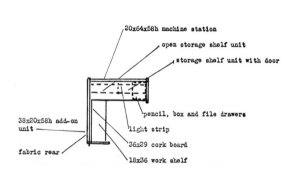

Knoll (left):
- 20x64x58h machine station
- open storage shelf unit
- storage shelf unit with door
- pencil, box and file drawers
- 38x20x58h add-on unit
- light strip
- fabric rear
- 36x29 cork board
- 18x36 work shelf

Oak finish. White paint or plastic finishes where applicable.

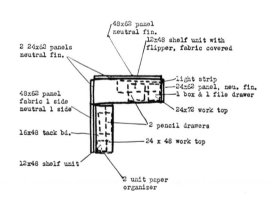

Herman Miller (right):
- 48x62 panel neutral fin.
- 12x48 shelf unit with flipper, fabric covered
- 2 24x62 panels neutral fin.
- light strip
- 24x62 panel, neu. fin.
- 1 box & 1 file drawer
- 48x62 panel fabric 1 side neutral 1 side
- 24x72 work top
- 2 pencil drawers
- 16x48 tack bd.
- 24 x 48 work top
- 12x48 shelf unit
- 2 unit paper organizer

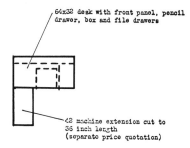

64x32 desk with front panel, **pencil drawer**, box and file drawers

42 machine extension cut to 36 inch length
(separate price quotation)

Oak finish. White metal and plastic finishes may be offered on drawers and front panels as available.

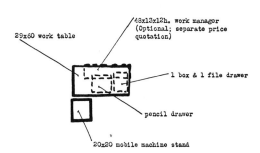

29x60 work table

48x13x12h. work manager
(Optional; separate price quotation)

1 box & 1 file drawer

pencil drawer

20x20 mobile machine stand

Opposite page and above: Work stations of comparable plan detailed in two different furniture systems to obtain comparative pricing and to permit assembly of similar mock-ups for user evaluation. Three pairs are shown, each planned in Stephens System and Action Office. Dial Financial Corp. offices; John Pile, office planner.

Special Problems

When news of the *Bürolandschaft* concept first began to circulate among office planners, the most common first reaction was "absurd!" or "it will never work *here*." Designers experienced with conventional planning were quick to point out problems that they felt sure made the approach impossible. While it has become clear that the approach is by no means impossible, the problems most often identified as impossible are very real and need to be carefully considered and controlled if an open plan office is to work well and be free from irritations. Each of these problems is also a problem to the conventional planner, but the ways of dealing with it, or the acceptance of the failure to deal with it, have become so commonplace in average offices that little thought is given to the issues involved. Because the open plan is still new, the problems it raises attract attention, and there is a corresponding opportunity to find effective solutions.

Privacy

The first and most obvious objection to an open plan is that it destroys privacy. Everyone, we are told, will be totally exposed, will be distracted by seeing what everyone else is doing, and will hear and be overheard in a way that will make business impossible. Private offices are commonly provided for people with important or sensitive tasks, and there is a genuine fear that eliminating them will make work difficult or awkward.

Recent research seems to confirm that a natural human desire for territory identifiable as one's own is present in every staff member and that its denial leads to feelings of unease and hostility. In conventional planning these matters are resolved by providing private offices for upper management and some levels of middle management; having shared offices, tiny cubicles, or some similar compromises for more junior staff; and reverting to open general or pool offices for clerical, bookkeeping, drafting, and similar functional groups. Those offered spacious private offices are usually quite contented even though their work effectiveness is possibly impaired by the isolation that results. Those with shared offices have not, in fact, any privacy; those in cubicles may have the satisfactions of territory but usually must put up with windowless and claustrophobic cells. The general office workers have not any privacy at all. Efforts to provide at least a minimal, private cubicle for everyone (by no means uncommon) generate a warren of tiny spaces in which people with tasks that involve cooperation are pointlessly isolated. A well-planned open office can avoid all such problems, but in so doing requires care in dealing with some real issues. These include:

1. All privacy is a matter of degree. The conventional private office with a door is almost always occupied with the door open. A closed door generates an excess of isolation, and users sense this and limit door closing to very special situations. In fact, the fixed walls generate an excess of isolation, but this is not realized because they are accepted as a norm. Sound in private offices can be overheard outside and in adjacent spaces in any normal system of office construction. Sound from outside penetrates a quiet private office in a way that can be quite irritating. The degree of isolation necessary to deal with these matters is only available to the most luxurious quarters of top executives and tends to isolate them in a way that has unfortunate consequences to their role in an

organization. To hide or be hidden totally is not conducive to a strong relationship with other members of the organization.

2. Open planning eliminates the privacy of total isolation, but still offers a variety of levels of limited privacy. It is useful in this discussion to identify kinds of privacy as "visual" and "acoustical"; in each area it is possible to make the separation:

| Seeing | versus | being seen |
| Hearing | versus | being heard |

It is helpful to be able to see other people and activity in progress within one's own areas of concern as long as the view is not distracting. As a practical matter, being able to make visual contact in order to know who is where at any given time can save many wasteful walks from place to place, futile phone calls, and interruptions when someone engaged in a conversation, call, or task is visited by an unannounced co-worker. Seeing vast areas filled with many people, some not known or related to one's own work, can be distracting, but it can be prevented by reasonable placement of screen barriers, wardrobes, plants, and similar obstructions. Direct eye-to-eye sightlines can be avoided by careful planning, and it is usually possible to arrange work stations so that the straight-ahead view in the normal work position does not include other people. No one should see active lines of major circulation from a normal work position. In planning terms, this means that each work station should be checked for related sightlines and that adjustments should be made to avoid problems.

The matter of being seen is somewhat different. There seems to be no valid reason why an office worker should feel it necessary to be hidden, truly invisible, at normal work. Being seen with a particular co-worker or visitor may, perhaps, in certain situations arouse curiosity or comment, but it is hardly possible to imagine an office facility constructed for a level of secretiveness that would avoid all visibility of such communication, and it is reasonable to ask what sort of office politicking would require so much secretiveness. Intelligent placement of work stations and screening elements will avoid an embarrassing sense of being overlooked. Visual privacy for genuinely sensitive meetings can be dealt with in other ways, discussed in the following point.

Acoustic privacy—not being overheard, on the one hand, and not being annoyed by overhearing, on the other—is a matter tied into the general acoustical climate of the office space. This is discussed as a separate problem, but in terms of privacy, it means that the open office must offer at least as good acoustical isolation as the conventional private office or cubicle. In practice, this is not hard to achieve. The seeming privacy of the private office is partly spurious, and the total acoustical environment of the open office can easily do as well or better in screening out intrusive noise, stopping the intrusion of overheard conversation, and ending worries about possibly troublesome overhearing of sensitive conversations. The solutions lie in part in the technical area of acoustics and in part in the provision of certain privacy alternatives.

3. Almost all office spaces include some special spaces for conferences and meetings. Open offices can include these spaces with varied levels of privacy and make them available to all appropriate levels of staff as needed. Open conference areas scattered through the work space offer places for meetings away from actual workplaces. Conference or meeting rooms with closed door privacy can be provided for meetings that may be either noisy or sensitive in ways that make open meeting areas unsuitable. Provision of some small, closed door private rooms not assigned to any individual but available to anyone as needed can be very helpful.

Above left: Open conference area defined by movable, curved screen. Dial Financial Corp. offices; John Pile, office planner. Photograph by Norman McGrath. Above right: Fully enclosed conference room on right in an otherwise open office. Glass partition preserves a sense of openness. Arco Chemical offices; Morganelli-Heumann, interior designers. Photograph by Richard W. Payne.

Above left: A tiny quiet room for private conversations, concentrated work, or private phone calls. Dial Financial Corp. offices; John Pile, office planner. Photograph by Norman McGrath. Above right: Work-related and personal clutter that might be offensive under other circumstances can be acceptable and useful when confined to well-defined individual territory. Offices of JFN Associates, Chicago. Courtesy JFN.

The term "quiet room" is sometimes used for such spaces. They serve the individual's occasional need to work under conditions of total quiet and isolation and are available for small meetings or person-to-person conversations in which a sense of total visual and acoustical privacy is needed. If such spaces are located in a way that makes access not too publicly visible, with an "in use" light sign to prevent interruptions, they become a haven available for the very occasional needs for isolation that can occur, not only for top executives, but for any members of an organization.

Similarly, in addition to the usual telephone provisions, it is useful to provide a few fully private phone stations or "booths" where people can make calls which they feel are too personal or private to be possible in the open working space. Providing these possibilities for full privacy has the effect of reducing tensions about the issue of privacy. They may be used less than might be expected, but the fact that they are available will minimize feelings of distress about absence of privacy.

4. The sense of personal territory, an area where one can arrange things as desired and control one's own environment to a degree, may be more a question of managerial policy than of physical realities. A private office with standard equipment and proscriptions against all change can be more hostile than an open work station with freedom to arrange matters as desired within certain limits of reason and practicality. Panel systems and work station systems of equipment tend to offer to each user a fairly well-defined space in which personal preferences about equipment and its arrangement and about the selection and organization of personal clutter can be exercised within a kind of containment that prevents this personalization from becoming a source of chaos in the total office installation. At the upper, middle-management, and executive levels, the spaces provided in open planning offer as much freedom for personalization as do conventional office spaces. It is hardly possible to provide for the individual who demands an office imitative of a Gothic chapel or an Empire bedroom, but there can be valid questions about the appropriateness of such demands in any kind of office space.

Status

The concept of status, made a byword by Vance Packard's *The Status Seekers*, is certainly an issue in the sociology of office life. Its impact on planning, closely bound up with privacy issues, is inescapable. Modern technological society likes to pretend, particularly in the United States, that it is truly democratic and egalitarian. The evidence that this is in part a pretense is everywhere in the desire for such status symbols as overinflated automobiles, expense-account dining, and executive office quarters designed more for show than for work. Ambition to rise in an organization is generally encouraged by management and rewards are offered in terms of compensation, privileges, and incidentals. such as physical accommodations.

Every organization must come to terms with its own views about status ranking versus democracy. Management and planner must arrive at agreed on policies about how visible, how rigid, and how organized the display of status is to be in any particular office installation. Friction will most often arise when stated goals and realities are far apart or when the planner fails to understand or accept the realities present in an organization. A desire to eliminate or minimize show of status may be ideologically sound, but it will not be effective if attempted as a planning goal without full acceptance both in words and in real attitudes by the user organization. In conventional planning, the size, location, and level of privacy of the individual office or workplace is a key element in status display. The bureaucratic organization is inclined to institutionalize policies about such matters as codifying square footage provided, size of desk, number of chairs, etc., not on the basis of need but solely on the basis of rank. Extremes of such codification are a source not only of any number of jokes, but also of very real resentments and hostilities.

Open planning tends to make status designation through office accommodation less obvious and so in organizations that are in fact status-oriented, it may generate complaints from those at levels where status display is normally expected who may feel deprived of anticipated symbolic rewards. The manager who through years of loyal effort has just become entitled to a private office may feel embittered when advised that the new facility will include no private offices. The vocabulary of open planning can, in practice, provide designation of status to whatever degree an organization may wish. It is desirable to avoid reverting to the conventional practices of indicating status through area provided, through amount and solidity of screening, and through location (window wall or corner) since these considerations, if used for status symbolization, will often work against rational planning. Giving the top executive a windowed corner may make it impossible to place him where the communications matrix study would suggest. Excessive area used for status designation is simply wasted. An excess of screen panels creating a pseudo-private office simply makes a joke of the principles of open planning. The most valid indications of status are those that arise out of the actualities of work activities. A top executive will tend to require space for formal and informal meetings at the workplace because daily activities include a variety of meetings. Adjacent assistants and secretaries are placed for communication ease, but generate space characteristics different from those of general work areas.

There is nothing to prevent the introduction of more luxurious furniture, rugs, accessories, or works of art if the management style wishes to make such symbolic elements part of the status designation policy, but the benefits of open planning will be felt most strongly if the rigidities of bureaucratic status designation are minimized or limited.

Acoustical Considerations

A number of the privacy issues (and some status issues also) discussed above are connected with the acoustical problems of the open plan office. The most common and most valid reason for desiring a private office is the sense that "the noise out here is too distracting." A busy open office, full of ringing telephones, clacking typewriters, and noisy conversations makes thought, conversation, or any form of creative work difficult. The originators of landscape planning recognized these problems and made special acoustical treatment a first requirement in any open plan. Noisy machinery must be removed from the work space, acoustically effective materials on floor and ceiling are essential, sound reflective surfaces must be minimized, and sound absorbant surfaces introduced (in screen and on walls) as needed. This general prescription has the effect of dropping the level of office noise to a moderate hum of activity which because of its random character is not intrusive or disturbing. With experience, it has become possible to be much more specific about acoustical problems and to develop ways of dealing with residual problems that the general policy does not always cover.

An ideal acoustical environment will make it easy to understand speech at close (normal conversational) distances, but will make intelligibility decline at middle distances so that conversations will not be easily heard at remote workplaces. If the space is too noisy, voices will be raised in conversation and so will become intelligible at longer distances and will add to the general noise. If a space is too quiet, normal speech will be intelligible at considerable distances. An ideal background sound level will be between 40 and 50 decibels, with a frequency mix in the voice range that tends to arise naturally in a work space.

To prevent high noise levels, there must be carpet of good noise reducing qualities and a ceiling with an excellent NRC (noise reduction coefficient) rating. Too many ceiling lights, especially those with hard lens surfaces, reduce the effective acoustical surface of the ceiling (task lighting and acceptance of lowered intensity levels help in this respect). The absence of partitions prevents the trapping of noise and allows sound to dissipate much as it does in the out-of-doors. Too many screens, panel-surrounded work stations, or solid furniture elements which may seem to aid privacy can actually be harmful when they add partitionlike hard surfaces in the space. Screens and panels should have sound-absorbing surfaces, not so much to block transmission (a purpose which they cannot effectively serve), but to prevent their acting as sound reflectors. Perimeter wall and window surfaces also introduce sound reflection and make the areas near them (often used for workplaces requiring maximum privacy) less satisfactory than central, open space. Curtaining, acoustical materials or sound-absorbant panels may help.

To keep sound levels high enough to mask conversation, overall density needs to be kept up; 125 sq ft (12 sq m) per person is optimum in this respect. When density falls below this level, the space may become too quiet. Individual seats at work places should not be closer than about 10 ft (3 m) unless the individuals work together so closely that full audibility of each other's conversations is acceptable. Where person-to-person distance is 18 ft (5.5 m) or more, speech intelligibility will fall off to such a degree as to present no problem (unless background sound is too low). Even in areas where density is fairly high, there may be times (lunch hour, for example) when many people are absent, with the result that background sound falls off. To deal with such times and with areas where low density makes for extreme quiet (often in managerial or executive quarters where privacy is at a premium), some kind of artificial background sound can be provided.

Background music or PA systems are not satisfactory for this purpose. The most usual approach is to provide a special system with central noise generators capable of producing a random gray or white noise having a frequency mix that masks conversation. This sound is delivered into the work space by speakers concealed above the ceiling, which ideally have local volume control for tuning of the system by acoustical experts. The sound produced is similar to that of an operating air conditioning system—a gentle hiss or rustle that is not noticed while it is present, although its absence (when the system is turned off) is quite noticeable.

The installation of such systems involves a number of problems. In many cases normal air conditioning and other random noise make its use quite unnecessary, but this can only be ascertained after the space is completed and occupied. After move-in, discovery that the acoustics are unsatisfactory and late installation of a sound system are troublesome and call attention to what will seem an unfortunate error to occupants. To install a full sound system to "be on the safe side" is possibly quite wasteful since the equipment is costly, and even when needed it may be called for in only a few areas. Also a central system cannot deliver a different frequency mix to each area, but can generate only one mix for all spaces.

Two alternatives are now in use. One is a self-contained sound generator concealed in the ceiling, but located only where needed and individually tuned to the need of the particular space. Installation of such units after move-in is much simpler than introducing a complete system, and a major economy may result if only a few units are required. A second approach introduces sound generator units as small accessories installed in plain view at work stations wherever desired or needed. Each unit has individual controls that may be operated by the adjacent staff to adjust to conditions as they vary at different times. Such units

Acoustic conditioner, a movable, local background sound generator that is part of the Action Office system. Courtesy Herman Miller, Inc.

can, of course, also be installed in concealed locations, which are known and accessible to users. This approach has the advantage of placing control of background sound in the space occupants' hands, but may have some disadvantage in seeming to call attention to an unsolved problem that requires an unusual gadget for control.

Layout Grids

A problem that does not impinge on open plan users, but that requires attention by planners involves the desirability of introducing some kind of geometrical grid for planning. The free and random placement of equipment in the early European landscape office was often said to create a "chaotic" appearance which was disturbing. Even if this is not perceived as a problem, truly random placement of equipment is difficult to dimension on drawings and to set up in a space accurately according to a drawing. Since no patterns are visually evident, items moved out of place (for cleaning or convenience) are not easily recognized and put back in place. What started out as an irregular arrangement having logical bases gradually turns into totally random arrangement which is truly chaotic and which cannot be kept accurately recorded on plans.

Conventional offices are often planned on a modular grid, based on the module of building construction, partitions, or the ceiling system, or at best, if all are coordinated, on a universal module that relates all elements. While a system of this kind is not necessary in open planning, it may be helpful. A plan grid may use a square module, with or without a 45° diagonal overlay or a 30° to 60° grid which generates triangular and hexagonal relationships. Other geometries (other angles, interlaced circles, etc.) are theoretical possibilities but present problems that discourage their use. An ideal grid will relate to floor wiring distribution systems and to equipment dimensional modules.

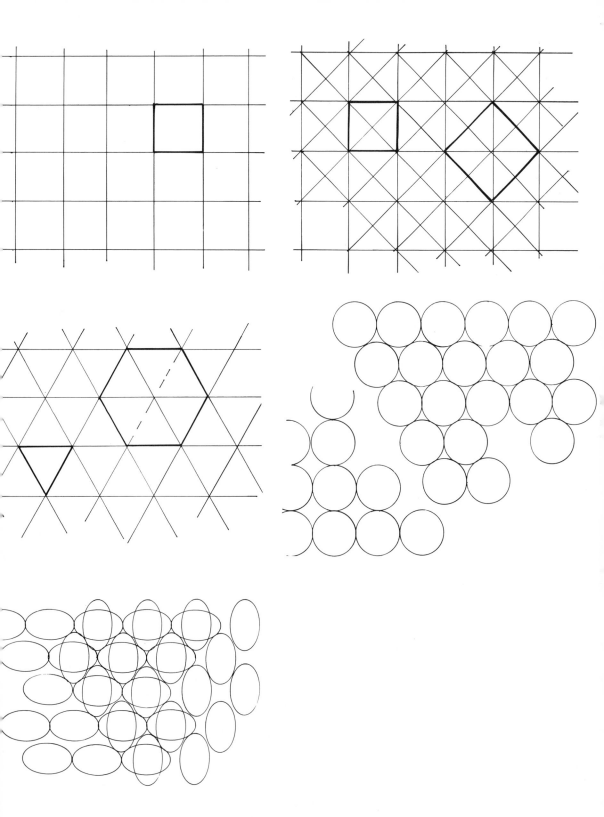

Layout grids. Top left: Square module. Top right: Square module with 45° superimposed diagonal. Middle left: 30/60 triangular relationships generating hexagons. Middle right: Circles in two patterns. Above: Overlapping ellipses.

Plan drawings are made over the grid chart and locate all elements on a grid line or at least in relationship to grid points and angles. In such planning, standard work station configurations become easy to develop; equipment can be placed in the space with a minimum of complex, surveylike measurements. Equipment to be moved or put back in place can be easily lined up by reference to visible lines established by the grid. In addition, many designers feel that some degree of harmony or order is generated in a space with a grid layout, even when the grid is not overtly expressed in any floor or ceiling pattern. The use of a grid layout need not, of course, be rigidly applied; it is possible to depart from its control in any areas where this may turn out to be desirable.

Color/Graphics

Open planning raises a few minor questions on issues that relate to what is often called "interior decoration": the selection of colors, textures, and finishes that will be visually attractive as well as practical. In conventional planning, it is easy to approach each room as a unit and develop a scheme for each, possibly in accordance with the preferences of the occupant where the necessary individual consultation involved seems justified. In open planning, since space is not cut into rooms, color and materials must be consistent throughout large spaces. Although decorative schemes could change in different parts of a large area, this would make flexible replanning more difficult. As a result, it is normal practice to make carpet color uniform throughout each open space and to restrict colors on panels and furniture to a small number of choices that are all reasonably harmonious together.

Two pitfalls may emerge. If color is kept very neutral to avoid color clashes, the resulting space may seem monotonous and dreary. If intense color is chosen for the carpet and a group of strong, related colors are used for other

Decorative graphic elements used to aid orientation and differentiate spaces. Offices of Hallmark Cards, Kansas City; Harper and George, interior designers. Courtesy Herman Miller, Inc.

elements, the color theme may seem too insistent. In multifloor schemes, it is often suggested that each floor have a color theme. This may be pleasant to the visitor, but users may be bored or irritated to be assigned to a green floor or an orange floor, even if that may be a favorite color. The best solutions usually involve neutrals for major areas (such as carpet) and then introduce strong color in small areas (such as screen panels or chair upholstery) in related groupings or clusters that change from one part of the space to another. Intense color can offer variety in quiet rooms, service areas, washrooms, stairs, elevators, etc.

Identification of spaces by names and numbers on doors is not possible in open offices. In large facilities it may be helpful to introduce graphic panels, color codes, or hung signlike elements to help identify various group work areas. In practice, the need for such visual clues to aid staff in finding their way does not seem to develop. They may make it easier to direct visitors to a particular location, they may help to give more sense of identity and territory to working groups, and perhaps most important, they may help to make a space seem visually lively and interesting.

Other Services and Lounges

Plumbing-related services—toilets and drinking fountains—are usually provided within or adjacent to the building core. Open planning does not introduce any modifications in these services when compared with the norms for conventional planning.

Coat-hanging space and space for other personal belongings (packages, overshoes, etc.) involve problems that are not always solved well in conventional offices. Each office worker will need, especially in bad weather, a place for outer wear and for personal belongings that must for some reason be in the office temporarily (for example, lunchtime purchases to be taken home or sports gear for an after-work activity). In many conventional offices there is a half solution for such problems through a few closets or coat hooks, while an overflow simply adds to the general clutter of small office spaces; visitors' coats often end up hung on chairs or on door knobs. In open planning, the lack of partitions to hide closets, clutter, or both forces some more thoughtful solution. A centralized hanging and shelf space near entrance points would serve in a totally honest society, but the realities of modern life mean that protection must be possible either through locks and keys or easy surveillance.

A logical lock-and-key approach is the provision of individual lockers, but the common association of this approach with school days or factory work makes it unpopular, at least in the U.S. The most favored alternative is the use of wardrobe or cabinet units that are large enough to hold the coats of a number of people, but small enough to be movable and to relate visually to acoustical screens. Furniture systems of the storage-wall type usually have provisions for such cabinets, but most open systems must be supplemented by cabinets specially made for the purpose. Acoustical materials on backs and ends can be helpful in absorbing sound and in providing color and texture variation. Visitors' coats can hang in extra units near a reception point or in excess space provided in units near workplaces. It is important that there is, in total, enough hanging space for all staff plus visitors on a typical winter day. Locks can usually be omitted if units are located so that they are visible to several workplaces.

The original concept of *Bürolandschaft* included the provision of *Pausenraumen*—lounges or rest areas available to all staff at any time for short breaks with a coffee machine always in operation. This was, perhaps, more of an innovation in Europe than it seems in the current American scene where the tradition of frequent (and often lengthy) breaks has become so well established. Where lounges have been provided in American open plan offices, they often are little used. Provision of coffee and drink machines on each floor will tend to cut down on long trips to a distant source, and a table or two close by with an easily cleanable floor covering may be useful; but the elaborate lounge of the early German examples seems not to be needed or particularly desired by American office workers. The size and location of the office will govern the need for providing a full lunch facility, but open planning does not inject any requirements in this respect that differ from those of conventional offices.

Wardrobe closets from the Zapf System. Courtesy Knoll International, Inc.

User Acceptance

9

It is a fact of life that moving is not pleasant. Even a desirable move is a chore, and establishing the fact that a move is desirable may not be easy. Most human beings resist change and the resistance increases when a known circumstance must be exchanged for one that is strange and unfamiliar. The fact that open planning is still, to most office personnel, a strange and unfamiliar concept makes it natural that its consideration for a new facility tends to stir up worries. The planning of a new office, even a totally conventional new office, always stimulates certain stresses. The office politician sees a chance to maneuver for more space and advantageous location for himself and his group; the office paranoid begins to fear deprivation. Rumors spread that suggest that the worst is in the offing. When word of open offices gets out the rumors become more ominous. Everyone will be crowded into one big room. Bosses will watch everyone constantly.

Since changing to a new location will almost surely present some problem to almost everyone, such problems become matters for discussion and worry. As surveys of needs, equipment, and communication patterns are made, word spreads that efficiency experts are about to eliminate jobs. An atmosphere of nervousness and hostility can develop, with negative attitudes becoming attached to every aspect of the project in a way that can hamper its realization and slow the inevitable period of adjustment to the new space. These attitudes are by no means limited to junior staff. Managers and top executives are as much threatened as clerks and typists and can be much more obstructive.

User Attitudes

Office workers have complex views of their jobs and the places where they work, which are not always easy to discover and explain. The job may be a challenge, a pleasure, or a burden. The office may be seen as a purgatory, a social center, a second home, or some combination of any or all of these things. The fact that it is about to be changed, changed without consent, and perhaps changed in some strange and incomprehensible way is a very real threat. It is also a real fact that even change for the better involves some degree of trauma. It takes time and effort to adjust to new circumstances even when they are of one's own choosing. Imposed new circumstances are sure to meet with some resistance.

Researchers in Europe, trying to discover whether early open plan installations were really workable, conducted tests which even included such physical reactions as blood pressure and brain waves. They found that the workers newly relocated in open plan offices did show signs of various strains that took months to disappear. As a crosscheck, they then transferred some user groups back into the conventional spaces that they had previously occupied and were interested to discover that the stress reactions were just as great. It was not the kind of office that was the issue, but the fact of change itself. Knowing this and knowing that the unfamiliarity of open planning makes it particularly susceptible to debate, the planner and user organization project management should make plans early to deal with the resistances and adjustment problems that are sure to arise.

Preliminary Briefing

The most effective counter to rumor and resistance is, as might be expected, full and accurate information made available at the earliest possible time. It is not practical to involve all members of a large office staff in preliminary discussion of when and where to relocate, but as soon as a particular plan is under serious consideration, some way of briefing staff should be found in an effort to get ahead of the flow of rumor. Whether a work staff should be polled to discover attitudes about alternate courses of action (for instance, stay here, move nearby, or move to the suburbs) is a delicate question. If the poll results will really influence decision making, it may be wise. If in the end the decision will ignore poll results, it may be better not to conduct it.

Once planning is under way, it is very desirable to arrange briefing sessions or seminars which are not conceived as pep talks in any way, but as genuine opportunities to explain the logic of the planning process, report on its progress, and invite questions as they may arise. Several different types of briefing sessions may be planned for managers, key staff members, and total work groups. Groups to be briefed should be kept small; a mass meeting in a hall is not at all appropriate for obtaining the kind of involvement desired. In large organizations briefing can proceed from small groups of top managers, who can in turn brief middle managers who report to their own staff. Involvement of professional planning staff in all such meetings tends to be very helpful.

User Participation

The idea of involving users at all hierarchical levels in the planning process through representation on planning teams is a key concept of the Quickborner Team's planning theory. Many managers and planners see this possibility as no more than a pointless source of delay and nuisance. It cannot work well if this attitude is present, but in organizations where democratic attitudes and participatory decision making are being seriously encouraged, such techniques will aid in obtaining user acceptance and enthusiasm and will often generate helpful suggestions and proposals that can improve the final result in specific ways.

Where participation of this kind is undertaken, floor plans with work stations in place and identified by occupants' names should be made available, explained in some detail, and left with user groups for study and discussion. Helpful suggestions will sometimes be raised, sound planning will usually be accepted with some enthusiasm, and far less trivial or troublesome interference will surface than might be anticipated or feared. If models of the space are made, it is very helpful to display them so that users not familiar with the architects' or planners' graphic vocabulary can gain an understanding of the plans. A full-size demonstration set-up (not described as a test space in a way that suggests uncertainty) of several typical workplaces with equipment under actual consideration can be very helpful. Constructive suggestions as well as acceptance and enthusiasm can be generated by an attractive demonstration of this kind.

Supporting attitudes and participation by the top executives involved in the project are very important. Any hint that "they" do not really approve the planning approach, are reserving something better for themselves, or are simply foisting it on junior staff to save money will encourage hostile rumors. Visible support and participation in the planning process will tend to raise enthusiasm.

Move-In

Shortly before moving in to the new facility, additional briefing is needed. Advance visits to the space can be made by staff representatives or interested groups. Immediately before the move, special briefings should discuss the practical problems of packing and unpacking, moving into new files, etc., but should also deal openly with the expectation of some dissatisfactions. It is very helpful to make it clear that a period of adjustment is anticipated and that everyone must expect to suffer some brief discomfort. Habit changes appropriate to the open plan can be discussed (lowered voice levels, new procedures in visiting others, phone use, use of quiet rooms, etc.) and the ways in which changes and adjustments are to be arranged can be explained.

After move-in, the making of corrections and changes must proceed rapidly and smoothly, and should be accepted as a normal part of the process, to be dealt with efficiently and cheerfully. There will always be pessimists present who will interpret every small problem as evidence that the whole project is a mistake and a disaster. It is important to contain the sources of these attitudes and make it clear to the majority that they are only the reactions of slow adjusters. In this period also, attitudes of top managers are crucial. An irritated and impatient chief can infect a whole organization with dissatisfaction and anger. Sensible and positive efforts to make everything right for everyone as quickly as possible, visibly expressed and acted out by managers, makes the process of settling in go smoothly and rapidly.

Real Problems

At move-in and during the week or two following, a number of real problems are likely to surface. They should not cause dismay, but need to be dealt with promptly. Typical problems are

Wrong equipment. Some people will find they have insufficient storage space; some will have too much (but will not be likely to report that fact). Small items such as letter trays or blackboards may be needed. Since system components will often take months for delivery, it is wise to order a small overage of parts (screens, shelves, etc.) so that minor problems can be adjusted quickly.

Telephones. The new facility will often generate unexpected difficulties in handling phone answering, message taking, identification of rings, sharing of instruments, etc. There seems to be no way to avoid some changes as soon as real experience exposes the problems.

Lighting. Where ceiling lighting is used, some work stations always seem to be underlit, with shadows cast by screens, shelves, or other such problems. Task lighting is less likely to suffer from such problems and is easier to adjust. Having a small stock of extra lighting units on hand is helpful.

Acoustics. Some people will be disturbed and some caused disturbance by unexpected ways in which voices travel. Some areas may turn out to be too quiet so that conversations are too easily overheard. Too much general noise happily almost never develops. Artificial background noise is usually the only effective technique for use in too quiet areas. Where voice disturbance appears in areas with adequate background noise, some replanning may be necessary to relocate loud talkers so that they face into absorbent surfaces and are located at an increased distance from others. Some individuals who tend to speak loudly may need to be coached (tactfully) to lower voice levels, and will usually tend to do so as they become accustomed to the new acoustical environment.

Clutter. Some people enjoy bringing personal items into the office to make it seem more homey, and there is no reason why the typical workplace should not make provision for display of family snap-shots, small souvenirs, and similar items, within reason. Briefings can include some discussion of reasonable limits on this kind of personalization. Ugly plastic plants, tasteless novelties, and pinups can be discouraged without giving offense, and most users will agree that the (actual) case of the worker who kept a cage of live gerbils at his workplace

A giant redwood root cluster worked into a sculpture by J.M. Blunk establishes a visual focus at the main entrance point of Weyerhaeuser headquarters in Tacoma, Washington. Skidmore, Owings, & Merrill, architects and interior designers. Photograph by Ezra Stoller, ESTO; courtesy Skidmore, Owings, & Merrill.

suggests that there are limits to tolerable clutter. Providing attractive ashtrays, memo pads, etc., will discourage bringing in unattractive ones and will help to establish a quality standard that everyone can then be encouraged to maintain.

Quality works of art in varied scales (from large paintings or sculptures to small framed graphics) can be assembled and made available for hanging in locations where they will help visual character and provide stimulation. Availability of works of suitable scale will discourage the display of bad art, often brought from home with the best of intentions.

In addition to these realistically based problems, every project seems to encompass a few problems that have no base in reality and that are therefore not accessible to rational solutions. An occasional individual will choose the open plan as a focus for resentments and resistances that go far deeper than the realities of any office plan. Efforts to deal with this kind of protest by providing larger area, more screens to increase privacy, etc., are doomed to failure and can generate secondary problems as the efforts to cope with the resister are observed by peers and colleagues. Excessive effort to deal on a realistic basis with problems which are, in truth, irrational can be destructive. It is certainly necessary to make sure that the complainant's problems in terms of equipment, acoustics, etc., have been dealt with in reasonable fashion, but resistance that remains adamant when all such matters have been brought under control must, in the end, be dismissed. Any large project will include a few such resisters who have made the open plan a vehicle for some kind of larger protest which has not found an earlier outlet. It is important that planner and organization management understand the character of such resistance and accept the impossibility of controlling it through practical action. The person who hates the new office (open or conventional) must in the end decide to accept it, suffer it silently, or move on to a situation which does not give rise to protest.

Planning in Continuing Use

10

Of all the possible benefits of open planning, the one most certainly identifiable is flexibility. The possibilities for making a drastic rearrangement overnight, or at least over a weekend, with no significant costs for construction cannot be matched by any other method of developing office space. Given reasonably easy ways of dealing with electrical and telephone changes, planning changes become almost totally problem-free and can take place whenever organizational realities may require.

Uses of Flexibility

Organizations are often not ready to take full advantage of the flexibility that open planning offers. After years of occupancy of rigidly organized space, it has become habitual to accept the layout as it exists and adapt to its realities for better or for worse. Any conventional office that has been occupied for some years will be found to be full of absurdities that result from plan rigidity. A department will all be in one place except for a few people who are off in some distant location. Junior people will be occupying some palatial office or meeting room because of its location, while elsewhere a ranking executive will be making do in a tiny cubicle. A's files will be located conveniently to B, and vice versa. The secretary to X will be on the opposite side of the building.

Worst of all, reorganization of work groups, formation of new teams, and other desirable changes will have been deferred because the available spaces are not suited to the changes that are needed. Open planning makes it easy to break out of such problems, but doing so requires some new habits and changed ways of thinking. At move-in time the new office will, if it has been well planned, suit the organization as it now is and will have eliminated the accumulated illogicalities of the old office. There is then no immediate and obvious need for change and the old habit of regarding the space as a given fixed circumstance will resurface. Staff and management may have to make an effort to remember that the flexible office is prepared to adjust to such changes as:

Addition of new staff. Expansion space has been provided on the basis of the space surveys conducted at the beginning of the project, but it has usually been distributed through the space evenly (so that it will not be obvious) in the form of overwide circulation routes and oversized meeting spaces. When a new employee is hired, a new work station can be set up (ideally from excess furniture components in inventory) in the exact place where it is required.

Staff reduction. The opposite situation arises when a work station is vacated. If the situation is temporary, nothing need be done, but if it is to last a long time, the vacant workplace can be removed to stock inventory and the space closed up by adjusting adjacent units.

Reorganization of work flow, working groups, or teams can be made much more effective if the floor layout is adjusted accordingly.

New equipment (data terminals, CRT units, etc.) may need changed workplace layout and may change the pattern of work and staff organization. Prompt change of workplace and layout for this reason is an easy possibility.

Changing privacy requirements at individual workplaces can be dealt with easily with the addition or removal of panels or altered orientation of work surfaces.

Changes to deal with such matters can often be improvised on an ad hoc basis by the staff and managers involved, with the necessary physical changes made over a weekend by the maintenance staff.

Flexibility Problems

While making changes on a casual basis is perfectly possible and will help in keeping up with needs for minor change, there will also be a tendency for this to cause a drift away from original plan concepts. Such changes are usually improvised on the spot without a study or a paper plan and are usually not recorded on a plan in a systematic way. Gradually, the original plan logic is lost, and it becomes clear that more systematic replanning will become difficult since the status quo is not a matter of record on paper. The impact of an accumulation of minor changes on the communications patterns that were the subject of the original survey and matrix study is also difficult to assess. It is not practical to undertake a completely new communication study as each minor change is made, but it becomes clear that when changes outnumber retained situations, the validity of the plan must come into question.

Deciding to forbid ad hoc change, however, negates the value of flexibility or else requires the constant involvement of professional planning aid in a way that is costly and often inconvenient. There are a number of steps that can be considered to deal with these problems while maintaining the fullest usefulness of flexibility.

Dealing with Flexibility

The size of the organization and the frequency with which change takes place will help to determine which of the following steps will be helpful. Some combination of them will usually make up a sound policy for an organization.

1. The planner or planning team should have continuing involvement with the project for a significant period of time after move-in. This is a period of frequent change and adjustment, and it is important that the changes that take place during this time be carefully planned and recorded on plans.

2. During this early period a decision should be made about whether the planner is to be retained on a continuing basis as a consultant for on-going revisions or whether an in-house planning person or unit will take over the function. Convenience of location and consideration of comparative costs will be factors in this decision. In most cases the planner will agree that being involved forever in minor change is hardly necessary or desirable. An in-house service may only require part-time attention by one person or may involve a substantial facilities planning staff according to the size of the project and the frequency of contemplated change. In any case, it is essential that the in-house planner be both knowledgeable and sympathetic to the plan concept in use. The original planner should have a good relationship with the in-house person (no sense of rivalry on either side) and should participate in some degree of training in how change is to be dealt with. A gradual transition can take place with participation of the original planner diminishing as the in-house person becomes skillful and confident.

3. It is wise to establish a clear policy about levels of revision and how each is to be dealt with. A typical plan might provide for:

Minor change can be improvised as needed and effected at once by user and maintenance staff. This might include adding or subtracting a pencil drawer, book shelf, or light. The only formal requirement should be that the shift in equipment be made a matter of record (a problem discussed below).

Work station change refers to adding, subtracting, or totally rearranging a particular work station or altering several work stations without changing their area or location. The planner or in-house plan service should be involved; they should sketch the proposed change and specify the parts to be drawn from or returned to inventory or ordered from a manufacturer. Such changes should be made in an evening or weekend and should take place within 7 to 14 days after they are requested. A duty of the planning function is to keep on hand a sufficient inventory of parts to make this possible without long delays waiting for parts delivery from a manufacturer.

Area revision means a replanning of a total work group or department (or more) to take account of work reorganization, new equipment, or new work flow patterns. A limited new communications study may be called for; careful replanning on paper is necessary with review and approval before the change is undertaken. This level of change may easily require purchase of new equipment, and this must be scheduled will in advance. It should still be possible to do the work over a weekend, but 30 to 90 days should be allowed from initiation of the change to its realization.

General revision, a total replanning of the space, may never be required if more limited changes are made as needed and if these changes are made with care and planning skill. A sweeping change in the use of the facility, such as a complete change in the functions accommodated, might require a full general replanning. In this case, the project will be similar to the original planning and a professional planner or planning firm should be involved. Since decisions about basic systems have been made for the original installation, these do not need restudy, but reuse of equipment on hand and needs for new equipment can present complex detail problems.

Periodic review on a regular schedule, perhaps every 18 or 24 months, is good practice. This involves a brief consultation with the original planner, a walk-through of the space, and a review of plans in an effort to discover and correct a drift away from the original concept that can result from minor changes. Occupants of a space are often not aware that a gradual accumulation of minor problems can add up to a total decline in the quality of the space in use. This is a good time to consider accumulated minor needs for change and to put into effect any such changes along with minor clean-up corrections of accumulated problems.

Equipment Inventory Management
Management of any office facility requires keeping an inventory of furniture and equipment in use and in storage (if any). Because systems are often complex in open planning and because frequent change is encouraged, inventory management can become very complex. The planner developing changes will find it particularly troublesome to discover that there is no record of how things are currently located, what components make up each work station, and what stock of excess components may be on hand. It is essential that a system of record-keeping be developed, put into use as the facility is opened, and kept up to date.

A simple system that will work well is described here. Computer memory may be put to use in the case of large projects, but the visual control possible with the system described here can be very helpful in planning work. In this system, a form is designed and printed up which can be used to represent a single piece of equipment or component. An index card or IBM card (the latter

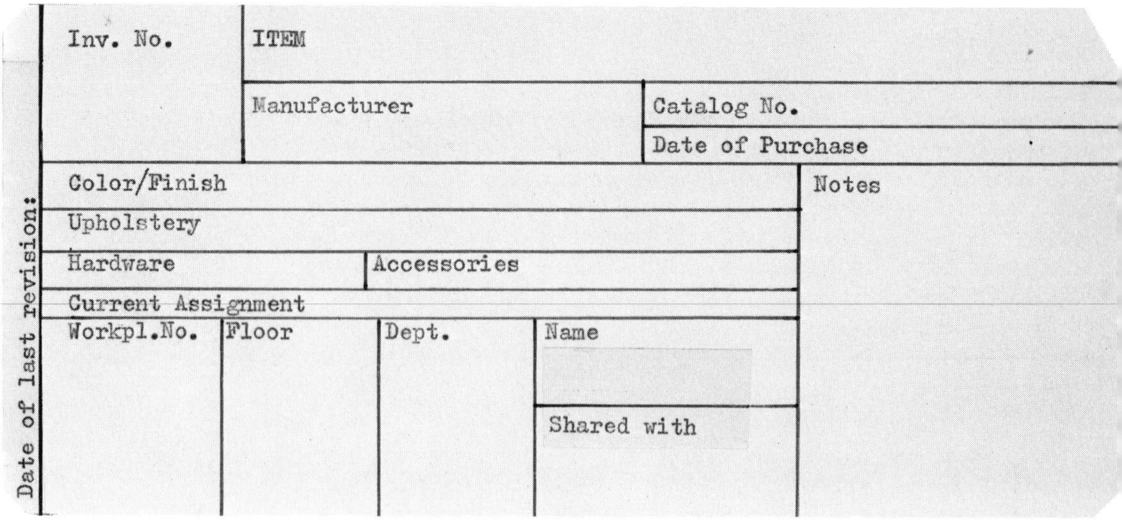

Date of last revision:

Inv. No.

ITEM

Manufacturer

Catalog No.

Date of Purchase

Color/Finish

Notes

Upholstery

Hardware

Accessories

Current Assignment

Workpl.No.

Floor

Dept.

Name

Shared with

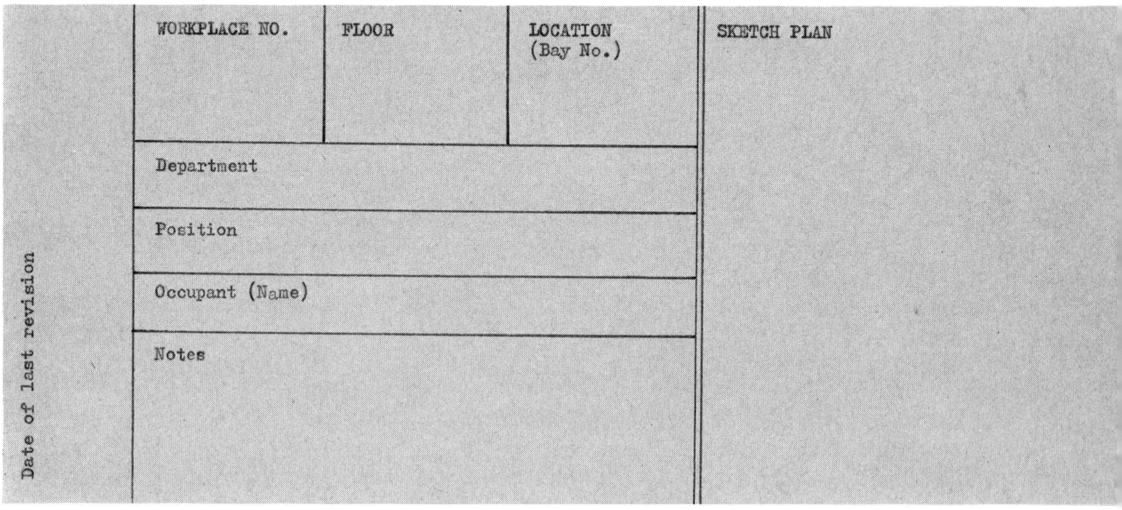

Date of last revision

WORKPLACE NO.

FLOOR

LOCATION (Bay No.)

SKETCH PLAN

Department

Position

Occupant (Name)

Notes

Above: Printed envelope representing one work station. It contains a group of cards (top), each one representing a particular piece of equipment.

particularly if computer management is contemplated) is suitable. A possible layout is illustrated on page 150. As the original installation is made, each piece of furniture or other equipment is recorded on two duplicate cards (different colors for each copy are advisable). Furniture units made up of interchangeable components should be listed, with a separate pair of cards for each component or accessory.

A second form should now be developed; it can be an envelope or file folder used to represent the individual work station, room, or other space (such as open conference area). This envelope is labeled with the "address" of the space and its assignment by department and individual person's name. A suggested form is shown on page 150. Into each envelope go the cards that represent the equipment installed at that location. The duplicate cards, with the number and identity of the station (envelope) where the item is, are filed by name and number of the equipment item in question. There now exists a complete record of what is on hand and where it is as well as a record of what each work station or other unit is comprised of. Extra equipment in inventory occupies a special group of envelopes. Where an equipment item is shared by two work stations, two pairs of cards should be made out with an indication of the sharing user on each and with a prominent marking (a special color, signal sticker, or stamp) that calls attention to the shared status. Cards for the shared unit should be in the envelope for each user space. The inventory card can be the two copies taped or stapled together. Inventory cards should show manufacturer's name and catalog number and color or finish for each item. At the inventory file, a manufacturer's catalog sheet should be kept for each item (or a comparable special form may be used) giving dimensions and complete data on what the item is. A tiny sketch diagram on each card is helpful in keeping this data visually available.

The planner working on a change will now find it easy to discover exactly what is at any given workplace and what items are in storage and available for use. A proposed plan revision can be drawn up, new work stations planned, and extra "dummy" cards made out for equipment required. Cards representing equipment at work stations that are being relocated or rearranged and cards from stock inventory can then be compared with the dummy cards to discover what new equipment must be ordered and what will become surplus. It is often possible to reduce the need to order extra equipment by making minor plan changes (exchanging right- and left-hand units, for example) when this equipment card comparison is made.

If this system seems complex and troublesome, it should be remembered that after a year or two of use with frequent plan changes it is possible to arrive at a situation in which no one has any idea of what items are where—a situation in which even small changes require endless searching for items needed or on hand. These are time-wasting and irritating steps and generate a sense of confusion that makes flexibility seem more of a burden than an asset.

Flexibility will turn out to be a tremendous asset to any organization, especially one that is dynamic and growing, but its full and easy use requires an understanding that change must be expected and that it will require organized staff and methods of work.

Conclusions

11

Does Open Planning Work?

By now you will hardly be surprised to learn that the general answer to this question is a yes. Many thousands of staff members working in many hundreds of installations for extended periods, in some cases as long as 20 years, make it clear that some early prophecies that the whole idea was a total disaster which would be given up within months were quite wrong. It is no longer an issue open to question that open offices are working well for many people in many organizations. If one proceeds to more complex questions—such as "does open planning work better than . . .?"—answers become more complicated. Is open planning always best for every office? Probably not. Do people work better in open offices, are they happier, is open planning cheaper? All such questions can only be answered with some discussion.

The difficulty in trying to offer clear yes or no answers lies in the fact that most such questions are concerned with comparisons. *What* open plan is to be compared with what conventional plan? Open installations have been in use for years; and early ones are not the same as recent ones. European practice is varied and differs from most of what has been done in the United States, and U.S. practice is varied and constantly changing. Some open offices are totally open; some so subdivided as to make the designation "open" a purely technical term. The quality of planning and the quality of installation vary from project to project. A badly planned open office will be just as bad as a badly planned conventional office, and many offices that are open or landscaped in appearance have not been planned with the logic that the concept is based on. There is no way to tell by inspecting an installation whether the planner proposals have been followed or whether, as can often happen, some manager with the power to do so, has altered planning logic to suit personal whim. It is also a fact of life that neither planner nor occupant organization management is likely to be willing to confess to major mistakes.

It is possible to extract some consensus from the many reports, studies, and evaluations of open installations that have surfaced. Without attempt to offer full documentation of these conclusions, it seems to be clear that:

1. Most open plan offices work at least as well as conventional ones. At best there are some very real advantages; at worst the advantages and disadvantages reach an approximate tie.

2. There are situations in which open planning is not likely to be successful. These are organizations in which work is done in isolation and/or in which private consultations are of primary importance. A law office is a prime example, with the possible exception of its clerical areas.

3. The anticipated gains in efficiency resulting from communication study are hard to evaluate and may not be as striking as anticipated. Modern office work is not so much based on work flow or paper processing as was the case in the past. As a result efficiency in office work is hard to evaluate. It seems clear that there are no losses in this area, but the gains may be marginal.

4. When well-executed, open offices are usually well liked by most users. Junior staff generally feel that there is a striking improvement over conventional space.

Executives and top managers are usually so well treated in any case that they are also content. A possible core of resistance may appear among middle levels where the hoped-for private office is denied. Every effort should be made to ensure that these people understand the rationale of open planning and to make sure that their workplaces are free from realistic problems.

5. Objections made to a new office situation are often, when closely studied, protests against other aspects of the work situation, which are displaced onto the physical facility. A study by an environmental psychologist discovered that a large open plan installation made by a major corporation was cordially hated by its occupants. Further study disclosed that the hatred was actually hatred of the rigid, authoritarian company management. Any new office would have been hated (as was the old office). The study was supressed!

Another corporation studied a generally satisfactory installation to discover the reasons for some marginal dissatisfactions. It was found that the resistance was actually to the facility's new suburban location which some staff found inconvenient, but felt unable to protest directly.

Because open planning is new and unfamiliar, it becomes an especially vulnerable target for such displaced protests, and its use tends, for the same reason, to magnify the human resistance to all change. Such resistance is most evident during the first year of occupancy, just when studies and evaluations are most likely to be done.

6. The promised flexibility of open planning is fully realized and may be its most important advantage. Easy and rapid change is in startling contrast with the agony of conventional office remodeling. This virtue shows up in adaptability to organizational change and in reduced cost of change—both values more visible and significant to managers than to typical office workers.

7. Open plan offices *may* be less expensive than conventional equivalents in both first cost and in continued operation, but that is not necessarily so. It is not wise to count on this as a certain advantage, although it is an advantage that can be assured if that is made a project requirement. Questions of costs are explored in more detail below.

Cost Comparisons

There is no clear way in which to establish equal quality standards for a conventional and an open plan office. As a result, planning concept and quality are hard to isolate as factors in generating costs. Open plan spaces must be carpeted; would a comparable conventional office have areas of tile flooring? If so, would these be provided by the building owner under lease agreements? How much fixed and how much movable partitioning would the conventional office use? How many doors? In comparison, how many screens and how many panels would be specified for the comparable open office? What light levels and what type of lighting would be used in each case? In estimating long-term costs, how frequent and how extensive are the changes anticipated? Will open planning lead to a greater density of occupation, or will density be deliberately reduced to provide for a better space cushion for expansion? All these issues have impact on the cost of an open installation and on the conventional system costs that will be evaluated in a comparison. The choices made will determine whether and to what extent an open plan can be expected to show economic advantages.

In a rough way, it seems obvious that most of the economic issues fall on the side of open planning. No partitions will always cost less than any partitions. Carpet may cost more than tile, but carpet is becoming a required standard even in conventional offices. Occupancy density in an open office will scarcely ever be less than in a conventional office and can be 10 to 20 percent greater—it may *need* to be that much greater for acoustic reasons. The ease of change weighs economically in favor of open planning as the frequency of anticipated change increases. On the side of conventional planning, it can only be noted that the cost of furniture *may* be less and the cost of plants will probably be significantly less.

In relation to a particular project, the only valid cost comparison results when a representative portion of space is planned in detail each way, and a careful, realistic, and unrigged cost comparison is made on the basis of specific decisions that are held to in the respective cases. First cost, in such a study, is only one factor. Cost over an anticipated occupancy life of 5, 10, or more years is the only reasonable comparison basis.

A very thorough study of this type was conducted in 1967 for the U.S. General Services Administration by Brooks Barr Graeber & White with Pitts Mebane Phelps & White. The results appeared in a report, "Office Landscape, a Feasibility Study." The subject was a U.S. Department of Labor building to be constructed in Washington. The Quickborner Team participated in the development of typical open spaces that would be compared with spaces planned for the same occupancies in conventional fashion. The kinds of comparisons developed included:

	Conventional	Landscape
Density of occupancy (sq ft per person)	150	135
Installation cost for initial occupancy (floor covering, furniture, partitions, blinds, etc.)	$4.18 per sq ft	$3.47 per sq ft
Annual costs of maintenance (relocations, cleaning plants, etc.)	.89 per sq ft	.46 per sq ft
Replacements per year (floor coverings, partitions, etc.)	.152 per sq ft	.127 per sq ft

If the density figures are taken into account and the first and annual costs used on a 5- and a 10-year basis, the cost per person per year compares as follows:

	Conventional	Landscape
Five-year basis	$281.70	$172.94
Ten-year basis	219.00	112.65

In this study, it is assumed that all floors in the conventional plan will be vinyl tile with a 30-year life and all landscape floor will be carpet with a 10-year life. If carpet was to be used in all or any part of the conventional plan, the comparison would be even more favorable to the landscape approach. Lighting is assumed to be the same in both cases, and furniture costs (exclusive of screens) are also assumed to match. Modifications of these assumptions might vary the conclusions.

Finally, it should be noted that this comparison takes no account of the fact that the greater density in the landscape facility will result in a savings in rent or construction costs and in building operations cost proportional to the area ratio.

Such cost advantages as this comparison suggests can be eliminated by decisions to use the advantage to make equipment more luxurious, provide a greater cushion for future expansion, or in other desired ways. But the pos-

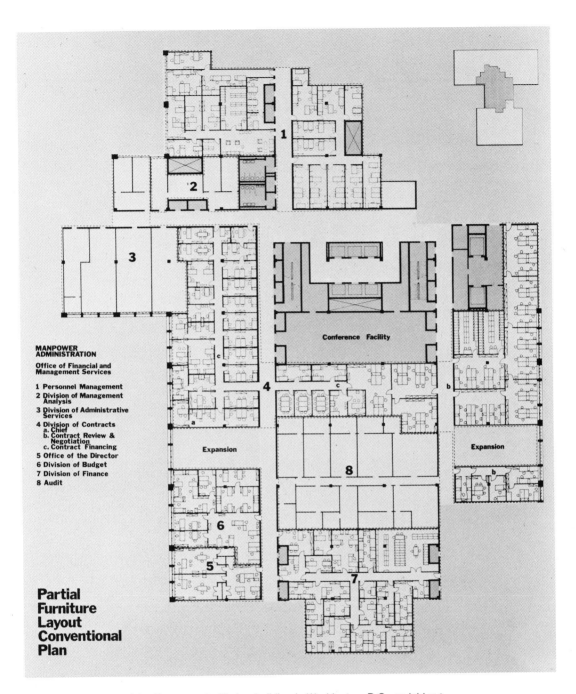

MANPOWER
ADMINISTRATION

Office of Financial and
Management Services

1 Personnel Management
2 Division of Management
  Analysis
3 Division of Administrative
  Services
4 Division of Contracts
  a. Chief
  b. Contract Review &
     Negotiation
  c. Contract Financing
5 Office of the Director
6 Division of Budget
7 Division of Finance
8 Audit

**Partial
Furniture
Layout
Conventional
Plan**

A portion of one floor of the Department of Labor building in Washington, D.C., as laid out
with conventional planning.

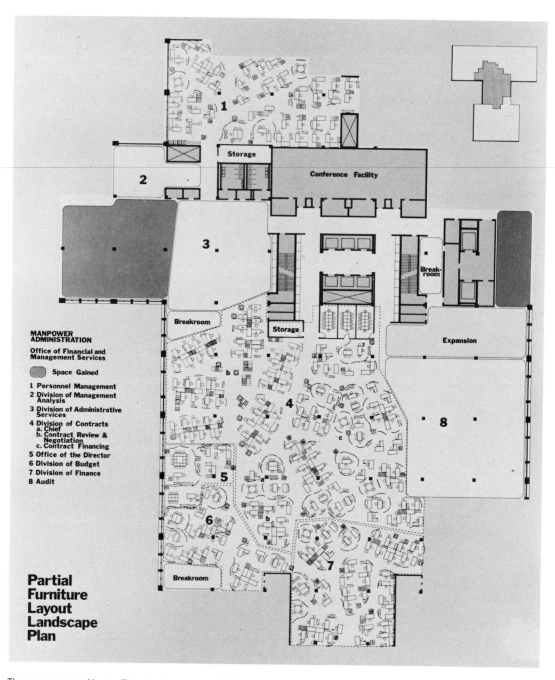

MANPOWER ADMINISTRATION

Office of Financial and Management Services

Space Gained

1 Personnel Management
2 Division of Management Analysis
3 Division of Administrative Services
4 Division of Contracts
  a. Chief
  b. Contract Review & Negotiation
  c. Contract Financing
5 Office of the Director
6 Division of Budget
7 Division of Finance
8 Audit

Storage

Conference Facility

Break-room

Breakroom

Storage

Expansion

Breakroom

Partial Furniture Layout Landscape Plan

The same area with an office landscape layout. These are hypothetical plans developed to establish a basis for direct comparisons.

sibility of making a significant saving is clearly present if the validity of this kind of comparison is accepted.

Project Evaluation

It is common knowledge that the projects which appear to be most attractive in photographs and which are best publicized are not necessarily the ones that are most successful in the experience of occupants and users. There is a new interest in attempting project evaluation after one or more years of experience in ways that will generate useful information about the success of planning approaches, equipment types, and various details which will aid in making future projects more successful. The rather new discipline called "architectural or environmental psychology" is concerned with such evaluations in terms of the individual space user's perceptions and satisfactions.

User satisfaction is, however, a somewhat uncertain criterion for evaluation of office projects. Is the satisfaction of the individual employee—the degree to which he or she likes the space—a true correlate with how well the space performs in all senses? In larger terms, the office is no more than a device to facilitate the more general purposes of the organization, whatever it may be, and these purposes can be quite varied and possibly unclear. User satisfaction of certain kinds may make the office more effective in performing its intended functions (by reducing absenteeism, staff turnover, or the vague dissatisfactions that make people less effective than they might otherwise be), but it is not clear that it is an end in itself.

Managerial satisfaction is a similarly unclear issue. It is made up of the personal satisfaction of the managerial personnel actually working in the space, their collective sense of how well the facility serves their performance goals, and whatever objective measures of output in terms of work done that anyone can invent to apply to the particular kinds of activities that the office performs.

In addition to its specific and real functions, an office serves some symbolic roles as a physical representation of the organization it houses. It is viewed in this way by visitors, job interviewees, its own staff, and its own management, whether they think about it directly or not. An office that is dismal, cramped, messy, and depressing makes a statement about the organization which has created it and tolerates it. An office which is pompous, grandiose, luxurious, and ostentatious makes a different statement, possibly better in some ways, but also subject to negative interpretations in other ways. Each office worker, each manager, and each planner might have a slightly different list of descriptive words for the ideal office, but terms that would often turn up include:

Rational

Convenient

Organized

Adaptable

Comfortable

Expressive

"Attractive" or even "beautiful" come to mind as possibilities on such a list, but they mean so many different things to different people that they seem ineffective as descriptors or criteria.

In the end, one might hope of any built space—home, office, factory, store, hotel, restaurant, or whatever else—that it would offer help and support to its occupants and users. It should be a place which, on arrival, offers some sense of lift—or reassurance and stimulation. On leaving, it should provide a memory trace with vestiges of these positive values and encourage a willingness or desire to return in order to experience the same favorable feelings once again. Too many offices make arrival a depressant and departure a relief.

The final test must be the extent to which this pattern can be reversed. To work in a place which is in itself helpful, which aids work process and also contributes something to a sense of participation in a sound and healthy world is, unfortunately, a rare experience. There is no reason why it cannot be commonplace.

Open Plan Project Examples

The collection of plans and photographs that follow will give an idea of the kind, size, character, and range of open offices in current use. Other illustrations of many of these projects appear earlier where they relate to the discussion. An attempt has been made at logical grouping of the projects, although exact classification is sometimes difficult.

Office Landscape Projects. These projects were developed by or in direct consultation with the Quickborner Team. They illustrate *Bürolandschaft* as conceptualized by its originators in a rough sequence from early projects in Germany to recent projects in the U.S.

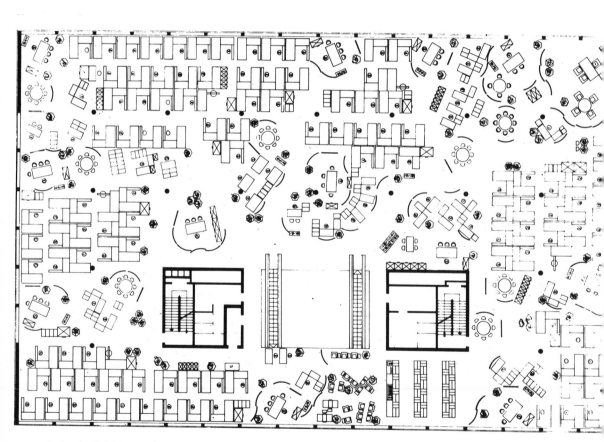

A classic Quickborner Team project in Germany: Orenstein-Koppel at Dortmund-Dorstfeld, 1963. This is a plan of the second floor (see page 19 for first floor plan). Note that major portions of the plan retain conventional, geometric patterns. Board chairman is in the upper right corner. Courtesy Quickborner Team.

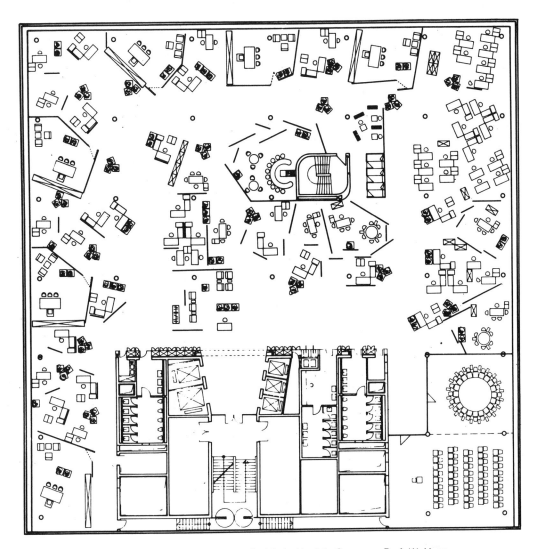

An executive floor in a multistory project. Osram Gmbh. in Munich, Germany. Prof. W. Henn, architect; Quickborner Team, planning. Courtesy Quickborner Team.

Above: One of three floors of a Ford Motor Co. office building in Cologne. Observe unusual building perimeter walls and staggered pattern of column locations. Courtesy Quickborner Team. Opposite page top: First floor plan, Krupp offices at Essen with main circulation lines shown. (See also additional plan on bottom page 25.) Planning by Quickborner Team. Courtesy Quickborner Team. Opposite page bottom: An early landscape project in the U.S.: Corning Glass Co. at Corning, N. Y., 1966. A Quickborner Team project. Courtesy Quickborner Team.

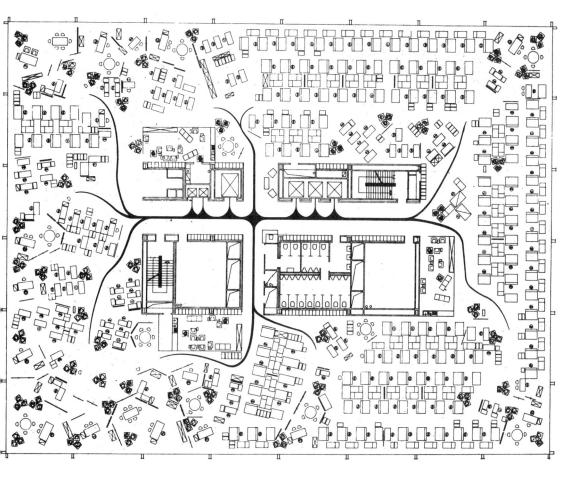

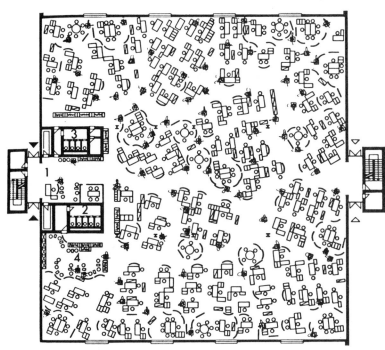

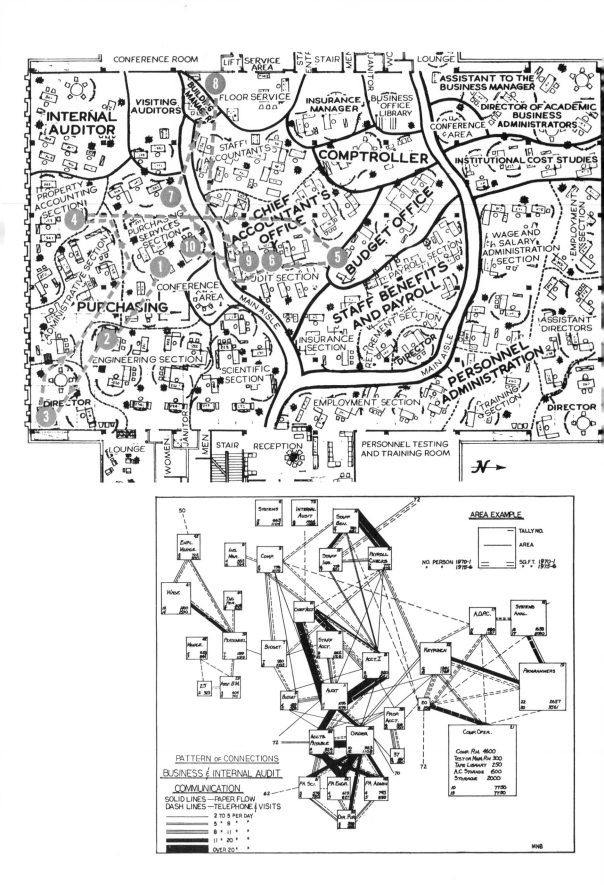

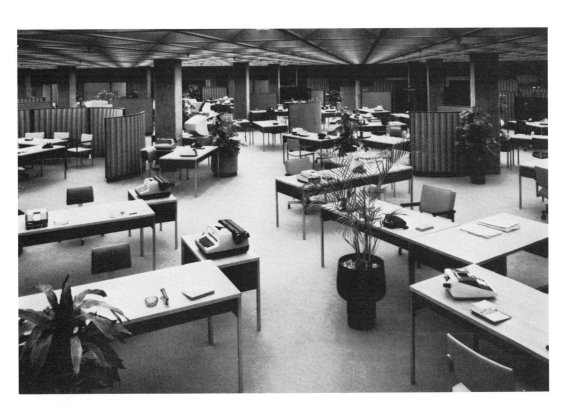

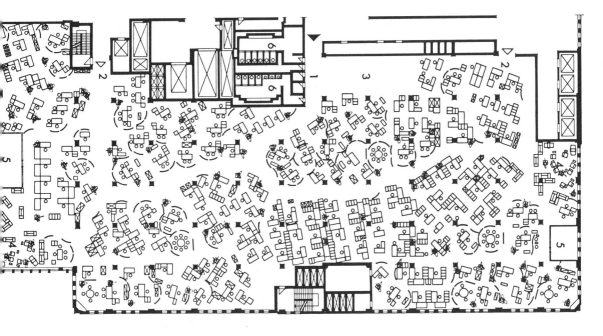

Opposite page top: Administrative Services Building for Purdue University. Plan with departmental areas and circulation paths outlined. Numbers indicate pattern of work flow for a particular procedure. Opposite page bottom: Communication chart for the same project. Top: General view of Purdue work space. A Quickborner Team project with Walter Scholer and Associates, architects; 1970. Courtesy Quickborner Team, Inc. Above: Eastman Kodak, Rochester, N.Y., an early test in the U.S., 1967, by the Quickborner Team.

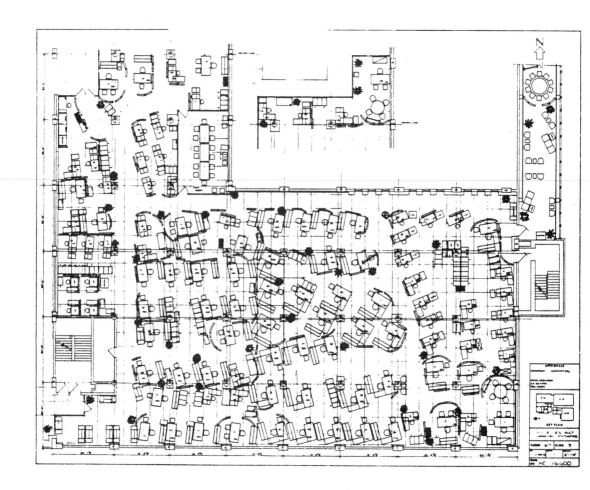

Top: Kodak is an extensive user of landscape planning in various facilities. A typical plan of a more recent project. Courtesy Quickborner Team. Above left and right: A typical work space and a more private, managerial area with extra conference space. Kodak at Rochester. Courtesy Eastman Kodak Co.

Action Office. This portfolio of the office system developed by Robert Propst for Herman Miller includes a variety of projects.

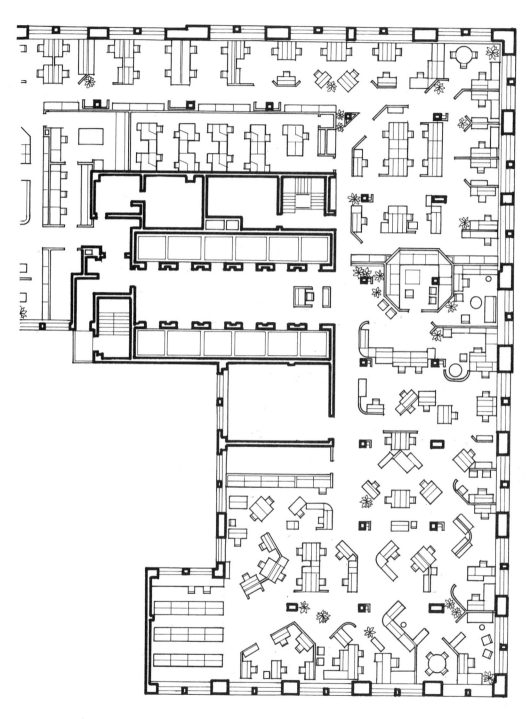

Young & Rubicam, Business Affairs Department, New York. Action Office put to use in an orderly plan with expectation of constant change. Joseph A. Grimaldi Design Associates, office planning and interior design.

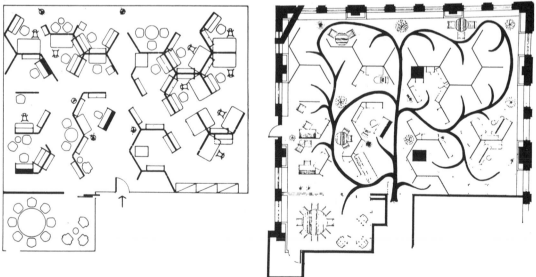

Top: The Young & Rubicam space. Electrical and telephone service by poles from ceiling channels. Photograph by Norman McGrath; courtesy Herman Miller, Inc. Above left: Chicago offices of JFN Associates. Action Office used on a hexagonal modular grid. Above right: Traffic flow shown on plan with typical work station layout. Courtesy JFN Associates.

Workspace (top) and conference area (above) in JFN office. Courtesy Herman Miller, Inc.

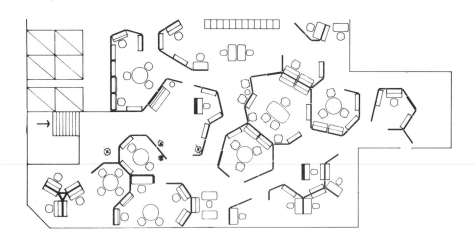

Top: Another JFN project using Action Office, in this case in a free, almost random arrangement. Courtesy JFN Associates. Above: President's office, Luminous Ceilings, Inc. Courtesy Herman Miller, Inc. Opposite page: Half plan of typical floor, Citizens and Southern National Bank, Atlanta, Georgia. Aeck Associates, Inc. architects. The unusual round plan accommodates a modified hexagonal grid. Courtesy Herman Miller, Inc.

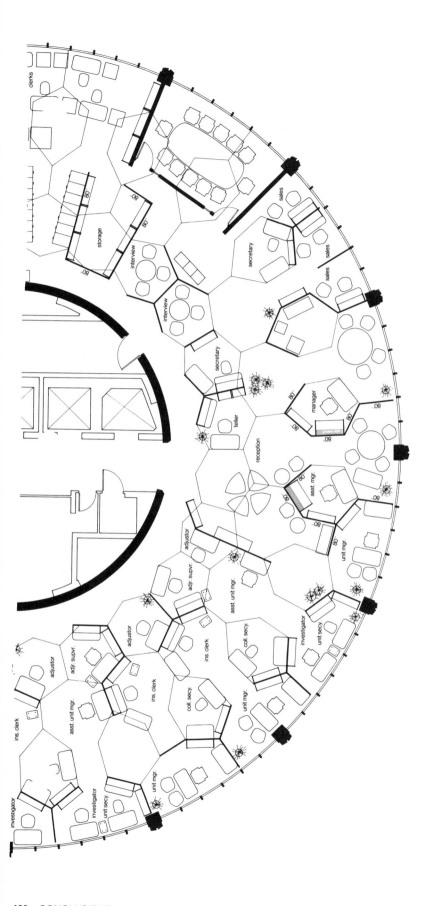

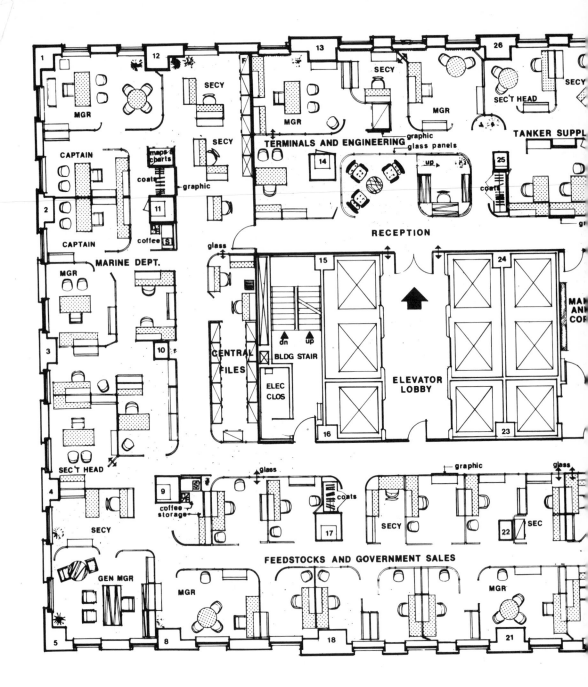

Plan, Asiatic Petroleum Corp. offices, New York; Di Iorio and Co., planning and design. Courtesy Herman Miller, Inc.

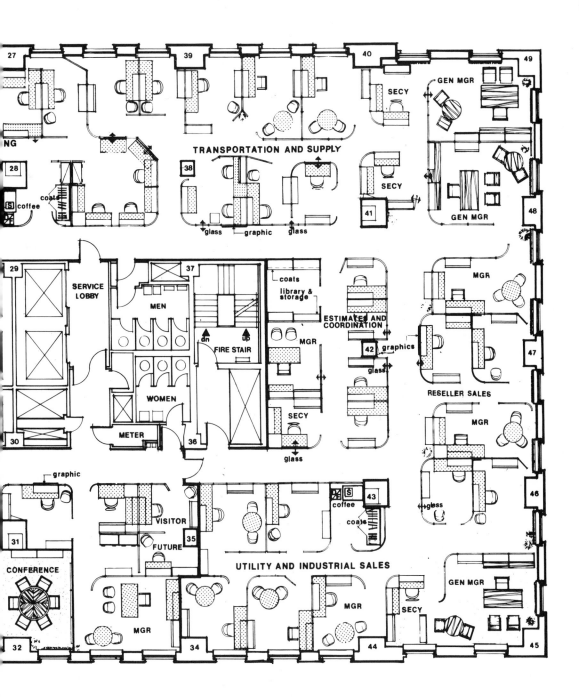

Top and above: General view of Asiatic Petroleum space. Courtesy Herman Miller, Inc.

Work Stations. Several different manufacturers have produced basic equipment for offices that are otherwise open in concept.

Top and above: Work stations from the Knoll Stephens System in use in the Weyerhaeuser Co. headquarters in Tacoma, Washington. (See top page 13 for plan.)

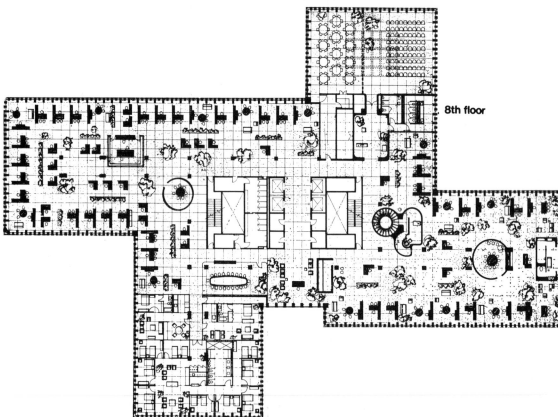

8th floor

Top: An executive office at Weyerhaeuser, open but still private in feeling. Skidmore, Owings, & Merrill, architects and interior designers; Sydney Rodgers Associates, space planners. Photograph by Ezra Soller, ESTO; courtesy Skidmore, Owings, & Merrill. Above: Typical floor plan, McDonald Corp. headquarters, Oak Brook, Ill. Salvatore Balsamo and Associates, architects; ASD Inc., space planning and interior design. Dining and meeting rooms are on this floor as well as the unusual think tank. Eppinger Furniture Co. TRM work station units are the dominant furniture.

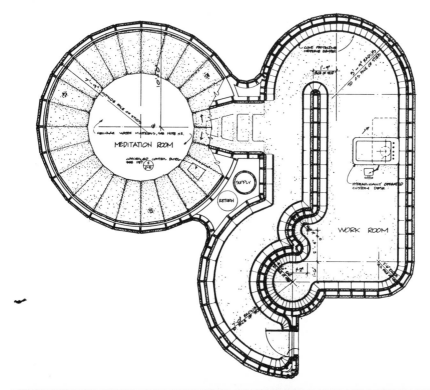

Top and above: Plan and view of the communicating passage in the think tank space for meditation and quiet work.

Above: Typical open work space area. Photographs by Balthazar Korab; courtesy ASD Inc.
Opposite page: Typical floor, Montgomery Ward headquarters, Chicago; Minoru Yamasaki, architect; Sydney Rodgers Associates, interior planners.

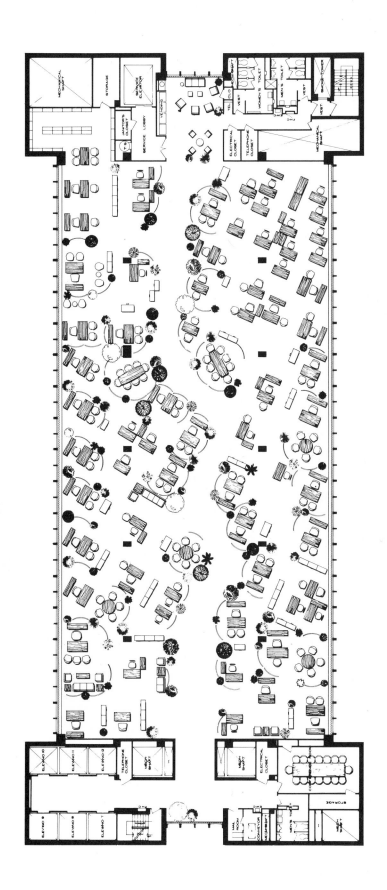

Top: General offices at Montgomery Ward use Steelcase 9000 series furniture. Above: Eppinger TRM units are executive office furniture and dividers at Montgomery Ward. Photographs by Hedrich Blessing; courtesy Rodgers Associates.

Top, middle, and above: Work stations of three types in use in three different functional areas: desks and screens in open general offices, work stations in computer programmer areas (Steelcase 9000 furniture, Rose screens), and Knoll furniture, including Stevens storage clusters in executive areas. Dial Financial Corp. headquarters in Des Moines, Iowa; John Pile, planning and interior design. Photographs by Norman McGrath.

Other Open Plan Projects. These examples combine landscape ideas in various ways and include variations and innovations as the planners involved preferred.

Top, above, and opposite page: Custom-designed desks and dividers in open office areas of Gilman Paper Co. in New York. Ducts and lighting are exposed, some ceiling areas are mirrored. Executive offices are conventionally private. SLS Environetics, Inc., planners and interior designers. Photographs by Louis Reens; courtesy SLS Environetics.

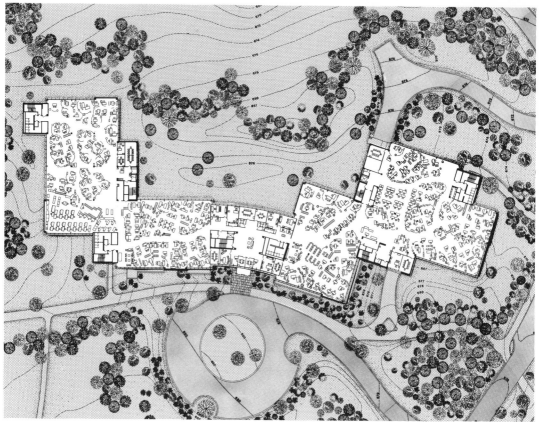

Top: Open drafting area in the Houston offices of Caudill Rowlett Scott. The unusual degree of openness to the exterior increases the sense of space. Photograph by Jim Parker; courtesy Caudill Rowlett Scott. Above: Plan of administrative building for Uniroyal, Inc., Oxford, Connecticut. The Eggers Partnership, architects; Sydney Rodgers, office planning and design. Opposite page top: Typical interior of the Uniroyal space. Photograph by Gil Amiaga; courtesy Sydney Rodgers Associates. Opposite page bottom: A typical floor (one of nineteen) in the Port of New York Authority offices in the World Trade Center. Yamasaki and Associates, architects for the building; Ford and Earl Design Associates, interior designers. Open plan except for the offices of top officials and related conference rooms at diagonally opposite corners of the floor.

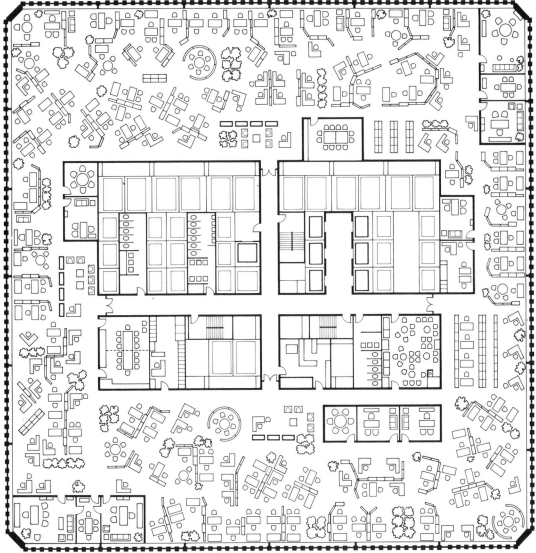

Top: A typical general office space with major furniture from GF, Inc. at the Port of New York Authority offices. Photograph by Balthazar Korab; courtesy GF. Middle and above: A particularly handsome open plan office in England. Noble Lowndes Annuities, Croyden, planned by Heal's Contracts Ltd. Photograph by John Maltby; courtesy Heal's.

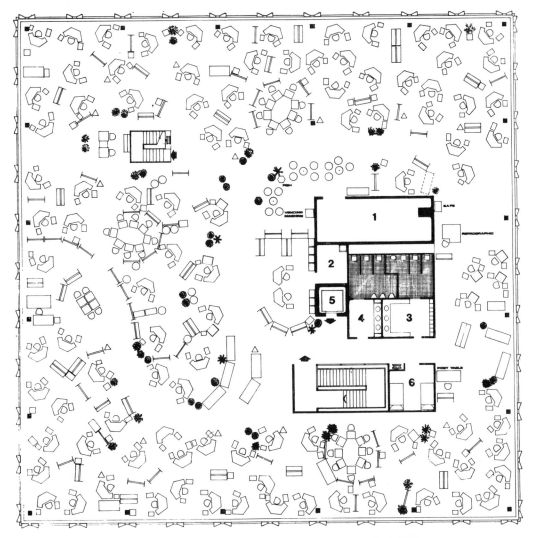

Top and above: A British government office (Directorate of Telecommunications) at Kew built as an experiment with open planning. Whitehall Development Group, architects. Work surfaces are of an unusual form—segments of a hexagon—which permits grouping in clusters of varied form.

Top: Typical plan in open offices designed by S. I. Morris Associates for Transcontinental Gas Pipe Line Corp. in Houston. Angular relationships of 45° are used throughout to establish a controlled layout geometry. Above: Typical Transcontinental office area with work stations designed by SIMA for the project. Photograph by Rob Muir; courtesy SIMA.

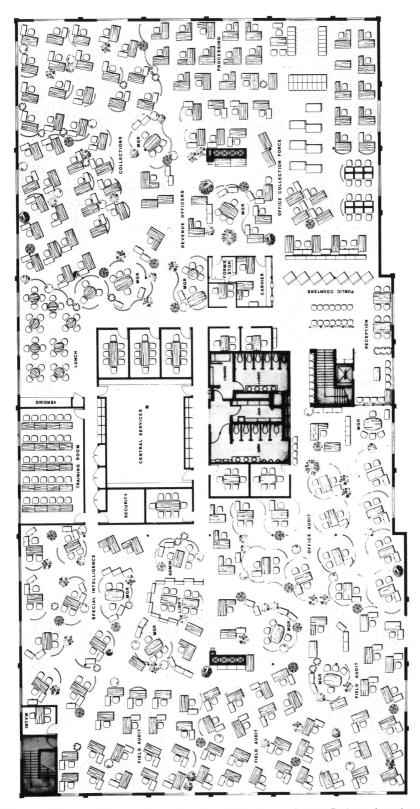

U.S. Internal Revenue Service office in San Jose, California, by Sydney Rodgers Associates.

Waiting area (top), general office space (middle), and private office-conference area (above) in IRS San Jose office. Courtesy Rodgers Associates.

Appendix of Technical Standards

Density

The amount of space allocated per office worker is an important factor in establishing the character of the office, its costs, and its efficiency. Too great a density leads to the obvious problems of crowding, but too little density can be a source of acoustical problems and may lead to a depressing sense of deadness, with large, vacant areas appearing useless and neglected. Executive and upper managerial areas usually have low densities for reasons of status and possibly for certain real functional needs (such as generous conference and waiting areas). It is impossible to arrive at one ideal average density because the mix of workplace types varies greatly in different organizations, but the following list will give some idea of the range of densities in current practice:

Project	Sq ft (sq m) per person
Buch und Ton	125 (12)
International Harvester	136 (13)
British Petroleum	137 (13)
Dial Financial Corp.	137 (13)
Port of New York Authority	145 (13.5)
Corning Glass	151 (14)
Ford Motor Co.	157 (14.5)
Du Pont (test space)	160 (15)
Kodak (1968)	174 (16.5)
Krupp	195 (18.5)
Osram	227 (21.5)
Orenstein-Koppel	232 (22)

Note: 125 sq ft (12 sq m) per person is often quoted as an ideal density from an acoustical point of view; the concern is that *lower* density will fail to create sufficient natural background noise.

In estimating area requirements and costs, it is usually best to arrive at an area average for each work station type rather than attempting to select an overall density average. This may be done by planning the required work stations in detail or by selecting figures from a table of typical ranges such as the following:

Workplace type	Sq ft (sq m) range
Top executive	250-450 (24-42)
Executive	200-350 (19-32)
Manager (department head)	100-250 (9.5-24)
Supervisor	100-150 (9.5-14)
Engineer/programmer	80-150 (7.5-14)
General office worker	55-90 (5-8.5)

Clerical/stenographic	50-80 (4.7-7.5)	
Executive secretary	80-150 (7.5-14)	

An allowance for circulation of about 25 percent, or 37 sq ft (3.5 sq m) per person, should be added to the above. Other functions (filing, conference, reception, etc.) must be added also.

For comparisons between conventional and open planning, standards established by two U.S. government agencies may be of interest. The GSA (General Services Administration) *Guide for Space Planning and Layout* gives area standards for each civil service rank designated by the grades GS 1 to GS 18 inclusive. The Department of Labor space directive establishes slightly different standards on the same basis, and it was used for comparison purposes in a study of landscape planning. The following table lists these standards:

	Conventional		Landscape
	GSA	Labor	Labor
GS 18 & above A	500	600	440
GS 18 & above B	400	425-475	306-410
GS 16 to 18	300	300	244
GS 14 & 15 (1)	250	250	192
GS 14 & 15	150	150	120
GS 12 & 13 (1)	150	150	85
GS 12 & 13	100	100	63
GS 7 to 11 (1)	75-100	100	54-105
GS 7 to 11	75	75	45-63
GS 1 to 6	60	75	45-63

Note: (1) indicates supervisory responsibility. Circulation not included in any of the figures of this table.

Costs

Rapid changes in the cost of all the components of an office installation make it impractical to suggest dollar figures for use in estimating. It is possible, however, to suggest an approach to cost estimating which is relatively simple and which will also serve for making comparisons between conventional and open office plans. The steps involved are

1. Set up a limited number of categories of workplaces such as:

A. Executive

B. Manager

C. Staff worker

D. Sales/engineering/accounting station

E. Clerical/stenographic

2. Assign an appropriate average area to each (see density statistics above). Count personnel in each category and multiply by area assignment to obtain an area total for work stations.

3. Add areas for other functions such as files, conference areas, and circulation using the following figures:

File cabinet	20 sq ft (1.9 sq m)
Wardrobe (serves 12)	25 sq ft (2.4 sq m)
Small conference area	100 sq ft (9.5 sq m)

Large conference area	as estimated
Reception area	as estimated
Lounges	as estimated
Circulation	35 sq ft (3.3 sq m) per person or 25 percent of total area

4. Using total area (plus any allowance for expansion), estimate costs on a square foot basis for the following:

Carpet and other floor coverings
Ceiling acoustical treatment
General lighting
Background sound system (if provided)

deducting any portion of these costs provided in rental space under provisions of the lease.

5. Estimate furniture cost for each workplace type on the basis of the furniture system selected. Multiply each workplace estimate by the number of such workplaces and total the result. Add allowances for furniture for file, conference, reception, lounge, and other special purpose areas. Add cost of wardrobes (1 per 12 employees). Add allowance for plants and planters (allow one plant per two employees). Add allowances for window treatments, wall-mounted acoustical treatment, and any other items not otherwise included.

6. Total all the above to generate a working estimate. A work sheet for this purpose may be arranged as follows:

Workplaces

Type	Number	Area per person	Total area	Equipment cost per person	Total equipment cost
A					
B					
C					
D					
E					
Etc.					

Other Functions

Name	Number	Area per person	Total area	Equipment cost per person	Total equipment cost
Files					
Conference					
Reception					
Etc.					

Circulation (total area allowance _____)

Area-Based Item

Floor covering	@ $____ per sq ft
Ceiling treatment	@ $____ per sq ft
Lighting (general)	@ $____ per sq ft
Sound system	@ $____ per sq ft
Other	@ $____ per sq ft
Total allowance	@ $____ per sq ft

X _____ Total square footage
_____ Total area-based items

Summary

Total workplace equipment costs	$_____
Total other function equipment costs	$_____
Total area-based items	$_____
Total miscellaneous items (plants, window treatment, etc.)	$_____
Project total	$_____

If a comparative figure for conventionl planning is desired, plans must be developed to establish the amount and kind of partitioning that will be used and a selection of furniture, lighting, and other equipment must be made. An estimate can then be made on a basis analogous to that outlined above. To avoid total planning of a large project, it will serve to plan some portion that represents a fair cross section of typical situations and to use this as a basis for comparison with the same area taken as a fraction of the total open plan project. To make such a comparison fair, it is important to be sure that the sample area is truly representative and that realistic assumptions are made in quality of furniture and equipment. Comparative estimates can be easily rigged to favor either plan type by setting up the comparison in a way that generates a desired result. Any comparison offered for consideration should be carefully checked to ensure that no such rigging is involved.

A study of first costs is, of course, only one aspect of the total cost. A valid annual cost comparison requires a reasonable estimate of the facility's expected occupancy life, an estimate of the frequency and cost of workplace moves and other changes and alterations, and estimates of maintenance and replacement costs for furniture and furnishings. A work sheet for such a comparison might be set up as follows:

	Conventional	Open plan
Annual space cost (rental or amortization of construction cost)*	$_____	$_____
Installation first cost amortized over estimated project life	_____	_____
Workplace moves per year times estimated cost of each move†	_____	_____
Annual maintenance costs (cleaning,‡ plants, etc.)	_____	_____
Replacements (partitions, floor coverings, upholstery, etc.) per year	_____	_____
Totals	_____	_____

*Observe that the area required for each type of plan will be different with open planning, usually requiring at least 10 percent less than conventional planning.

†Cost of moving a workplace will vary with type of equipment proposed for each case. Figures for relocating a conventional office can average as much as $550; those for moving an open workplace as little as $10.

‡Open office cleaning is more efficient by about 20 percent as a result of easy movement of equipment and cleaning staff.

Lighting

Intensity of lighting is easily measured and is expressed in terms of the footcandle. Over the years, many attempts have been made to establish standards for desirable intensity for various tasks with a tendency, historically, for standards to be constantly raised. Recent rises in energy costs have led to a general reevaluation of standards and a discovery that acceptable levels can be considerably lower than was supposed a few years ago. The following table suggests reasonable current standards:

Motion picture auditorium (during picture)	1 footcandle
Storage areas and passages	5
Stairways, shipping areas	10
Ambient light in office area	10
Intermittent reading and writing (minimum)	20
Reading newsprint (minimum)	25
Bookkeeping, typing, accounting	30
Prolonged reading, study, close work	50
Task lighting at workplace	50-70
Drafting	50-100
Sewing black thread on black	500
Hospital operating table	2000
Noon daylight in shade	100-1,000
Noon daylight in full sun	6,000-8,000

The quality of light for visual tasks is more complex to define and measure. One useful criterion is brightness contrast: the ratio of brightest to dimmest areas in a certain situation. Seeing is easiest where brightness contrast is minimized. Suggested standards are

IES standard luminence ratio	3:1
Seeing task to background, no more than	5:1
Seeing task to general surround, no more than	20:1
Light source to general surround (maximum)	40:1
Maximum anywhere in visual field	80:1

Output of various types of light sources (called "lamps" in the industry; "bulbs" or "tubes" by most laypeople) varies greatly and is usually given in lumens. The lumen is the amount of illumination necessary to light an area one foot square to a level of one footcandle at a distance of 1 ft (30 cm). Lumen output of common light sources is

Incandescent	20 lumens per watt
Mercury vapor	50 lumens per watt
Fluorescent	80 lumens per watt
Multivapor	85 lumens per watt
Lucalox	100 lumens per watt

The lumen output of a lighting fixture indicates the footcandle level it will deliver through the use of the following formula:

$$\text{Footcandles} = \frac{\text{lumens output x CU x LLD x LDD}}{\text{area to be illuminated in sq ft}}$$

In this formula CU indicates the coefficient of utilization, LLD indicates lamp lumen depreciation, and LDD indicates lamp dirt depreciation. These are values that can be found in tables provided by fixture manufacturers for each available type of light fixture. The CU takes into account the characteristics (shape, colors) of the space to be illuminated, while the other two factors are characteristics of the lamp and fixture in question.

Color of light called "white" is quite variable and is usually expressed as a "color temperature" in degrees Kelvin (°K). A high figure indicates a cold (bluish) color, a low figure a warm (reddish) cast. Typical values are

Daylight, noon sun	5000-6500°K
Daylight, overcast	5300-7175
Fluorescent, daylight	6500
Fluorescent, warmtone	3000
Fluorescent, standard white	3500
Incandescent (according to wattage)	2400-2800

Cost of lighting depends on electric power cost, type of light source and lighting installation, and footcandle levels required. Since most office lighting is fluorescent and installed in fairly consistent ways, it is possible to arrive at figures for wattage per square foot requirements for typical light levels as follows:

Common building standard	3 watts per sq ft = 39 footcandles
Good conventional installation	5 watts per sq ft = 70 footcandles
Task/ambient installation	2.5 watts per sq ft = *
Task/ambient, practical minimum	1.25 watts per sq ft = *

To convert these values to estimates of lighting costs, solve the following:

$$\frac{\text{Watts per sq ft X area}}{1000} \text{ X hours of annual use X energy cost} = \text{total annual cost}$$

Energy cost is expressed in charge per KWH.

Since heat produced by lighting must be removed through air conditioning, any comparison of different lighting approaches must include a calculation of the impact of different energy consumption on air conditioning costs. In making this comparison use the values:

1 kw energy used in lighting = 3413 BTU (heat)

1 ton air conditioning will remove 12000 BTU per hour

1 ton air conditioning requires approximately 1.2 kw energy

*Providing 70 footcandles at task, 40 on task area back panels, 10 in circulation and other nontask areas.

Therefore, removal of 10000 BTU per hour will require 1 kw for air conditioning; removal of the 3413 BTU produced by 1 kw of lighting will consume 314 watts for air conditioning. Looked at another way when comparing two lighting proposals, each 1000 watts not required by the more economical system will save an addition 314 watts for air conditioning. The saving in energy cost for lighting alone can be increased by 31.4 percent to give an estimate for the total saving, including reduction in air conditioning required.

A complete comparison also requires comparison of first costs and maintenance costs for both lighting and air conditioning equipment.

Acoustics

The most useful unit in discussion of sound levels is the decibel (DB). Sound or noise can be described as having an intensity of a certain number of decibels; reduction in sound resulting from acoustical treatment of barriers (partitions, for example) is stated as a loss or reduction of a certain number of decibels. The following table lists the decibel level of various types of sound:

Threshold of hearing	0 DB
Quiet garden (rustling leaves)	20
Quiet residence	30
Soft whisper at 5 ft (150 cm)	34
Quiet office	40
Ideal office background sound	40-50
Average busy office	45-65
Window air conditioner	55
Speech at close range	60
Typing area in office	65-70
Typical factory interior	80
Threshold of hearing damage with sustained exposure	85
Heavy city traffic	92
Subway train	95-100
Home lawn mower	98
Jet aircraft 500 ft (150 m) overhead	115
Symphony orchestra (maximum)	145
Jet engine (maximum)	170

Effectiveness of sound-absorbing materials is usually stated in terms of the noise reduction coefficient (NRC): the percentage of impinging sound at standardized frequencies that will be absorbed. This term thus has a range from 0 to 100. Typical NRC values are

Ceiling of plaster or metal pans	.40-.60
Acoustical wall or screen panels	.55-.65
Desirable for carpet with underlay	.65
Desirable for acoustical ceiling	.90
Most efficient ceiling treatments	.95

The effort to predict and control acoustical conditions in a way that will establish adequate speech privacy, avoid irritating and intrusive sound, and still achieve a pleasant and comfortable acoustical environment has led to the development of several additional units of measurement defined in complex ways. Without explaining derivations of these terms, it is possible to note the following:

NC (noise criterion) curves. A series of lines on a graph plotting sound pressure in relation to frequency. Each curve carries a number; a range of 25 to 55 is useful. Measured or predicted noise levels are plotted on the graph. The lowest curve with all plotted values below it establishes the NC of the space in question.

NIC[1] (speech privacy noise isolation class). A single number indicating the acoustical effectiveness of any ceiling/screen combination. The higher the figure the better the possibility of speech privacy. Typical values are

Open sky	23
Efficient ceiling/screen combination	18-20
Average ceiling/screen combination	16
Gypsum board ceiling only	11

SPP (speech privacy potential). A single number indicating the effectiveness of a particular open office environment in providing speech privacy. SPP should equal or exceed 60 in order to ensure satisfactory speech privacy.

Layout

In conventional planning, it is customary to establish typical office layout plans on the basis of rank level, designated A, B, etc., down to perhaps F or G. These types, with minor variation for window or door location, can then be combined to make up a cellular plan. The very openness of open planning makes much greater variation possible and works against the rigidity of repeated, standardized units. It is still possible to set up a series of typical equipment selections that can be used with enough consistency to avoid the need to plan every work station as a unique identity. How the chosen equipment will combine depends on the dimensional and detail characteristics of the furniture systems chosen. Many furniture manufacturers offer suggested packaged layouts to help the planner use a particular system.

The layouts illustrated below are in no way standards, but merely suggested points of departure for developing work stations in a particular furniture system to suit the requirements of a particular installation. Dotted lines indicate optional or shared elements. Diagrams are at ⅛ in. = 1 ft 0 in.

A. Senior executive work area

B. Executive work area

C. Department head or middle manager

D. Supervisor or special work function station

E. Work station with extra storage and visitor chair

F. Basic work station

G. Other commonly required elements:

1. General storage and wardrobe units

2. Lateral files

3. Movable acoustic screens

4. Open or semienclosed conference area

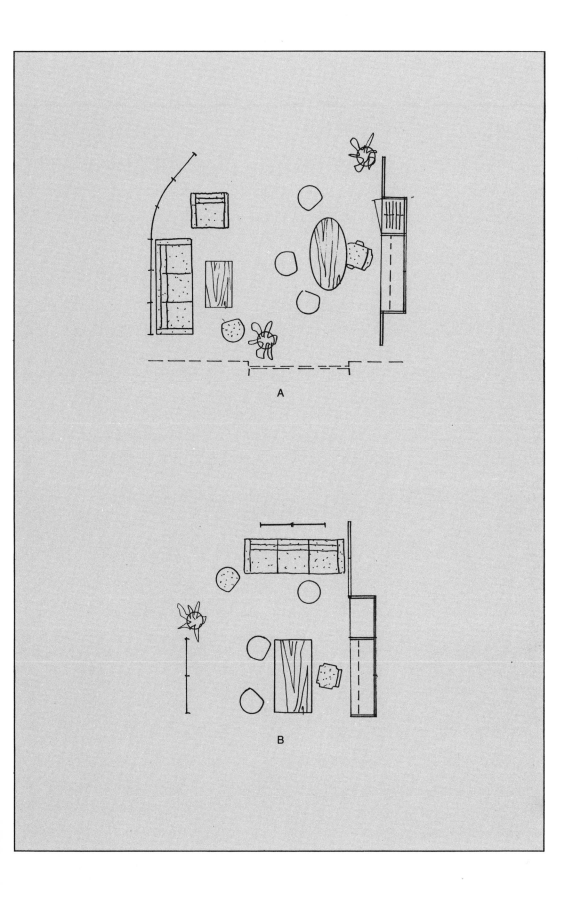

A

B

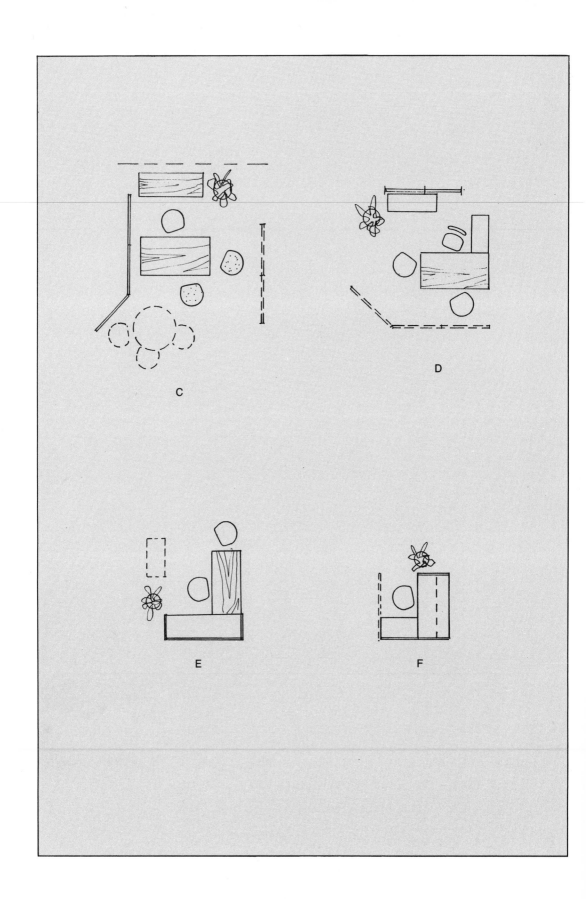

C

D

E

F

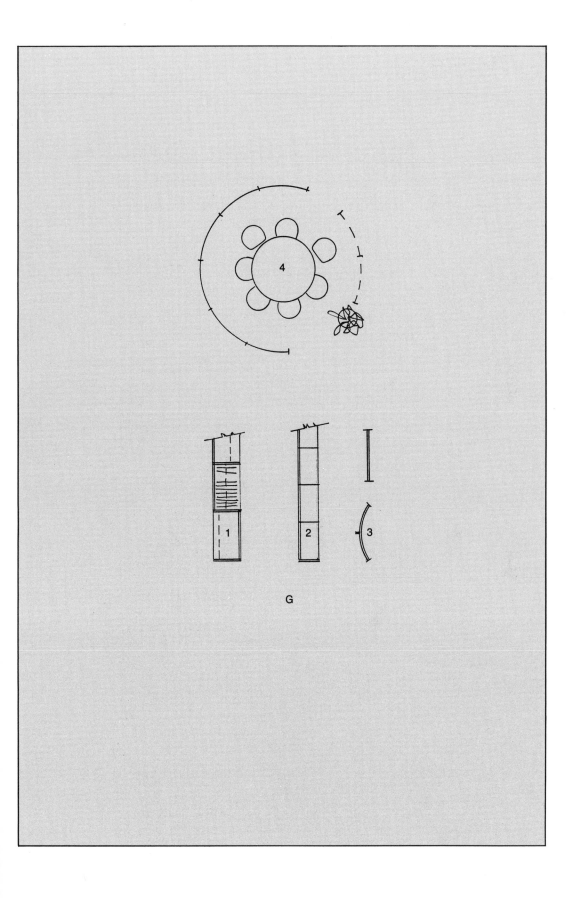

G

Glossary

Absorption (sound). Dissipation of sound wave energy within a material. Sound waves on striking a material are partly reflected, partly absorbed. The absorption coefficient of a material indicates the percentage of energy that will be absorbed.

AC (alternating current). The most usual form of electrical energy as supplied by utilities for general use.

Acoustical conditioner. A device for generating background sound (VOV(locally.

Acoustical screen. A movable screen with surfaces of a material that offers good sound absorption.

Action Office. Trade name for an office furniture system using work surfaces and storage units supported on movable panels. A product of Herman Miller, Inc., that has been widely imitated.

Adjacency. Location next to another unit. An adjacency study lists levels of need for adjacency between persons or departments in an organization.

Air-handling fixture. A lighting fixture for ceiling installation with capability to act as a distribution outlet or return for HVAC air.

Ambient light. Light generally present throughout a space (as distinguished from task light concentrated at a particular work area).

American plan. A European term describing the open, general office spaces used in large business offices in the U.S. early in the 20th century.

Area diagram. A chart using simple, usually rectangular, blocks to show areas (to scale) needed by units of an organization. Also called a "block diagram."

Background sound. The random sounds present in an occupied space generated by user activities and mechanical equipment (especially air conditioning) and when provided by a background sound system (qv).

Background sound system. A system of electronic sound generators and speakers providing artificial background sound to aid in masking unwanted sounds, such as conversation taking place at a remote workplace.

Brightness contrast. The ratio of brightest point to dimmest point within a field of vision. Limiting brightness contrast is important to good seeing conditions.

BTU (British thermal unit). The amount of heat needed to raise the temperature of 1 lb of water 1°F (Fahrenheit, approximately). The most common unit for designating amount of heat or cooling.

Bubble diagram. A chart showing relationships of individuals or groups within an organization in freely drawn shapes (bubbles) which may be overlapped or contained one within another.

Bürolandschaft (German), literally, office landscape. The usual term for the particular type of open planning developed by the Quickborner Team.

Central filing. The concentration of all files in one location, normally associated with a special system for easy retrieval, delivery, and return of material to the files.

Cluster. A grouping of closely associated workers or work units.

Communications survey. A study recording the number and kind of communications between individuals or groups in an organization.

Convector. A device for delivering heat to an occupied space by convection, usually provided at the lower edges of windows or fixed glass areas.

Core. In planning, an area in which such fixed elements as stairs, elevators, toilets, and ducts are grouped. In many buildings the core is centrally located, but the term may still be used for such grouping in non-central locations.

CPM (critical path method). A sophisticated method for planning a process in relation to time schedule. Often used to aid scheduling of building or office installation projects.

CRT (cathode ray tube). The television screen-like display on which data (words, numbers, or images) can be displayed; used in connection with a computer.

Decibel (DB). A unit of measurement of sound intensity.

Density. The concentration of occupants within a space, usually designated in number of square feet per person. In comparing density figures, it is important to note whether or not circulation and core spaces are included in the total area figure used.

Factorial (number). Written in mathematical notation with the symbol !. The term 5! (read "factorial five") is the product of multiplying together each of the successive number digits from 1 to 5, that is, 1 x 2 x 3 x 4 x 5. Thus 5! equals 120.

Fluorescent. Capable of glowing with a visible light when in the presence of invisible radiant energy, such as ultraviolet wavelengths. The tubular lighting tubes in common use are designated "fluorescent tubes" because a significant portion of their light output is of this type.

Footcandle. The most common unit for measuring intensity of illumination. It is defined as the level of light produced by a standard candle at a distance of 1 ft (30 cm).

Grid. A regular geometric pattern superimposed on the floor plan of a space to establish a patterned order in the placement of elements. Grids are most often made up of squares or rectangles, occasionally of triangles or hexagons, but the term is also used in the rare situation in which a pattern of circles or elipses is used.

Grossraum (German), literally large room. A term for the large open space occupied by an open plan or office landscape facility.

Hard area(s). Parts of an office plan constructed in fixed materials that make rearrangement difficult or impossible. A core (qv) is always hard. Conference rooms or other special purpose areas may be hard also.

HID (high intensity discharge in lighting). A category of light source which is neither incandescent nor, strictly speaking, fluorescent. Mercury, sodium, and metal halide lamps are of this type.

HVAC. Common abbreviation for systems providing heating, ventilation, and air conditioning.

Incandescent. Capable of glowing as a result of heating. The most common form of electric lighting makes use of the familiar light bulb in which tungsten glows when heated by the flow of current in a near vacuum.

Index of interaction. A figure indicating the amount of communication a particular individual or unit within an organization has with all other units of that organization.

In-house (within the organization). In-house office planning is provided by planners who are regular, salaried employees of the organization as distinguished from consultants.

Interaction study. A study of communication patterns between individuals or units of an organization based on the findings of a communications survey (qv).

Landscape (office). Literal translation of *Bürolandschaft* (German for "office landscape"), the most usual term for open planning based on the concepts of the Quickborner Team.

Link value. A numerical indication of level of communication between two individuals or units of an organization as discovered in a communications survey and used in an interaction study.

Low brightness (fixture). A type of lighting device which appears dim or dark when viewed at normal angles, but which delivers a normal intensity of illumination.

Lumen. The most common unit of lighting quantity; the amount of light flux which will illuminate one square foot of area with an intensity of one footcandle.

Masking sound. Sound present in a space of a kind and intensity which covers or obscures other, undesirable sounds. Intelligibility of speech can be blocked by sufficient masking sound developed as background noise or provided artificially by an electronic sound system.

Matrix. A chart in which all the relationships (with respect to a particular value) between two lists of items are displayed. The two lists may be the same or different. The mileage chart often provided on a road map is a typical matrix chart.

Modular grid. A grid (qv) based on a dimensional module which may be a multiple and/or submultiple of other dimensional units used in the same planning process.

Network (based) planning. Process and/or schedule planning that charts all or many step relationships and dependencies (as distinguished from linear or sequential planning which recognizes only one line of relationships).

NRC (noise reduction coefficient). A numerical unit of measurement of the degree of sound absorption provided by a particular surface material. A high NRC indicates a high level of absorption effectiveness.

OC. Abbreviation for "on center" used in giving dimensions. For example, columns in a building may be 24 ft oc (center to center).

Open plan. A common term for office space that uses little or no fixed partitioning. An alternate term to "office landscape" which has more general applicability when office landscape is reserved to designate planning based on Quickborner Team concepts.

Pausenraum (German), literally, room for pausing. A lounge or rest area invariably included in *Bürolandschaft* office plans.

PERT (program evaluation and review technique). A sophisticated form of network planning for organizing process flow and time schedule in complex projects and monitoring the progress of the project in relation to that plan.

Plenum. Hollow space above a hung ceiling which can be used for circulation of conditioned air (most often return air) and as a space for concealment of ducts, wiring, pipes, and similar utilities.

Pool. A general office space without partitioning for stenographic or other clerical workers. Informally often designated a "bullpen."

Quickborner Team. The management consulting firm, based in the German town of Quickborn, usually credited with the development of office landscape planning.

Quiet room. An enclosed room offering closed-door privacy and total quiet for the occasional situations requiring acoustical isolation.

Raceway. A wiring duct, usually part of an underfloor system for electrical and telephone system wiring.

Rank order. In order of numerical value from least to most.

Reverberation. Successive reflections of sound (echoes) which cause a sound to continue with gradually decreasing intensity for some time after its original production has stopped. Reverberation time is the period required for reverberation to drop at an inaudible level.

Spectrum. The range of wavelengths of energy present in a particlar flux of radiation; most often visible light. Light which appears white or colorless when passed through a prism will be broken into a band of various colors corresponding to the wavelengths present.

Spectrum, continuous. When all visible wavelengths of light are present, the resulting spectrum will be a rainbowlike range of all colors (although the intensity of various colors may vary).

Spectrum, discontinuous. The spectrum produced by certain light sources (fluorescent and HID, for example) made up of strong bands of particular frequencies with little or no energy in the frequency bands between.

Stacking (plan). The arrangement of space assignments on the various floors of a multifloor office facility. A stacking plan may take the form of a list, tabulation, chart, or diagram.

Status. The visible expression of level of rank or position through physical arrangements (such as space assignment, location, choice of furniture or equipment).

Task lighting (also called task/ambient lighting). Lighting provided locally at work (task) locations at levels of intensity required for the tasks in question. Other light in the space is limited to lower levels adequate for circulation and limitation of brightness contrast. Such general lighting is the ambient light in the space.

Territoriality. A human concern (shared by other animals) with identification of space for exclusive or at least personally controlled use.

Three-times estimate. A means of accurately estimating time required for a given process that requires three figures representing a probable maximum, a probable minimum, and a most probable time. A similar triple estimate is useful in estimating quantities other than time, for example, costs.

Underfloor duct system. A system often used in modern office buildings to provide access for AC and telephone wiring to points remote from walls or columns. Raceways (qv) are imbedded in the floor construction in a regular pattern, and access plates are provided where wiring connections are required.

White noise. A mix of sound frequencies which is unobtrusive and random, but which provides good masking of speech and other office sounds. "Gray noise" is a term for a similar sound mix of slightly different frequency content.

Selected Bibliography

The following is a selected listing of books and articles that deal with open or landscape office planning, plus a few general works on office design. A complete listing of all useful material on office function and planning and on such special aspects of office design as lighting and acoustics is not attempted. Magazine articles presenting theoretical material on open planning are listed, but pictorial reviews of typical projects are not, except where they touch on general issues. Much of the basic literature on open planning is in German; in this list, a German text is indicated by the symbol (G) after the title.

Alsleben, Kurd. *Neue Technik der Mobilarordnung im Büroraum* (G). Verlag Schnelle, 1960.

"America's First Landscape." *Office Design*, March 1968.

Archibald, R., and Villoria, R. *Network Based Management Systems*. New York: John Wiley & Sons, 1967.

Armstrong-Wright, A. T. *Critical Path Method*. New York: Longman, 1969.

Bach, Fred W. "A Systems Approach to Ergonomics." *Modern Office Procedures*, October 1974.

Brooks Barr Graeber & White and Pitts Mebane Phelps & White. *Office Landscape: A Feasibility Study*. U.S. General Services Administration, 1967. (Not publicly available.)

Cihlar, C. (ed.). *New Concepts in Office Design*. New York: Business Press, 1966. (An anthology.)

Duffy, F., Cave, C., Worthington, J., et al. *Planning Office Space*. London: Architectural Press and Nichols Publishing, 1976.

————, and Wankum, A. *Office Landscaping*. Anbar Publications, 1969.

Fetridge, C., and Minor, R. *Office Administration Handbook*. Chicago: Dartnell Institute of Business Research, 1974.

Friedmann, A., Pile, J., and Wilson, F. *Interior Design: An Introduction to Architectural Interiors*. 2d ed. New York: Elsevier, 1976; Japanese edition, Shokokusha, 1973.

Gottschalk, Ottomar. *Flexible Verwaltungsbauten* (G). 2d ed. Verlag Schnelle, 1968.

Hamme, R., and Huggins, D. "Acoustics in the Open Plan." *Office Design*, September 1968.

Heyel, C. (ed.) with second chapter by Bach, F. *Handbook of Modern Office Management*. New York: McGraw-Hill, 1972.

Hjelm, Ake. "Subjective Spaces of Landscaping." *Office Design*, March 1968.

"International Office Design." *Office Design*, November 1967.

Joedicke, Jürgen. *Office Buildings*. New York: Praeger, 1962.

Kommunikation: Zeitschrift für Planungs- und Organisations-Kybernetik (G). Verlag Schnelle (particularly issues 1, 2, and 4 of September and November 1965 and March 1966).

Lappat, A., and Gottschalk, O. *Organisatorische Bürohausplanung und Bauwettbewerb* (G). Verlag Schnelle, 1965.

Lorenzen, H., and Jaeger, D. "The Office Landscape: A 'Systems' Concept." *Contract*, January 1968.

Mittag, Martin. *Verwaltungsgebäude Krupp Rheinhausen* (G). Deutscher Bauzentrum Verlag, 1964.

"Mixed Reactions to First U.S. Office Landscape." *Contract*, April 1968.

The Office Landscape: A Report on User Experience. Office Landscape Users Group, 1970. (Transcript of a symposium conducted by the Administrative Management Society.)

"The Office That Changes Gracefully." *Office Design*, July 1968.

Orenstein-Koppel im Grossraum (G). Privately printed, undated.

Palmer, Alvin E., and Lewis, M. Susan. *Planning the Office Landscape*.
New York: McGraw-Hill, 1977.

Pile, John. "Clearing the Mystery of the 'Office Landscape,'" *Interiors*, January 1968.

————. *Interiors 3rd Book of Offices*. New York: Whitney Library of Design, 1976.

———. "The Nature of Office Landscaping." *AIA Journal*, July 1969.

———. "The Office Landscape: Does It Work?" *Progressive Architecture*, June 1977.

Planas, R. E. "Integrated Planning Concept." *Building Operating Management*, June 1973.

———. "Yes: We Introduced It in This Country." *The Office*, July 1969.

Polites, Nicholas (ed.). *Improving Office Environment*. New York: Business Press, 1969. (An anthology).

Propst, R., and Wodka, M. *Action Office Acoustics Handbook*, Herman Miller, 1975.

———, Wodka, M., and Kelley, J. *Action Office Energy Distribution Handbook*. Herman Miller, 1976.

———. *The Office: A Facility Based on Change*. New York: Business Press, 1968.

Saphier, Michael. *Office Planning and Design*. New York: McGraw-Hill, 1968.

Schnelle, E., and Wankum, A. *Architekt und Organisator* (G). Verlag Schnelle, 1965.

Shoshkes, Lila. *Space Planning*. New York: Architectural Record Books, 1967.

Sommer, Robert. *Tight Spaces*. Englewood Cliffs, N.J.: Prentice-Hall, 1974.

Wheeler-Nicholson, Douglas. "Maybe: An Americanization of the Open Plan." *The Office*, July 1969.

Index

Numbers in italics
refer to illustrations.

Edited by Sarah Bodine and Susan Davis
Designed by James Craig
Printed in 10 point Times Roman